Through a Looking Glass

Through a Looking Glass

An Englishman kidnapped by the Colombian guerrilla

by

David Hutchinson

The Memoir Club

© David Hutchinson 2008

First published in 2008
Reprinted in 2013 by
The Memoir Club
Arya House
Langley Park
Durham
DH7 9XE

British Library Cataloguing in
Publication Data.
A catalogue record for this book
is available from the
British Library

ISBN: 978-1-84104-174-2

Dedication

To my family and friends,
and the selfless priests who got me out.
How can I ever repay the debt?

Contents

List of Illustrations

Toucan in the rainforest
Howler monkey
Poster asking to free Ingrid Betancourt
Green tree snake on palm tree
Meandering lowland river
Orchid – Cattleya
Anaconda
Piranha
Wild pig or peccary
Baby cayman, common in many lowland streams and rivers
Chiguiro with babies, found in the Ilanos plains
Red and blue macaw
Freshwater stingray
Leishmaniasis sores on leg
Local bus, known as a *chiva*
Army roadblock to check passengers and bus
One of hundreds of village churches in Colombia
Young girls playing outside
Che Guevara at the start in Cuba
Che Guevara after being captured in Bolivia
David after his release

Preface

'I suppose that you will write a book?' smiled *Comandante* D----, dressed in his camouflage uniform, in the Colombian jungle clearing, later, much later. '*My Experiences in the Jungle.*' He smiled at that title.

He was a pleasant man, who had come to see us, on a visit to his troops, who were guarding us, the prisoners. I only saw him once. But I read about him again, when I was free. The Army had gone to war into the jungle, and a story had been printed by the *El Tiempo* newspaper of Bogotá. It said that there were four thousand soldiers in combat and in the list of FARC units confronting them was the *Frente* 40, under *Comandante* D----. He was a fighting *guerrillero*. I was a captive.

People wonder whether the FARC is a political movement, after forty years of fighting and surviving and living off crime. Yes, it is. This is the book that the *Comandante* anticipated. Does it worry him? Any political movement must welcome a story about it and not be angry at the written word. There is a philosophy behind their political violence; claims and convictions; beliefs, not just brigandry. Many who went through an experience like mine are dead and many more are still in captivity, in great hardship. I think of them. I got out alive. I have to thank my friends and family, who form the 'double helix' of this story. It is about them as well as about me. I saw one side; they saw the other.

This political violence is not going to end soon. I sympathize with the Presidents of Colombia who have to negotiate with these unreasonable people. Being poor does not mean that you can be as bad as you like and blame society. I love to live in this beautiful country and am privileged to have as friends such a large number of marvellous Colombians. Colombia deserves better. This is a true tale and just relates facts. I would be flattered if it contributed to the 'oral history' of Colombia, and even more pleased if it stopped some people coming to the wrong conclusions about what is happening. But I want the reader to read it, and I don't want to push my conclusions in his face. He must work out what he thinks and help the right people take the country into a peaceful future.

Foreword

Rt. Hon. Michael Portillo

When David Hutchinson, an Englishman in Colombia, is seized by the FARC guerrillas and held for ransom, he feels a burning sense of injustice. While being marched over mountains and through forests he faces the perils of insects, illness and injury. While in captivity he marks his sixtieth birthday. He combats boredom through conversation with guerrillas and fellow hostages, innumerable games of chess, and eventually two novels sent to the jungle by his family. On his release he suffers traumatic effects, and is ruined by the cost of raising the ransom.

It is a remarkable story. Few have Hutchinson's experience of what the guerrillas are really like. Many of them appear simple and ignorant. Some are volatile, others kindly. They fight to overthrow their government through violent revolution. Their idealism has become submerged by the drug-dealing and kidnapping that finance their struggle. Hutchinson sees no justification for their viciousness or for wrecking his life.

He acknowledges that he is a lucky one. Large numbers who were taken hostage remain prisoners of the guerrillas today, many years later. Countless others were murdered. Kidnapping has ravaged Colombia and destroyed thousands of families.

It is paradoxical that Colombia, that has long abjured the death penalty, should be the victim of so much killing. It is ironic that a republic that, unusually for South America, has rarely fallen into military dictatorship should be so torn by revolution. It is tragic that cocaine — for export — should have polluted the state and society to their roots.

Colombia is a nation determined to fight back. With a combination of enlightened social programmes and measures to improve security it is bearing down on the drug-trafficking, kidnap and murder.

Hutchinson was in the wrong place at the wrong time. He was an unlucky foreigner in Colombia. But his book touches on the anguish of a whole nation. I fervently wish the people of Colombia a future that brings reconciliation and peace, and liberty for all the victims of abduction.

Photo credits

Matthew Leighton
(www.leightonstudios.com)

Cover IMAGES AND DESIGN

INTERIOR PAGES
Toucan
Army road block . . . to check passengers and bus
Mountain cloud forest
Colombian Orchid Stanhopea
Tree frog in heliconia plant
Green tree snake on palm tree
Walking cattle to market in the Llanos
Loading mule with provisions
Aerial view of the Andes mountain range
Juan Pablo Montoya – Colombian Fl racing driver
Lizard basking in sunshine
Waterfall
Fossil in rock
Local shop, trading in basic food supplies
Fully loaded DC3, with marijuana, failed to take off in time
Orchid Cattleya
Meandering lowland river
Fresh water stingray
Young girls playing outside
Western cordillera rising through morning mist
Mountain jungle hill side
Map of kidnap walk
One of hundreds of village churches in Colombia
Local bus know as a *chiva*
Mountain hills near the 'Savanna of Bogotá'
Bogota's bull ring
Sunrise over the savanna of Bogotá
Map of Colombia

Frailejones, found only in Colombia and the Northern Venezuela highlands
Andean mountains near Bogotá

Brian Moser
Colombians harvesting *coca* leaves in the jungle
Coca leaves drying in hut after being harvested
Colombian *guerrilleros* walking through village as locals look on
Colombian *guerrillero*

Jean Marie Perier
Poster asking to free Ingrid Betancourt

A guide to the characters

The guerrilla is the rebel force, as the Army is the force of the State. In the guerrilla are the *guerrilleros* or *guerrilleras*, the rebel fighters. Their officers are *comandantes*. The Spanish word originally meant what we would think of as 'skirmishers' as distinct from the main body of troops, and in the time of the Napoleonic Wars was identified with informal fighters against the French (uniformed) troops invading Spain. Now it means clearly informal fighters, whose slogan is 'When the Army advances, we retreat; when the Army retreats, we advance.' They don't usually defend their bases or camps, but fade away. They often take off their battle clothes and put on civilian clothes and are unidentifiable.

There are several guerrilla groups in Colombia, of which the main one is the FARC-EP, *Las Fuerzas Armadas Revolucionarias de Colombia-Ejercito Popular*. The other main one is the ELN, *El Ejercito de Liberación Nacional*. There are others active and again others who have in the past negotiated peace and more or less disappeared. They keep apart under separate leaders, but probably talk informally. The Colombian government negotiates with each group separately.

The FARC is led by the following real people, but I use their pseudonyms (*noms de guerre*):

Tirofijo ('Manuel Marulanda'), born Pedro Antonio Marin
'Raul Reyes', ideologue and spokesman (real name – Luis Devia – an ex-trade unionist)
Joaquin Gomez
'Alfonso Cano', born Guillermo Leon Saenz, supposedly the eventual successor to Tirofijo
'El Mono Jojoy', born Jorge Suarez Briceno, the military commander of the Eastern Front (*Frente Oriental*), nearest to Bogotá
'Grannobles', his brother
'Romaña', the kidnap king of the *Frente Oriental* (the Eastern Front)
'El Negro Acacio', the *comandante* in Guaviare province, in charge of the drugs and arms trade over the Brazilian frontier (now dead?)
El Negro Antonio, formerly of the front that controlled Viota, in the River Bogotá valley

Ricardo Palmera, alias 'Simon Trinidad'
and many others.

The names (disguised) of the *guerrilleros* who were my captors are:
Milton, the top *comandante* of the *Frente*
Oscar, a senior *comandante*
Ferney, another senior *comandante* and the boss of Pedro
Pedro, the *comandante* of the *comision* (special unit)
Janeth, 'La Bruja' (the Witch), his 'wife'
Hanibal
Hernan
'Pancake'
'La Negra'
Vladimir
Juan Carlos
Ismael, thick and strong, like army tea

Guerrilleros of the second group:
Edwin 'Cat's meat'
Sandra, his wife
Olmedo, number two, with the parrot on his shoulder
Adriano, the ex-convict
Carolina, the chubby one
Polo, the old drunkard
Patas Chitas, the 'indio'
Bad Boy
Yasmin, la negra
Carlos, the musician
Yesica
Jonhatan
Ramiro, the bigger indio
The red-nosed Reindeer, the second *comandante*
Jaime
Andres
Colacho

The last three *guerrilleros*
The little prince – *principito*
Amelia
Dog
and Pipo the peccary

PART 1

The First Eleven Days

CHAPTER 1

Kidnap

A VOICE SAID FROM BEHIND ME, '*Usted es el señor Hutchinson*? Are you Senor Hutchinson?'

I was standing in front of the lift in the underground parking of the apartment building where I lived in Bogotá, the capital of Colombia.

'*Si*,' I said.

Why did I not say, 'No'? Hindsight is wonderful. Did he not know what I looked like?

Four or five men grabbed my arms and threw me on the ground. They dragged me out of the light, for the garage has a light, activated by a sensor, and a camera that shows up on a television screen in the hall porter's cabin, by the front door to the building – a security system, such as is essential in Latin America. I was pulled along the floor, into the back room where the rubbish bins are kept. There is no automatic light there. I flailed about and kicked out in the dark. A rag dampened with a stinging chemical was pushed into my face, and I turned my head aside. My muscles do not match those of the Governor of California, so my struggles were of no avail. I was squashed on the floor. My hands and legs were tied with twine behind me. It was very uncomfortable. With a heave, the invisible men threw me into the boot of my own car, my dear ancient 1982 maroon Mercedes 250. They say that cars never die in South America but are patched up for ever. My kidnappers were about to prove that wrong.

This was 1 May 2002, a holiday in Bogotá. I had spent the morning doing some work at home and the afternoon playing golf with my friend Raimundo and his lovely, although unpunctual, wife Titina. We had dinner at a restaurant in the picturesque old square of Usaquen and I drove home at 8.30 p.m. alone. My wife was out of the country, staying with her family in the Philippines. I was doing some building work on my apartment and had a painter in during the day. I am always asked if I had had any indications that I might be a target for kidnap. No, I had not noticed anything. I was a retired man, of no wealth, an employee all my life, not a businessman, but it was not a chance kidnapping, a 'road block' or *reten* (called a 'miracle of the fishes' after Christ's successful fishing event) nor a car-theft. There they were, inside the garage of my building and asking for me. How remarkable that the man who spoke first pronounced my name with the correct English accent. Normally Colombians cannot do that and they say 'Hotchinson'. And they had no car of their own. I could make out that they had

3

leather jackets, jeans, boots, black pistols and masks on their faces. They spoke in whispers, so that I could not recognise their voices afterwards (or now? Did I know any of them?). They took my golf clubs out of the boot, thought a bit and put them back, with me on top. Why? One of them put a revolver in my face and said that I should keep very quiet or else he would kill me. The lid was slammed. One of them knew how to drive. But they had not come in their own car. They might have waited for me on the road up to my apartment building and grabbed me on the road. That is common.

The engine roared. An anguished shout came to me, through the back seat. 'How do you get the brake off?' I had a sticking plaster over my mouth. Indeed a Mercedes has a knob on the dashboard rather than a brake lever. I passed on this fact via the sticking plaster and the back seat, and the car lurched forward and started to climb the ramp. Clearly the door of the garage was open. Ah ha! What does that tell us about the role of the porter? The car was on the road and soon speeding on the streets of Bogotá, but in what direction I knew not. It grew warm in the boot, which also was furnished with sharp edges of steel.

I remembered some lessons from the 'defensive driving' courses given by security advisers, ex-sergeants of the SAS. Kick out the back lights and wave your hands around. A car behind you can see you and can give chase or call the police. I had a problem. My hands were tied behind my back. I wriggled them and heaved. Yes, one hand came loose. I could loosen my legs too. But there is not much space to stretch out inside the boot of a car. Could I open the boot lid, jump out at a traffic light, and escape? It was dark outside. Not as dark as inside. I found the back of the lock and moved it about a bit. It did not open. I remembered that I had installed a central locking system, so that when the doors shut, they locked automatically and the boot as well. The only way to open up was by pressing the button on the control, hung on the key ring. I was defeated by my own security system! I unscrewed some screws. The car started to go over some unmade road. Was I going north, to Zipaquira, and the province of Boyaca? We started to go uphill.

'All right?' a voice asked.

'Umm, mmmm, argh, ergh,' I answered. Those wordless sounds were open to various interpretations, but told them that I was conscious, which is about as much as they wanted to know. And it was better that they felt that the plaster was firmly over my mouth, than loose. I did not want them to know that my hands were untied.

'So this is a kidnap,' I thought. And it was I who was the victim. Like everyone in Colombia, I had had friends kidnapped and read stories, but when it happens to you the reality is unexpected and brutal. You think that you will not get killed but you think of escape or rescue. You are rushing away from your family, in the hands of frightening, hard men with guns. This has never happened to you. You have lived in a comfortable world of affection, a warm bed, food, friends and stimulatings things to do all day. You have a diary of appointments. But all this is over in a second and you are in the hands of people whom you would never have met or chosen to meet; human beings, but not the ones you like. Wolves. Killers. Now my life was worth nothing, but I was not afraid. The instinct of survival had kicked in. I knew I must put up with the pain and discomfort and cold and make the best of it. A new life of hardship had started, but I would damn well stick it out. The string around my wrists hurt like hell as it bit into the flesh, and my body banged into the steel edges of the inside of the boot. I don't like pain, but I had to shut up and bear it. After about an hour and a half of driving, the car bounced over some ruts and stopped off the road. A man opened the lid, and cold fresh air flowed into my space, where I lay sweating. I had had to roll up my legs and wrists in all the string, as if I was tied up firmly. I saw stars in the sky, a house outlined, and some trees. A pistol was waved at me.

'Not a sound,' the man said. 'No one can hear you. Everyone here is with us. They all shoot to kill, if you do anything foolish.'

He looked in. 'Hey, he has undone the string,' he called to his companions. 'His hands are loose.'

I was worried. What would he do? But he did nothing. 'Mr Hutchinson, we trust you. You won't do anything silly, will you?'

'Of course not. Keep the lid open. I need air, please.'

I thought I could hear a telephone call being made inside the house. I could see a telephone line coming into the house from the road, something which is not very common in the Colombian countryside. We waited. The man shut the lid and went off. After a while I called out for the lid to be opened, as I felt that I was suffocating. I banged. The lid was opened and I explained. The gun was waved, but the lid was not closed. We were high in the mountains and it was cold. Bogotá is at 2,600 metres and every night is about 9 degrees centigrade, except for very sunny days with clear skies when there can even be frost. We were higher than Bogotá, I thought.

A dog barked, then an old 4 × 4 Toyota Landcruiser drove in. Several men came out of the house. I was picked up and carried to the Toyota and put in the back.

'Do you want to lie down or sit up?' I was asked.

I sat up and the Toyota drove out into the lane and up a dirt road, higher and higher. The Mercedes followed. We stopped and they all got out. It was much colder and the night was black and moonless.

'Are you cold?' an older man said. They put a black plastic sheet over me.

'Sit down lower, so that you can't be seen.' We waited for a long time. Had they gone away? I dared not sit up and look.

A man walked by and remarked to another '*Donde estan estos guevones?* Where are these buggers? They said seven o'clock.'

I could not tell whether it was night or day under the black plastic. A call was made on a mobile phone. We waited. At last, the door was swung open and the plastic was taken off. It was light. I saw a man in a uniform, with gumboots and a rifle slung over his shoulder. He had a thin Ronald Coleman-style moustache, a sharp nose and a thin brown face with straight black hair – a typical *campesino* from the *sabana* (savannah or high plain) of Cundinamarca or Boyaca, the provinces nearest to Bogotá. The kidnappers cut the string. I had no shoes on.

'Get out. You have arrived.'

The uniformed man had shoulder flashes that said 'FARC-EP'. I tore the plaster from my mouth and stood up in my socks.

'Do you know who we are?' said the FARC man. 'We are *Las Fuerzas Armadas Revolucionarias Colombianas – Ejercito Popular*. You are an economic prisoner (a *retenido economico*). We know all about you. You have twelve thousand million pesos and four houses in Bogotá. We shall ask for two million dollars. You pay and you go free.'

It was 7.15 in the morning of 2 May 2002.

CHAPTER 2

Pablo Escobar and the cocaine business

I AM AN ENGLISHMAN OF THE 'overseas' breed. I was born in the Indian frontier city of Peshawar, which is now in Pakistan, the country created out of India for muslims in the 1947 'Partition' and independence of India. Until then my father had been an officer of the Indian Army, which he had joined at the time of the 1929 Crash and Depression. In 1935 in Peshawar he had met my mother, whose Scottish/Austrian family had been in India since 1745. I had been to schools and university in England and had looked for a job abroad as soon as I could. The world had changed by 1967, when I was looking for work. A large chunk of the globe was under communist rule and the British Empire was being unwound. Latin America had escaped the war and was free and open to capital and emigration. I was accepted by a company with operations there and was not disappointed when I arrived in Argentina in late 1967. My work took me to many countries in different jobs. My Argentine wife, Graciela, died of cancer in 1983, and I married Nanette, a Filipina with Spanish grandparents. In fact she was christened Maria Cecilia, but all Filipinos are known by nicknames. She was lucky. She might have been a Peachy or a Ping-ping. Our children, John and Victoria and Gino, grew up in schools in various countries and prospered. From Manila I was posted to Papua New Guinea, that huge island between Australia, Singapore and Indonesia. Nanette cried all the flight in and later cried on the flight on the way out. The tropical climate and sparkling Coral Sea had won our hearts.

I was sitting in my office in this South Pacific island looking at the sea and my papers alternately, when a senior colleague rang from London. Would I like to go to work in Colombia? When Latin America is in your bloodstream, the prospect of returning meets with no rejection, nor doubt nor worry. 'Yes,' I said. Ah, faithful employee! I knew Argentina and Brazil and the neighbouring countries but not the northern Latin countries. Coffee, the Andes, salsa, the Caribbean.

'My dear fellow, you don't have to reply immediately,' came the dry Scots comment.

He said he would ring the next day. Well, fair enough, I should consult my wife, should I not? If I didn't, I should be in trouble. Nanette is a beautiful Filipina girl, brought up to speak Spanish at home. She is an adaptable companion, a genius at growing orchids, and a good sportswoman. I had always worked for international companies and travelled the world, and could expect one more job and maybe a pension before I got too old. So it was a day later that I said yes again. After the months spent getting visas, and meeting Jorge Uribe, the rotund and amusing consul of Colombia in London, to consularise packing lists for furniture, we found ourselves landing in Miami on 5 December 1989, to take the next morning's Eastern Airlines flight into Bogotá. The USA was in those days an opportunity to shop for electric goods that were difficult to get, or not as good, in Latin cities. The streets of central Miami are lined with shops, from which one is addressed in Brazilian Portuguese and Rio de la Plata Spanish, offering radios and watches and cordless telephones. We stayed in the airport hotel and came down for breakfast at six in the morning. Outside were blue sky and heat and the Caribbean on the horizon; inside, waffles and eggs and coffee and OJ (the orange juice one, not OJ Simpson yet) and the newspaper, the US *News and Daily Report*, the only one with colour printing. In the middle of the front page, a colour photograph showed a building in Bogotá in flames. I seized it and spread it, causing maple syrup to anoint the baseball results on the back page. The headquarters of the DAS – the Department of Security Administration, who administer security and foreigners – had been bombed with huge loss of life. It was surely the drug lords – what became a familiar word – *narcotrafico*. We had not even got into the aircraft to go to Colombia for the first time, and our new home was in the headlines for drugs and violence. The aircraft was not full.

This was not the first event in the war of the drug barons against the government of Colombia, of course. 1989 was a particularly bad year in that war. The candidate who was sure to win the presidential election of 1990, Luis Carlos Galan, from the city of Bucaramanga, good-looking, eloquent, tough, of the Liberal Party, was murdered in August, in a suburb of Bogotá. The killer was hired by the leading *mafioso*, Pablo Escobar, who objected to Galan's views on extradition of *mafiosos* to the USA, when the US Department of Justice was asking for them to stand trial in the USA. This campaign for extradition had been started, when Belisario Betancourt was President, by his brave Minister of Justice, Rodrigo Lara, whom Escobar had murdered by *sicarios* – hired gunmen – in 1984. The drug peddlers – known as *trajetos* or men from the 'magic kingdom' – wanted to stay in their country and to terrify the members of parliament and judges into avoiding convicting them. Pablo Escobar, from the city of Medellin, was the biggest of them all. He was said to be the richest man in the world, to have offered to pay off the entire foreign debt of Colombia, to have cornered the gold market in Chicago, and other tales. But it takes two to tango. Supply and demand had both grown as the passion for snorting lines of cocaine in the USA (and elsewhere) had absorbed the capacity for growing *coca* bushes in the Amazon rainforest. Analysts made a living by tracing the graphs of New York street prices of cocaine and comparing the curves to exchange rates, coffee price, and stock markets. Aircraft were shot down over the Caribbean in the night by pilots who might have featured in books by Tom Clancy.

The US Coastguard patrolled the offshore waters. The satellites disgorged transcripts of telephone calls (there were no mobile phones yet in Colombia) and faxes on the desks of analysts in the Pentagon and Langley and Cheltenham, while international banking became a nightmare of vigilance against money laundering as billions of dollars were collected from the streets of USA and Europe, by 'smurfs', who deposited them in small amounts in banks. Some came back into the producer countries, some was used to buy real estate around the world, some for aircraft and weapons, for the chemicals used to make *coca* paste out of the leaves (precursor chemicals), and some stayed in banks in a variety of countries. The USA was going mad. The president declared the drug lords a 'clear and present danger'. There was no way that the democratic leaders of the USA and Europe (although the experiments in Holland and Switzerland excited interest) were going to decriminalise drugs. The US Congress had to approve military expenditure budgets of half a billion dollars a year for Colombia – not to combat the guerrilla, but for drug eradication. This made Colombia the third biggest recipient of US military aid after Israel and Egypt. Such expenditure is not usual for the USA, nor do many countries get it, and is much less than the money spent by the Colombian government itself on the conflict. But it was a sign by the leading power of the world that it wanted to help and a sign that, alone, Colombia was not going to make progress.

The fight against drugs identifies three main activities: cultivation, consumption and money laundering. Stop the cultivation, and there will be no cocaine, no heroin (let's forget about marijuana, the drug of the 1960s). Stop the consumption, and there are no users. Seize the money and the business collapses. US policy had as an essential ingredient the spraying by the countries involved of the poppies and *coca* bushes with herbicide (glyphosate), usually from the air. The growing was illegal was it not? The policy also had crop substitution offers, which appeared to have some success in Peru and Bolivia. The area planted had to be reduced, and this could be controlled by satellite images. But did dumping herbicide on the land not affect the other vegetables and fruit trees, and did it not affect the health of humans? And as soon as you get involved in this type of discussion, it is easy to attack the rich countries for hypocrisy, since they are the consumers of the 'illegal substances'. The Wall Street investment banker, sniffing a line of 'coke' at home after dinner out, does not really feel that he is breaking the law. What harm is he doing to anyone?

For the poor peasant in the Amazonian forest the choice is obvious. There is a joke: 'Look, señor, when I was growing vegetables, I used to load then on to my mule and take them to the market and come back with a pocketful of money. Now I take a pocketful of *coca* to the market and load the money on to my mule. Ha, ha.'

And so from day one, I was plunged into this world of drugs. I knew that there was a guerrilla war too, but that does not impact you as you travel into the city, to work, to find a house to live in. Maybe the number of armed police and soldiers astonishes a visitor. Are the cities safe? I made friends and got on with my job. Drugs and guerrilla are not a daily problem. In fact, when investors are asked to rank their worries in order of importance, insecurity comes low down, well after the constant changing of laws and taxes, corruption in public administration, inflexible labour practices, expensive transport costs and inefficient customs and excise. However, the avoidance of contamination by dirty drug money, yes, that is a never-ending duty.

Within a week of my arrival, the second most notorious mafioso, Gonzalo Rodriguez Gacha, *el Mexicano*, was shot dead by the police from a helicopter on a farm in the north of Colombia, near the Caribbean. He was away from his home territory, which was near the emerald mining area, north of Bogotá. This caused his house in Bogotá to come on the market, the old house of the Shaio textile family, but improved with a swimming pool inside the sitting room, gold taps in the bathrooms and a billiard table with heated cushions to improve the bounce. His death caused a problem for the writer of the foreign community's Christmas pantomime, who had penned some immortal lyrics for a chorus, in which 'Rodriguez Gacha' was rhymed with 'Margaret Thatcher'. Should he drop the song? No. The show had to go on.

The drug show certainly went on for all my first years in Colombia. The bomb aimed at the police headquarters was followed by bombs in the streets. I was sitting lunching in the Four Seasons restaurant when one went off one block away. I watched fascinated as in slow motion the window of the restaurant slowly bulged in and bulged back, without breaking. The compressed air made my ears hurt and I felt sick. But I was alive. The drug lords had taken on the government. It was war, about drugs and about extradition of captured smugglers to the USA for trial there.

When Rodriguez Gacha died, it was clear that the Medellin cartel, under Pablo Escobar, and the Cali cartel, with the Rodriguez Orejuela brothers, Miguel and Gilberto (the 'Chessplayer'), had the bulk of the trade in drugs. The Cali cartel was discreet but Escobar was madly show-off. He had a farm called *Hacienda Napoles* on the Bogotá to Medellin road, with imported hippopotamuses and giraffes. Small planes landed there bearing people such as Vladimiro Montesinos, the Peruvian president's right-hand man. There was a block of apartments in Medellin with a swimming pool on every balcony. The BCCI bank of Pakistan opened a branch in Medellin and an agency in the *barrio* of Envigado, the heartland of Escobar, and took enormous deposits. But Escobar was always on the run in the end and trying to negotiate with the Colombian government. He handed himself in and was kept in a specially built prison, from which he easily escaped after a while. In order to find him, electronic surveillance was provided by friendly countries. At the end twelve aircraft were said to be in the air over Medellin simultaneously, listening.

On Thursday 2 December 1993, I was in my office in Bogotá. My security manager from London was in Colombia and had flown to Medellin, as luck would have it. He was checking on the risks to our staff there, bank robbery, kidnapping, the routes they drove on, their housing. The telephone rang. It was my manager from Medellin.

'Marta had a call from her home and went back to look after her children. The maid said that there were lots of soldiers on the roof of the next-door house, and shooting,' she said.

My secretary, Mireya, erupted into the room. 'The radio says that Pablo Escobar has been killed.'

'Where?'

'In Medellin.'

'Keep listening.'

It was the end of an epoch – the richest man in the world, drilled full of bullets on the roof of a house in the *barrio* of Los Olivos in Medellin. Did this mean that the drug war was won? Would less cocaine and heroin hit the streets of the US cities? Not likely. New generations would arise, but not so vain as to drink Dom Perignon from golden goblets, while their pet giraffes stroll around the garden.

And, by coincidence, there was Nigel, our international security manager, on the spot in Medellin, when the reign of the world's greatest criminal was snuffed out, due to his own carelessness.

Pablo Escobar had been heard making a telephone call from his hiding place to his wife, Maria Victoria Henao, and his chubby son, Juan Pablo, who were in the Hotel Tequendama in Bogotá. He spoke for long enough to be triangulated to the precise house where he was hiding. It was his death warrant. Why did he run and not surrender when the door was smashed in? He had certainly under-estimated the power of electronic surveillance. I was to learn a lot about that.

CHAPTER 3

The no-go area (*zona de distension*)

IS THE FARC A POLITICAL MOVEMENT? Yes. What does the FARC live off?
Extortion, kidnap, and most recently, drugs. This is how it gets money from us.
In fact the drugs may well be swapped for arms, avoiding money which leaves a
trail through the banks.

Before his presidency (1998–2002), Andres Pastrana, whose father Misael had
been president, had made a campaign promise to negotiate peace with the FARC
and indeed, before he took over, had flown into the jungle to see Tirofijo, its
founder. As part of the peace talks, he had agreed to set aside an area in the forest
around San Vicente del Caguan and the Sierra de la Macarena in the jungle, the
old heartland of the FARC since they had marched in 1968 from Tolima, east into
the forest. This was the *zona de distension* – the safety zone, roughly translated – a
no-go area for the Army. In theory the State went on with its activities there –
justice, education, mayors. The guerrilla could hang about safely, and invite all the
ambassadors and the journalists of the world to come and see them. The zone
would be the place where the government would come and sit down and talk
peace terms. Before he took over the presidency, Pastrana travelled to the future
zone and had words with Tirofijo. His campaign had offered talks and the enemy
was playing the game. Was it to be a game or a serious peace talk?

The government appointed negotiators. They went up and down by aeroplane
to San Vicente del Caguan. They started by seeing that there should be talks about
what should be talked about. If there was to be 'peace', what did the FARC want
for that? Would they be giving up a good life and money from crime and drugs?
Obviously yes. If they gave that up, what would they live on? Where would they
live? Could they have 'their own territory'? Could they stay in the *zona de
distension* for ever? The people of Colombia would never swallow that. And the
constitutional lawyers would say that the country of Colombia was a whole,
subject to the rule of law.

The requirements of the Marxist guerrilla in return for peace turned out to be
absurd. They wanted a Marxist state, public ownership, equality, punitive taxes.
They were against foreign investment. They were not prepared to enter
democratic elections under the current rules, and so on. The talks about the
subject matter of talks to arrive at agendas for discussions for a future state in which
they would be happy became elusive. They continued with their campaign of
violence and kidnapping, which rose to over 3,000 a year (just the recorded ones).

'But something good has come out of it,' protested the Ambassador, as we walked along the country lanes one weekend, his body guards not far behind.

'The world has become conscious of the problem. It is back on the agenda. Everyone can see that a Marxist drug-fuelled war in the backyard of America cannot be allowed to go on for ever. The entire world is going to help Colombia solve this problem.'

'But we don't see it like that,' I countered. 'I am not sure that people think that Pastrana is on the right track. He looks like a fool. We are the victims in Colombia and we are suffering. It is more and more insecure. The FARC is making a mockery of him and us. '*Tomando el pelo.*' (Pulling his leg.)

'And the Europeans are being taken in!' exploded Jimmy, our companion and long-term resident in Colombia. 'They support the guerrilla. They defend the criminals and make life impossible for the Army. They don't care about the kidnap victims. The journalists go and see these people, when the Army can't find them, and broadcast justification for their cause.' And he was a reader of the English *Guardian* newspaper at that.

Years of fury that Sweden and Germany and Mexico and other countries had allowed the FARC to have offices and websites in their countries welled up. These are no peasants oppressed by oligarchic landowners. Their crimes set them beyond the pale.

'You don't get anywhere like that,' threw back the Ambassador. 'The world is now involved and we have achieved that. Of course the peace process will take a long time . . .'

'And money?' I queried.

'And how do you get money? From our countries. You make people aware. They must come and see. The government of Colombia does not have enough money and military power on its own to win in a reasonable time scale. And there is the drugs angle.'

He was in favour of the decriminalisation of drugs. Leaving drugs in the hands of the *narco-traficantes* and guerrilla had not been a good idea. But it was a 'not in our lifetime, perhaps our grandchildren's' dream. The policy shift in the USA was too great, like turning a huge oil tanker in mid-ocean.

The peace process fell apart when a *guerrillero* kidnapped a small plane in which members of the Getchen family were travelling and made it land on a road near the *zona* and took away the passengers, They were being chased under Law 003 of the FARC, penalising political 'crimes', theft of public money, etc. This act of armed piracy took place outside the zone, in the middle of the peace talks. Pastrana blew up and put an end to the fruitless and humiliating talks, in February of 2002. The guerrilla took to the forest and hills and melted away.

Well, how much and how far they melted, I was to see for myself.

CHAPTER 4

The start

A T SEVEN FIFTEEN ON THE MORNING of 2 May the sky was blue in the mountains somewhere in Colombia. Where was I? There were hand-carved stone posts, with barbed wire stretched between them, to mark the fields. The fields were either planted with potatoes or left to grass for cows. In the rainy cool Andes the grass is emerald green and thick. Potatoes come from here. Europeans only knew the potato when the Spanish brought samples after 1492, when 'Columbus sailed the ocean blue'. The English accepted the Indian name of *patata*, but the French called it an 'earth apple', a *pomme de terre*. There are many varieties of potato native to the Andes, which are not known in Europe, and the best food of Bogotá, the *ajiaco* soup, is made of three different types.

The ground was hilly and damp. We were not above the tree line. It was pretty countryside. I could have been in Boyaca to the north or somewhere to the south of Bogotá, near Usme? I could not tell but I could see my Mercedes further down the lane.

'Could I have my glasses?' I asked. The *guerrillero* looked in the boot of the Mercedes and found them and gave me them.

'*Gracias*,' I said. How could I keep them safe and unbroken for what could be a long time? Anyone who uses glasses and has to rough it in wild country for a long time is constantly worried about keeping them unbroken. Where do you put them at night? How would you manage if they were broken and you could not see distant objects? I am myopic.

I had my watch on my left wrist. They could not get it over the string that tied my hands together, so it was not stolen. But all my pockets had been emptied. One of the kidnappers came up. 'Do you have a microchip? In your car? Or shoes? Open your mouth.'

I could not believe what he was saying.

He looked into my mouth. 'Do you have false teeth?'

'Yes, but they are fixed. I have bridges.'

He seemed satisfied that I was not hooked up to the Pentagon, and that a Harpoon missile was not going to take his head off. The fear of GPS-micro-transmitters (as in car security chips) is real and a danger. Electronic surveillance is looking for you, and listening to you, from satellites.

He could not find my shoes. I stood in the muddy lane in my socks. He told me to walk down the lane and around the bend and not look back. A girl in uniform with a rifle, a girl with an Indian face, flat and brown, with sloping eyes, told me to stand next to a bush and not look back. The kidnappers were driving the Toyota away. They did not want to be looked at. They live in Bogotá and I might bump into them if I got back to the city. When the Toyota had gone bumping down the lane, the *guerrillero* came back.

An old couple of peasants (*campesinos*), very short, knobbly old folk in felt hats, were walking up towards us. The old man started to talk to the *Comandante*.

'Can you help me? My skin itches all over. It is painful. I can't sleep.' He looked as if he had not changed his clothes or bathed for a decade. A leprechaun.

'OK, I see what we can do, *viejo*,' answered the *guerrillero*, the dispenser of people's justice, and people's medicine!

The old man went on complaining. It is true that medicine is expensive and that many poorer people have little or no access to medical care, beyond emergency hospitals. A bit more often to the bucket with a bar of soap might have helped. The *guerrillero* turned away and motioned me to walk on. The girl went in front. What could the old man do? He had seen me. He was not going to report it to the Army. This was guerrilla territory. But where was I? I plodded along the damp earth road in my socks. Soon we turned into a field and down towards some trees. Strangely enough, up and across the field came a man, with a bag over his shoulder. The *guerrillero* spoke to him and he put down the bag and opened it. He fished out a pair of tennis shoes, size 38. (This was my first meeting with the logistics organisation of the guerrilla. How do they get their clothes and food and toilet paper? We cannot have been far from the city and this was their shopping.) My feet are size 45. I put the tennis shoes on but as my heels would not go in, I took them off and went on barefoot. We entered the woods. Very soon we came across a tent, or rather a canvas bivouac roof, stretched between two trees and anchored by guy ropes, then others, and a clearing with a wooden hut.

'You sit here,' said the *guerrillero*, pointing into the first tent on the left. Its entrance faced a larger tent, where another man was cleaning a rifle. Camouflage equipment was piled on the ground. The Indian girl went on into the clearing. My tent was a simple one, with a plastic sheet on the ground. They are called *caletas* in the guerrilla. Bivouacs, we should call them. I was wearing what I had put on after my shower at the golf club – pale gabardine trousers, an undervest (Marks and Sparks from London), a cotton checked shirt, no tie, a grey woollen sweater, a brown sports jacket, socks and no shoes. Well, a pair of small tennis shoes, into which I did not fit. Did they really think that my shoes had micro-transmitters in them? These were clothes for the cool climate of Bogotá. My watch was still on my wrist but nothing remained in my pockets. The Indian girl came and gave me a blanket, without a word. At about eleven o' clock a young man brought me rice and some meat in a saucepan, with a spoon. *Guerrilleros* came and went along the path in front of my tent. I lay under the blanket and slept a bit, after my cold, bad night. My wrists were bleeding where the string had bitten into the skin. A radio played popular music from the hut. A deeper voice, with an educated accent and vocabulary, spoke occasionally. At five o'clock a supper of potato soup and some biscuits came. I peed in the bushes behind the tent. I lay down and the tropical night fell, after six, like a stone. It was a cold mountain night and I shivered under the single blanket. There was no pillow, so I laid my head on a tennis shoe. I was on the ground and it was hard and full of spiky prongs and lumps

In the dark, before dawn, a voice whispered behind me, 'I shall be here at five o'clock. OK?' In the confusion of what had happened to me, I imagined that the voice spoke to me. Was it a rescuer? Had the police tracked me down? How could I dream of a James Bond-type of rescue, a mad illusion, a dream of waking from a nightmare. Dawn came and the sentries changed, and there I was in the middle of a FARC platoon. My second day. 3 May. 'This will not be over quickly,' I thought. 'Patience.' What could I do? Nothing. I was a puppet in the hands of these armed rebels.

When you are a prisoner, you have time. My God, you have time! There is nothing to do all day, but eat and sleep and defecate. It is a basic animal life, like my dogs'. We had three yellow labrador dogs at home. I thought of my life, so rudely interrupted. Nanette was away from Colombia, and Ana, our maid, was in charge of me and the dogs. What would she be doing, after my disappearance? I thought, but mainly I adapted myself to my new life as a prisoner, cold and dirty and wondering what I would get to eat and listening to my captors; sleeping as much as I could; keeping warm; looking at the trees; seeking birds and insects to have something to think about and look at.

I was all right, wasn't I? I could live where these young men and girls lived, here in among the trees, couldn't I? I knew about the FARC, but like most Colombians, I had never seen a *guerrillero*, much less talked to one. God forbid. We had to avoid getting anywhere near them. We were careful about driving on country roads or walking in wild places. We did not want them to know we existed. Their war was absurd and they were dangerous. We worked and were paid our wages and employed people and paid taxes. They just destroyed and killed. How would they treat me? What was I guilty of? I watched and listened to them.

That second day, I was moved to another tent or *caleta*, the other side of the *comandante*'s tent, below the hut. This had been made for me. A space of earth had been slashed and cleared and flattened. The camouflage tent roof had been tied to trees or posts, and stretched. Grass or bracken had been cut and laid on the earth, and a plastic groundsheet placed on that. That was it. There were no walls. It was all right if it rained but damn cold. I looked down, through the trees, across an opening. A barbed wire fence separated me from a little clearing, in which was a plastic barrel, with a hose dripping water into it. This was their water supply, brought by this hose from a stream in the woods. I could hear the chatter in the hut, where they cooked. The man with the deep voice was called Felipe, an educated man, probably from a university, a Marxist. This was a platoon, and in the front line. The rest of the *guerrilleros* were young boys and girls. They played what looked like 'toss the penny', where you throw coins towards a sandy patch, and if you cover one, you take it. The sentries were down below, or back along the path.

The same *guerrillero* who had received me the first morning came to look at me. I could see that he was the *comandante*. The guerrilla is a Marxist organisation and does not go in for ranks, like major or colonel. If you have rank, you seem to be called *comandante*. But there are junior and senior *comandantes*. They know their hierarchy. He went away and came back with a chain and chained me to a tree, one end around my ankle, with a padlock, the other end padlocked to a stout tree. He also brought a pair of rubber boots, which they all wear. They were too small, size 43, and my toes were scrunched up, but the chain fitted inside. I stared out. I began to see little emerald humming birds among the bushes, finding flowers to suck at. I could get up and walk nearer to them and watch them. Meals were soup or rice, and biscuits. I kept some spare biscuits in the top pocket of my jacket, the start of a policy to have a little bit of left-over food all the time, just in case. The *comandante* saw that and asked, 'Why do you do that?' He was nervous that I was thinking of escape, perhaps. But I was chained up.

At night I could see lights below. I guessed that there was a main road down there and that we were not far from civilisation, from my home. The second night, I heard aircraft overhead and then bombs falling behind us. Boom, boom. Good God! One night I heard bursts of rapid gunfire, not far away, and feet running past along the path. The next night the bombing noise was audible again, behind the front line where we were. I knew that I had been taken into a war. The bullets and bombs of the military would be aimed at me. I was in the middle of the enemy.

Nobody came to see me or speak to me. I had to wash, so I asked to be taken to the hosepipe. My chain was unlocked and I asked for soap and a towel. I soaped my head and hosed it down. It was too cold to strip and bathe in cold water. I would stay dirty for the moment. The towel was green and old and bald. The nights were cold as I only had one small blanket, so I slept a bit during the day. When the sun was out, I found the sunniest patch of ground and stood in it. I wondered what the family was doing. I was unable to do anything. I could not escape, but I thought of how to get to the road, past the sentries, in the dark. All prisoners start by dreaming of escape. Not for nothing was I chained to a tree, like a dog.

CHAPTER 5

The family finds out

O N THE MORNING OF 2 MAY, the porters in the building where I lived changed over. The incoming porter, Luis, had been down in the underground garage, where the porters have their changing room and toilet. Colombians are hard workers. Schools start at eight and breakfast meetings can start at 7 a.m. Almost all of the children are picked up by school buses outside on the street, but some neighbours set off to work by car early. Luis had seen that my old Mercedes was not there, but there was no record of it having driven out when he looked in the log at the desk upstairs. He rang up and told Ana, the maid. She went to see. Back in the flat, she started to worry. I had rung her the evening before to say that I would have dinner with my friends and that she did not have to cook and so could go to bed, without waiting up for me. Why was the car not there? She rang the house of Raimundo.

'Don Raimundo, el señor came back last night?'

'Why?'

'His car is not here.'

'Yes, of course he came back. He dropped us at home and drove home at about half past eight. Is he in his bedroom?'

'I don't know?'

'Ay, *por favor, niña*. Go and look, and tell me. He is probably asleep.'

She put the telephone down and walked the corridor to the bedroom and knocked on the door. 'Señor David?'

No answer. She opened the door. No señor in the bed. The bed was undisturbed. She rushed back 'Señor Raimundo, *no está*. He is not here.'

Her heart was pounding, and it was not the altitude of Bogotá (2,600 metres above sea level). The drama had started.

Ana called a friend of hers to come round. Jorge, the architect who was doing some redecoration in the flat, also came with his master builder. Ana said that she was scared to stay alone and Jorge agreed to sleep over at our place. She called a neighbour, Camela, who rushed up the hill from her place. She called my son's friend, Maria Isabel, who rang my son John, in England. Raimundo, my golfing partner, called our friend Willy, who was the head of a hospital, and he started the process of ringing the mortuaries all over town. Was I murdered by thieves, especially car thieves? It is dangerous to be out alone at night. Had I got into a road rage argument?

More friends got involved. Jimmy, the imaginative one, said, 'Perhaps he went out for a drink in a nightclub and met a lady of the night who drugged his whisky.'

Bertie stopped that line of thought and said, 'Come on, I don't think so. He is doing this decoration in the house, isn't he? He must have gone out to buy some cement and bricks in the Siete de Agosto district rather late and been mugged.'

Alicia, my former secretary, and her husband, El Negro, drove around the roads to look for me. This was because there is an unpleasant form of robbery in Colombia using *burundanga*, which is a powder extracted from the flowers of the *datura* tree. If puffed in your face, you fall into a trance and follow your captors around like a labrador dog. They take you to a cash dispenser and you give them your money and then they take you home and you say, 'Help yourselves.' Then they leave you, sometimes naked, in a ditch by a road out of town. My architect, Jorge, had this done to him twice. It is possible that he liked to give lifts to young ladies late at night. He lost two cars and his reputation, if you can lose that twice.

But the ditches were Hutchinson-free. In these panic situations, everyone is suspect. And in Colombia one has a maid, there are porters on the building, there are neighbours on the farm, there are staff in the office, there is the beggar on the corner. Who dunnit?

John did not know the telephone numbers in Manila so he rang Gino, Nanette's son, in Boston, USA.

'Oh my God, I had better ring my mom.'

The telephone rang in the house in the San Juan *barrio* of Manila, in the Philippines. 'Hi Mom, it's me.' Gino was ringing his mother, my wife, across the world. 'How are you?'

'Well, thanks, *mabuti*,' she replied in Tagalog, the language of the Philippines. It was hot and sticky as usual and the airconditioners hummed. 'What's happened? *Anong nang yare?*'

It was six in the morning, a time for bad news.

'Hey Mom, I am afraid that I have bad news. John rang me. Tito David has disappeared.'

And he told her facts, as much as there were. She was thunderstruck, of course. It was difficult to take the news in.

'You had better fly back to Bogotá as soon as possible.'

Our friends from Colombia began to call her to tell her what they were doing and comfort her. It had been a terrible shock for her and she did not know what she was going to have to do. I was gone. But our friends were rallying around and investigating. I was not dead, or rather my body had not been found. John said that it was a nightmare come true. He had thought that it could happen. Kidnapping was a fact of Colombian life.

Nanette knew that she had to go home and take charge. So off she went to change her ticket at Cathay Pacific and start the round-the-world trail from Manila to Colombia. Her suitcase proved itself of independent mind and set off in another direction, but a week later turned up in Bogotá, probably via British Colombia, or Columbia University, New York or Colombo in Sri Lanka. John was already there.

On the email inward mail tray was a message from the daughter of old friends. 'I have finally made it to Latin America after all these years and will be travelling through Bolivia and Peru. I would love to see something of Colombia but everything I have read makes me a little nervous. What would be your advice? Should I fly into Bogotá and leave directly from there? Or would it be feasible to travel overland. Looking forward to hearing from you soon. Polly.'

John had to reply. A week before, I should have welcomed her and invited her to stay and travel around a bit. Now he had to break the news to her.

Leaning against the window of the porter's cabin of the building where I lived, 'Jorge' the porter, one of three who rotated duty, looked down at the street and the residents walking their dogs to the park and back. He was a part of the security that Bogotanos need to live in safety. He opened the front door and the garage, greeted the residents, and when the pizza delivery boy appeared on his motorbike, rang up to the apartment and told us.

A sly smile passed across his features. He thought of the money. It had gone well. No traces. How clever he was.

From out of my education came some lines of poetry. 'Quis custodiet ipsos custodes?' the Roman poet, Juvenal, wrote two thousand years ago. 'Who watches the guards?'

CHAPTER 6

The family mobilise

SINCE MY BODY HAD NOT BEEN FOUND in any hospital or morgue, it looked like a kidnap, but there was no hard news. The car had gone, and the porter of the building swore that I had never come home. All my stuff had been put back in the boot of the car. Nothing had been left on the floor of the garage. The family had to assume that I was taken by some gang on the street. But there was silence.

John had gone to Bogotá immediately. He left on a Thursday from work and was involved in Bogotá on the Friday. He remembers the nightmarish quality of the speed at which it all develops at the start. You are unprepared and feel that you are striking matches in the dark. The police and experts are telling you things and you have to take them in at once. Time seems so important and nothing can be left until later. The expression is 'rapid response'. The experts in drugs and kidnaps tell you how to pick up the telephone and how to respond. The bad boys will ring. When? Within a week, a thousand things had had to be done and had been done. In Bogotá, the police had to be told. Before that the family wanted to see the embassy and get advice.

'I shall do everything possible to help you,' said the magnificent Ambassador.

This would open up channels to both governments. How the hell do you negotiate with these people, behind the back of the police? Is it legal to pay ransoms? What money is there? Who is going to advise us? Friends started to telephone and offer help and money. Immediately it was clear that one's government will not contemplate paying money for kidnaps and neither they nor the security companies can negotiate nor make the payments.

A *denuncia* or report had to be made to the police, more precisely the specialised anti-kidnap police, the *Gaula*. Their feeling was that it was a kidnap. Within the week, they had had a report of a car like mine, stopped on its way to the frontier with Ecuador. They thought that it would have ended up in Peru, for sale, with false papers. It turned out to be a false lead.

Going to the offices of the *Gaula* is scary, as John found out. There are young boys and girls, with guns and leather jackets and computers. The wall has pictures of agents killed in action. They want to know everything. But you are thinking that they will not be negotiating. You will. How much should you hold back? They are there to solve crimes and finger the collars of the criminals. You sympathise. The population is not always on their side or ready to confide in them.

John on 8 May had seen the International Red Cross, who have contacts with the guerrilla. But who will go into the jungle with the money and bring back Father? The family had to talk to a top security consulting company. How does one manage this?

'One week gone, and oh what a week it has been,' emailed John to his sister in London.

How the heck do you establish the truth that the victim does not work for a large company, is retired on a pension, had only ever earned a salary, does not have money, and does not have insurance? If they thought that he was a millionaire or that a large company would stump up for him, they were wrong.

The press was going to be a problem. Or could be. A whole heap of publicity, when one is negotiating a ransom, could be fatal. A high profile was the last thing that was wanted. The BBC correspondent was understanding. He had contacts with the guerrilla, as is the annoying way things are. What if the story leaked out to irresponsible journalists? Could the family trust any journalist at all, and manage the story?

'Vic,' said John to his sister in London, 'don't get involved in amateur press relations, please.'

A week later, the problem was evaluating which security advisory firm would be a possible help. The BBC man had heard on the social grapevine that a Brit had been kidnapped. The news could leak out. A famous Tory politician had spoken in Madrid to Marta Lucia Ramirez, the Minister of Foreign Trade of Colombia, who knows me, and he was to have a chance to repeat the news to the President and Foreign Minister of Colombia in Madrid again in the next few days.

The decision to ask the press to shut up and that the press department of the Foreign Office would stonewall, if necessary, was a good one and enabled the family and the committee to get on with the job, without the glare of sentimental and emotional publicity. No one knew where I was.

Nanette and John went to see *Pais Libre* ('Free Country'), the organisation set up by Francisco Santos, of the Santos family who owned the *El Tiempo* newspaper, who had been kidnapped himself. The organisation offers free psychological counselling and sensible advice to families who are often desperate and frightened and don't know how to set about handling the negotiation. Their knowledge is vast. They could be our advisers, but they do not provide negotiators.

'You need a committee of friends to guide the process,' said David Buitrago. He was comforting. 'This is a kidnap all right. You have to wait for the call. As he is a foreigner, expect to wait for a month or more just for the first call. Be prepared. This will be a long process. They will ask for lots of money. They will be prepared to keep him for over a year.'

The best security company in England was asked to help by Jimmy and they said, 'Expect a year or more.'

'We can't tell Nanette', said Jimmy to Bertie in Bogotá. 'She can't be expected to take that.'

Friends told Nanette that there were radio broadcasts of messages to prisoners of the guerrilla, especially a four-hour programme on Saturday nights by Caracol Radio. Victoria heard of this too. Nanette talked to her friends. Would she be too nervous to broadcast? One of her friends said that she would read out a written message on behalf of Nanette. Would I have access to a radio?

A week after the disappearance, Victoria emailed our old friend in Paris. 'I have to tell you that Dad has disappeared a week ago in Colombia. We think it is a kidnap, as the police have found his car on its way to be smuggled into Peru, which is what the FARC often do with cars. We are told that they will feed him and release him, but they will torture the family with long silences and it may take over a year, but he will come out. They will want a lot of money and my mother will probably have to sell her house. Very sorry to give you this bad news, but you should know.'

This was a sanguine estimate of what lay ahead. But the truth is that many kidnap victims die, and those who are released are mentally affected for the rest of their lives. It is a vile and cruel crime.

CHAPTER 7

I move and make my phone call

AFTER A WEEK OF BEING CHAINED UP and in the front line, we moved. I had my towel, a toothbrush and toothpaste, and soap, and my blanket and the small tennis shoes. Nothing else. We marched back along the path and across a grass meadow and into a potato field.

'Don't tread on the potatoes,' a young *guerrillero* said to me. Good farmer's behaviour. On the other side of the field was a wood. On the edge of the wood, stood a man, with a brown leather jacket, open-necked shirt, and leather boots. His hair was blond and short and getting thin in front. I guessed that he was a local farmer. Was he on their side? I entered the wood and stopped. This man was next to me, standing and watching, nervously, silently.

'Hello,' I said.

'Hello,' he answered. I thought again.

'They got you too?' I dropped my voice.

'Yes, this morning,' he affirmed. We looked at each other. He was not one of them. Poor chap. He looked nervous. I felt like an old hand.

The *comandante* passed and peered at us. '*Peligrosas amistades,*' he remarked. 'Dangerous friendships.' What did he mean? I still don't know. He went on to organise the lads to make new *caletas*, a new camp, the first move that I had made. Was this because they fear staying too long in any one camp, in case they are spotted by the Air Force? We were under tall trees. It was early in the day. My companion was called Laureano and he was snatched on his way to the Abastos vegetable market to buy potatoes. He bought potatoes wholesale and delivered them to restaurants in his van. His father had a shop in a poor *barrio* of Bogotá, in the outskirts. We chatted.

'I have a good idea of where we are,' he said. 'I have been around this area buying spuds. This is Sumapaz, and I was brought here through Usme, in the south of Bogotá.'

Sumapaz is a high mountainous area on the Eastern Cordillera of the Andes to the south of Bogotá. You can get into it from Fomeque in the east or Fusagasuga in the west. It is not as high and snowy as Cocuy to the north, but it is higher than anything in the south until you get to Ecuador and it rises to over 4,000 metres. There is a big water reservoir there, Chingaza, close to Bogotá, but no one has been able to go there for some years.

24

After lunch, some people appeared at the entrance to the wood, where we had come from. Squatting on the ground or on logs were two nasty looking girls in black uniforms and a couple of men. They looked at us and talked. One had a radio and made a call. We were asked to come up.

'*Para adentro*,' said one girl. 'Take them inside.' She meant that we were headed for the back lines of the war, not the front line. A pretty girl, called Anita, with uniform and rifle, was told to take us and one *guerrillero*, young, tall, good looking. We set off back over the potatoes, and into a grassy field, with a gate in the corner leading on to an unpaved road of good dark earth. And next to the gate, there was my old Mercedes. Two civilians, nasty young men, were waiting there. We all got into the car, with one of these civilians in the driving seat. The other sat next to me and covered his face with his hands and shirt collar, so I could not see him well. Was he a man that I could bump into when I was free again? Not a *guerrillero*? A petty criminal. The driver could not get the car going and kept stalling it. We got nervous. What a berk!

'Let me drive it,' I called out, after he had stalled it for the tenth time.

'Shut up,' said the punk and showed me a pistol. At last the car moved forward and shot into the road. We lurched up the road, nearly ending in every ditch. A truck full of jute sacks of potatoes came down the road and we had to stop. Labourers hung from the sides and looked at us. They must have been used to living on the guerrilla frontier. The punk sneered, '*Sapos*. Informers.'

My car was getting a terrible beating and I knew that the clutch would not last long. The undercarriage was being bashed by the earth road, which was luckily soft. We got as far as we could, where the road ended at moorland, which stretched up to a mountain. A man was waiting. We got out and started to walk. The ground was covered in *frailejones*, ancient plants with soft silvery leaves and yellow flower spikes, which only grow above the tree line in cold mountains. We were climbing above the tree line into the *paramo* of high moorland. There was some discussion as to whether horses were coming to meet us and take us along. But none came. We walked, up and up. It got cold. It got dark. The moon rose. It got very cold. Anita strode boldly along, with pack and rifle, with the young tall *guerrillero*, better than we could. The man who had been waiting, a friendly middle-aged peasant, was not in uniform.

When we had got high up on the mountain, there was a stop and some conversation. The *guerrillero* wanted to go back. He came to me.

'Let's make a call,' he said, taking out a mobile telephone. Was it mine?

'But I don't have any numbers in my head,' I said.

'I have your notebook,' he said, and pulled it out. Whom should I ring? Should I keep my home number secret? Not possible. But I did not think that there was anyone at home. Nanette had gone abroad. Could I keep my friends out of it? It was after eight o'clock at night, and no one would be in their office. Who would be able to field such a horrible call? I peered at the notebook in the moonlight. I found the home number of my lawyer, a stout friend in thirteen years of corporate in-fights and foreign investment processes.

'We don't like to speak to lawyers,' the young man said. 'We don't want the police involved.'

'No, it is a friend. Anyway it is the night and whom else can I call, eh?'

'Don't you have family?'

'No, I am a foreigner. My family doesn't live here.'

'Can't you ring them abroad?'

'I would not have a clue how to and I don't have their numbers.'

'OK, we shall ring this lawyer.' I gave him the number and he dialled. I could hear the answer.

'Alo. No, I am the maid and los señores have gone out.'

'When will they be back?'

'In an hour or so.'

'Don't ring off,' I hissed. 'Leave a message.' These country boys are hopeless at using the telephone and get nervous.

'OK, I shall ring back,' he said and rang off. What a waste of a call. But the number worked. He kept my notebook. He shook my hand and walked back down the mountain to rejoin his unit. I was to see him again much later.

My emotions were alive and electric. I stood on the cold mountain. The call had gone in because we had a good signal up there in the heights. My old friend would get the message. He would know how to get things moving. Would he forgive me for making him speak to the guerrilla? His life was put at risk. I wrapped the blanket around my shoulders. Laureano had nothing, but he was wearing a leather jacket.

We reached the top of the moorland, and the *guerrilleros* gave a shout. They had heard something. A man came down towards us and we could see a couple of horses. It was too late to mount as the walk was nearly over, so we all marched on and down a path. We could make out a road, and a house. They shouted and a young man came out. A radio transmitter was produced and soon a 4 × 4 Toyota Landcruiser drove up. It stopped and we were offered fizzy drinks and a sandwich, civilian food, then in we climbed and set off on the road. It was unpaved, but wide and newly made by a bulldozer. In fact there were road signs, so it was a government road, to the top of the hill. But where were we? The road went down and we took a left fork and the temperature became pleasantly warm. We swung right and there was a new concrete bridge and, beyond it, the lights of a town. We stopped in front of a tavern. The man who had appeared with the horses turned round and told us not to do anything silly. He had a revolver. 'This town is a guerrilla town,' he said. 'This house belongs to my aunt. Wait in the jeep.'

He called out and the aunt appeared. He embraced her, went in and came back with some bottles of beer and biscuits. What a luxury, a cold beer. The climate was semi-tropical and pleasant, after the cold *paramo*. Bougainvillea vines climbed over the tavern with their purple flowers. I saw a bus station with the names of well-known bus companies. Music came from the town. There is no town in Colombia which does not pulse with music – *vallenatos, rancheros, salsa*. Anita was with us, outside on the street. An old man was sent off towards the town. He came back with a mule and a mare and saddled them.

'Right, mount. We say goodbye now. El gringo can have the mule.' Laureano explained that he did not know how to ride and felt nervous.

'Don't worry, chum. Push down with your toes in the stirrups and hang on to the saddle pommel, if you want. You won't fall off,' I encouraged him.

Easy for me to say. I liked riding. The old man led my mule, with Anita striding along. The aunt from the tavern led the mare. We crossed a wobbly suspension bridge and started up a rocky track. The moon had risen late. Normally this would have been a good adventure, and I enjoyed the scrambling of the mule up the rocks. The old man let me hold the reins and go free. Anita had the rifle over her shoulder to pot me, if I did anything silly. Laureano was cursing and finally was allowed to get off and walk. We entered a grassy field and there was an unfinished wooden hut in the distance. The old man walked over and shouted. A voice answered after a while and a conversation followed, which made it plain that the owner did not want a gringo in his house.

'He is not a gringo,' the old man said, but it was not the time of day for a geography quiz. The door was not opened. European, Chinese or African, it was the same to him. I could go to hell. The night was getting cold. We had gone far up the mountain. In another field was an even more unfinished hut, with a tin roof and no windows. We went in. There was a bare concrete floor. Food? 'No food. Get down and sleep.' Anita had a regulation pack and pulled out a sleeping bag. Laureano and I lay on the concrete.

'Take off your boots and share the blanket.' So we huddled up, back to back, to get some body heat. Christ, the floor was hard and cold.

In the morning, I saw that other *guerrilleros*, in uniform, had joined us in the night. I poked my nose out of the doorway .

'Get back in. You might be seen.'

'I want to pee.'

'Right, do it here, next to the wall.'

We were surrounded by fields of thick lush green grass. It was cattle country. The guerrilla made coffee and a soup of potatoes, then we set off uphill. The mare and mule and the old man had gone. It was Shanks's pony now, a hard walk uphill. We passed some gardens, where the rich earth had been dug and turned. They were planted with potatoes, blackberries (*moras*), and beans. Two men came out of a hut, but paid us no attention. Up and up we went. A path started, stony and wet, and we entered a wood. The cloud came moving up the hill and we lost the view. It rained gently. We sweated and my legs ached. Finally we came out of the wood and round a corner. Ahead, the hill went on up, but it was bare and rocky. More climbing. There was a noise and a mule appeared, coming down. Then another and another.

'Get out of the way,' one of the *guerrilleros* warned. Indeed, the unstoppable force of loaded mules crashing over the rocks was a danger. On the back of one was a sunburned young man, with a gap-toothed grin and a loud shout. '*Arre, mula, arre!*' They had bags of food, rice or whatever, on their backs, a heavy weight. This was our first sight of the mule trains that supply the guerrilla, along the spine of the Andes. No roads, just mules, and the muleteers.

I remembered the poem:

Do you remember an inn, Miranda, do you remember an inn?
The cheers and the jeers of the young muleteers,
    and the wine that tasted of tar
Do you remember an inn, Miranda, do you remember an inn?
The fleas that tease in the high Pyrenees,
    and the wine that tasted of tar

Well, that was Spain in the old days. Here were the children of Spain, the *criollos*, the *americanos*, the Andes.

About twenty mules crashed past. On we climbed. The sun came out and we had a splendid view of the hillsides. We could rest from time to time but they liked to keep going. I think I am fit, but, nearly sixty years old, I was not as fit as they were. In the afternoon we arrived at a hut, with a very muddy corral in front, and some mules up to their hocks in mud. We sat on the step of the hut and were given lumps of *panela*, the sugar loaf of Colombia – cakes of brown, unrefined sugar, from the press or *trapiche*, hard and dry, easy to keep and transport. It gives you sugar energy quickly, if you are on the march, and you can boil it up with any dirty water and have *agua panela*, hot sugary water. *Guerrilleros* and muleteers milled around. Then we were made to get up and walk up the hill some more, to a camp. It was hard, as my calf muscles had done enough already and were getting stiff. The camp was one tent, then others, and in front of one, some *comandantes*, senior men, who smiled at us. We stopped. A very young Indian girl, with a brown Chinese face and a long black plait, came with a canteen of *mora* (bramble)-coloured cold water. I drank it all thirstily. This is 'prepared water', cold water with sugar and fruit flavour mixed in it. The flavour comes in paper sachets, usually 'Royal' brand, which are easy to carry. I asked the senior man whether I could have some clothes. I was in the same clothes as ten days before. They were muddy and the trousers were all wet and the shirt collar filthy.

'We don't have spare clothes. Anyway you will be marching tomorrow and the clothes will dry on you. You don't want to stay here. It is dangerous.'

We were in the front line still. They were the target of the bombs that I had heard. And if the Army advanced in force, they would have to fight and run. They were all in uniform and armed with rifles. We were taken to a tent for the night. It was open all around and cold, but a girl brought us sleeping bags. These were light and thin, but warm and big enough. They had the Nike brand mark on them. I had my blanket, but Laureano had nothing else, apart from his leather jacket. This was a fighting camp so we had a *sentinela* standing looking at us, and *guardias* walking around the perimeter. We asked what happened if the Army attacked. The *sentinela* was very young, maybe 15 years old, and did not speak much to us. Military discipline. He said that the *guardias* fire at the Army and raise the alarm, for the whole guerrilla to fight, but the *sentinela* was responsible just for the prisoners. We would be led away. Or shot? Supper of rice and beans came, night fell and we slept, in the cold night.

Before dawn, the dangerous hour in battle, came coffee. The camp was awake in the dark. All was clear. We had breakfast of soup and biscuits and were taken down to the corral. They wanted us gone. It was dangerous and they were at war. We could keep the sleeping bags, and we were given a sack to put them in. At the corral, there was Anita, and with her a different type of man, an *arriero* or muleteer, older, large, with a big belly, and a leather hat. He had a big smile and a brown, wrinkled face, as brown and wrinkled as his hat. He mounted us on a mule each, but without reins, and set off with another *guerrillero*, leading each mule on a lead rein, called a *cabestre*. Anita marched. Off we went, up the hillside and along the hilltops. We climbed high, with huge views of endless mountains. There were no valleys, nor rivers, nor woods, just great bare mountainsides and then lakes in the folds of the peaks. It began to rain. We were given capes, called *carpas*, of shiny black plastic, with hoods. I had no hat. The mules plodded on at the pace of the men who walked with us. The visibility shortened.

The Andes mountains are the rain maker of the Amazon/Orinoco rain forest, the greatest of the world. The Amazon is the greatest river of the world, measured by the volume of water that flows through its mouth into the Atlantic. The rain is precipitated by the mountain wall. When it rains, the big rivers rise by eight to twelve metres. They flood the *varzea* forest, of which part remains dry forest and part becomes flooded forest – as the Brazilians say, *igarapés* and *igapos*. In the mountains the rain soaks the ground and runs off in streams and then into the rivers of the foothills, or *pie de monte*. But in the high mountain, the water lies around in bogs. This is tremendously important for humans, who live on the sides and below the cold mountain. These bogs hold and leak water, so that the streams flow all year. These bogs must not be drained, nor can cattle be allowed to tread on the spongy mosses, otherwise the water will flow off when it rains, destroy the hillsides and run out in the dry season.

We had to march across these spongy bogs of grassy tussocks, separated by pools. This was slow and tricky. When we walked, we had to leap from tussock to tussock, or step, up to our waist, into the muddy water. At the start we had mules. Mules have a legendary ability to 'smell' water. They lower their head and sniff and avoid deep water and step on the tussocks. Horses do not. On we went in the rain. The visibility was limited. We got to a place where, on the right, there was a pond, with green duckweed at the edges and, on the left, the remains of a camp – poles and rotten grass beds – of the guerrilla, used in the summer dry season. In the dry season, the guerrilla marches and camps up near the mountain peaks, but the Army also moves up to attack them. We went through the middle, and suddenly my mule sank up to its belly.

'Get off quick and run,' shouted the muleteer. The mule in such a situation heaves and kicks and flails to get out. You do not want to be kicked. I jumped off and rolled along the top of the bog and got clear. The mule got out by itself in a series of heaves and sucking noises. We stopped for lunch of cold rice and a chew of *panela*. I mounted and we went on. Two large lakes appeared. A discussion started and the muleteer decided to go right around them, a longer but more gradual route. It rained non-stop and we were inside the rain cloud above the tree line. There were rocks and low shrubs and *frailejones*. We were wet and cold and miserable, but at least we – the two prisoners – were mounted. The older man and Anita walked. My God, they were good walkers!

Now the track started to squeeze between big rocks and open out again. Between the rocks, one had to take one's feet out of the stirrups and put them on the back of the mule, to avoid nasty knocks to one's ankles. Mules plunge and climb and drop down hard, regardless of their passengers. One's ankles and shins get smashed on the rocks. Not that this was a dressage contest. There was no fancy riding. The secret was to hang on the tail strap, the one that goes from the saddle and under the tail. It stops you shooting over the animal's head when it plunges down and, when you go up over the rocks, you bend your knees and put your stirrups back, lean over the neck of the animal, and push down with your arm. This is riding without reins. We could not use the reins, as then we could gallop away. Ha, in theory!

But then we arrived at a narrow path, where I begged to be let off to walk. If I was out of the stirrups on a jerking mule, between rocks, I imagined falling and bashing my skull. So I was allowed to walk, once, twice. Then the third time, one of them held the mule's head and told me to dismount on the higher side of the slope. There was a rock, on to which I could step. My cape hid my feet and the rain was falling. I stepped on to the rock with my left leg and put the right foot down. It did not land on rock. There was nothing underneath. I fell slowly under the neck of the mule and rolled down the hill. I got up and looked. Oh hell, my left wrist was bent like the S bend of a water closet. It did not hurt, but it started to swell up. It had no strength. I looked at it. Was it broken? If it was, would the guerrilla shoot me like a steeplechaser that falls at Becher's Brook, in the English Grand National horse race? They could not mend it, could they? Was it going to hurt?

What a start to my captivity! Reduced to one arm.

CHAPTER 8

Into the hills and the cheese farm

I STOOD BY THE MULE, in the rainy mountain, and wondered what to do with my bent wrist. The muleteer looked at it. I took out a handkerchief and tied it round the wrist, and put the arm into my jacket, as a kind of sling. We walked past the narrow passage through the rocks and then he helped me back on the mule and off we went.

The muleteer's name was 'Ramirez', a surname. Being an older man, this was a mark of respect. We chatted. He said that the FARC believed in equality and was against the oligarchy and the government of the rich. They did not harm ordinary people. His father had been one of the original 1960s Marquetalia peasant rebels, and as a child he himself had marched to the Macarena, and grown up there.

Why did they kidnap? He said that not everyone was in agreement with kidnapping, but that was the decision of Tirofijo and the *Secretariado* – the Staff of the FARC. The war needs money. What about drugs? That was not a good thing, he thought. They were not originally a narcotics movement. I said that El Negro Acacio, in the Guaviare jungle province, must be the richest *guerrillero*. He looked uncomfortable and mumbled something about some *Frentes* being different from others. Here in the Sumapaz, the *Frentes* had nothing to do with drugs. They did not have much money and were fighting for their 'convictions', against the State.

In fact, the decision to grow the FARC and engage in direct warfare against the State, the police and the Army had been taken as late as 1990. The FARC had grown to something like 35,000 (probably overstated) men and girls in sixty-eight fronts and had abandoned having a recognised political party and fighting general elections. They had so many enemies and quarrels about drugs and money that their candidates were often killed. Nor did they have many votes. The road to power was to be by military force. So their logistical problems and need for money had ballooned.

'Why am I kidnapped?' I asked. 'I am a foreigner, living and working and employing people in Colombia. What good does it do to hurt people like me?'

'I am not in favour of this,' he admitted. 'I hope you will be home soon.'

Laureano carried on about himself. He was not an oligarch or rich. Ramirez, on his own, on a bare mountain, was frank and even sympathetic. He seemed to be a descendant of a purer peasant rebellion. But he was not running the modern FARC diversified business.

He was taking us somewhere. We started to descend the mountain, past big outcrops and down slopes. Then we had to dismount as the path went through narrow rock openings. We walked for a couple of hours down the narrow path, with water trickling along it. Trees appeared. At the bottom, we crossed a stream, and there was a farmhouse. It was set in a beautiful valley, surrounded by the high mountains that we had been in for three days. The stream came from the lakes that we had skirted. It was clear and cold and shallow and fast, here at the top of the valley. We walked across a grassy field and into a yard, where the mules and horses were stabled. They were unsaddled. My few possessions had been packed that morning into a hessian sack and carried behind the saddle of my mule. That was unloaded. We were let into the main room of the farm, a big kitchen, with a wood-burning stove. My God, were we wet and dirty and cold?

The 'owner' of this remote farm was an apple-cheeked young woman, with a small baby in a hammock. Her husband was away. There was a farmhand, a gap-toothed older man with a dirty cap. She made water with sugar and fruit powder, the guerrilla drink. We sat by the fire and steamed. There was no one else there. Anita went to set herself up in an outbuilding. The fire had a top with hotplates to cook on and a stone ledge, higher than the top, on which we could sit, boots off, socks steaming, and put our feet on the stove top, like a Russian stove. Ramirez was a welcome guest and in great humour. Laureano was given the only bed, with a mattress. For me they threw potato sacks and a sheep skin on the floor. We had hot potato soup and chunks of cheese, plain, fresh and almost tasteless. This was what the farmer's wife did, make cheeses.

My wrist had swelled up. They looked at it. She said that she could give it a *sobado*, a manipulation. I accepted and she squeezed away at it, trying to get the bones back in their sockets. It could not do much harm. I asked for permission to get my toothbrush and towel out of the sack outside and went out and undid the top and brought them back. Ramirez and the woman chatted away. I slept well enough. In the morning, I went out. A large boar was routing around in the stable. He raised his head and froth bubbled from his mouth, like a mad dog. He trotted off and I saw that he had tipped out my sack. The rotter, it was my soap that he had eaten. Ramirez came out and chided me for not closing the sack. Right! One up to the pig. This pig was going to cross my path again, always with disastrous results. What a boar!

'Come on,' called Ramirez, after our soup and cheese. 'We have a long day.'

'Oh dear, how long?'

'Not so long, really. Just up that hill.' He pointed behind the farm, the other side of the valley, from where we had descended. It was too steep for the mules, which were led. We climbed, stopping when our legs ached. At the top, we saw that it was a false top, and there was another ridge. Up that, there was another false top and another ridge to climb. But we could get on the mules for a while.

We looked back and on the other side of the farm valley was a lake, with a precipitous mountainside reflected in its waters. The stream ran down the valley and joined another that was born in the lake. The weather improved and it became sunny. We got to the crown of the pass between two hilltops, the *corona*.

'*Coronamos*,' said Ramirez, with satisfaction. 'Get off the mules, it is too steep here.'

The wind whistled over the pass. We lay down and chewed *panela*. This was high, over 3,500 metres, perhaps. It looked as if the streams flowed east. This was the water that gives birth to the Orinoco River, which flows into the Caribbean, through Venezuela. Ahead of us was another valley, with another river, flowing to the east. So we were walking north-eastwards? It had taken us at least three hours to climb up. I looked at my watch, which had not been stolen, but it had stopped. I turned it over. The back had gone and the works were open to the mud. It must have happened when I fell and bashed my arm, the day before. I started to tell the time by looking at the sun, as people had done since time immemorial, even in Switzerland. The way down was long, and I was tiring faster than the younger Laureano. It was a steep scramble, so that the mules had to go round a longer route, and we had to walk – across a bog, over some huge rocks, along a horizontal path across a steep slope, through some scrub, over a stream by jumping, across a wet field, another stream and we were at the valley bottom. We turned left before the river and went over a long bog and up a hill. I was last. I saw a hut and a corral outside it and some *guerrilleros*. Under a barbed wire fence and I had arrived, dog tired and filthy. A tall Indian-looking *comandante* greeted me.

'You are the gringo?' I nodded. Why argue about a word? I sat down. A girl came out with a sugar-water pan and I drank.

'Come in to the hut,' this man said, and, when I went in, there was a senior *comandante* sitting on a tree stump. He beckoned me to another stump. He was moustached, in his thirties, and wore a beret and full uniform.

'*Bienvenido a la revolucion armada*. Welcome to the armed revolution. *Como le gusta*? How do you like it?'

It was not easy to find an answer. Later I was told that he had come here from his camp especially to meet me. He took out a notebook and started to write down my details.

'Name?'

'Atchy, oo, tay, say, atchy . . . HUTCH . . .'

'*Momento*. AH . . .'

'No Atchay, ooo, . . .

'*Jota*? . . .'

This went on for a bit. 'Look, I'll write it.'

'I can write,' he bridled. Well, I was not in a hurry. Before nightfall, we had written down the name and address and telephone numbers. This was not a literate man.

'You have children?'

Er, watch it. Er. One has to think fast. 'No, I don't,' I decided to say.

'You have a wife?'

'Yes, but she is not in Colombia.'

'Family in Colombia?' he questioned.

'No. I am a foreigner and my family is abroad.'

'Is there someone we can speak to?'

'I suppose so. Or my embassy.'

'No, we don't speak to embassies,' he said firmly. And then more fiercely, ' I hope for your sake that no one has spoken to the police?'

'What do I know? I am here.'

'Well, how much are you going to pay us?' He had changed the subject to the one that interested him.

'I am a retired old buffer. I have a small farm and a second-hand car.'

'You have a home in Bogotá?'

'I rent a small flat.'

'So how much?'

'Er, the car, so much . . . (I mentioned a figure in pesos of about eight thousand dollars). No one wants to buy a farm, because of the insecurity. There seem to be people who go round the country killing and kidnapping. Eh? So a farm is worthless. But I reckon that I could . . .' my mind was racing about in every direction, 'raise about er, er, one hundred and fifty million pesos. It would take time, and I can't promise it. I am here. My family is not in the country.' I babbled on.

He laughed a hearty laugh, indicating that I was a proper caution. 'We know all about you. We do our work before detaining people like you. You have four houses in Bogotá and that is worth four billion pesos. You pay us two billion, OK?'

'Not really possible, *comandante*. That is all untrue. I told you what I have.'

'You will have to be our guest for a long time, then.'

He laughed like Pancho Villa or the Mexican bandido in *Treasure of Sierra Madre*, by John Huston, starring Humphrey Bogart. His moustache bristled. He was enjoying himself. The peasant chief had the gringo in his power. My negotiating skills, honed by snoozing through management courses at business schools, were of little avail. I knew that I was not going to negotiate, that I myself should not negotiate. It was the family outside who would have to do that. Did it matter what I said? What had he said? His information was wrong. Good. He did not know anything about me, not even my name. Better. He was just filling in the hotel guest register? Not so good. But he was the most senior *guerrillero* that I had seen. Who was he? Was he one of the faces on the WANTED poster in the US Department of Justice office? Was this Romaña? Or Flaminio? Or Oscar Cancharina? I did not know all those names yet, but they were whispered in the bivouacs of prisoners in the mountains.

'What *frente* am I the prisoner of?' I asked him.

He did not proffer an answer. '*El Frente Oriental* of the FARC; that is all you need to know,' he warned. The *Frente Oriental* (Eastern Front) is a large army composed of many smaller *frentes*, 51, 53, 55 being infamous.

He did not want to see Laureano. He was waiting for me. The interview was over. The process for ransom had started, I supposed. It was 12 May. I left the hut. I needed a change of clothes and a bath. Twelve days in the same clothes, without a bath! Even for an Englishman brought up in a boarding school, that was too much. A stream ran down behind the hut. The *comandante* with the Indian eyes told me to take off my clothes and a *guerrillero* would wash them. I could have new clothes. Socks, underpants, a khaki shirt, a track suit bottom. I did not want my woollen sweater washed, as it would be ruined. We were taken to the stream and we washed in the freezing running water. I had the green towel from the first camp. I washed my hair. It was cold, but it was good to be clean again and to get into clean, if old and used, clothes, leaving the washed clothes hanging on a barbed wire fence to dry. In the hut, there was a wood fire, on which were placed blackened pots, for cooking water, rice, soup. I began to distinguish the *guerrilleros*, girls and boys. The Pancho Villa man had gone. Ramirez had left with his mules. Anita walked across the stream and up the hill in front. She was off to a training course in a big camp. I warmed my toes at the fire.

Prisoners on the march have no time to think of anything but the hard physical slog. Then you arrive and have to eat and sleep. Perhaps you can wash? That is all I had done, walk and sleep on the ground and get up and get my legs moving again and keep going. I was as overweight and unfit as any nearly 60-year-old desk worker. I had been called up in a war in which I had no interest and no reason to participate. But when you are called to meet one of the *comandantes* and they talk of 'your money or your life', you know you are in danger and in the presence of killers. War is said to be 99 per cent boredom and 1 per cent sheer panic. I could understand it.

After a while it was time to move from the hut. A boy led us over a swamp and towards some trees. We turned a corner and saw some *caletas* – bamboo beds on poles with plastic sheets for roofs. On the edge of the bed in the top *caleta* sat four bearded men in uniforms, one old man with a white beard, one short man with a dense black bristly beard, like Captain Haddock of the Tintin books, one tall man with a black beard, and a young man with a camouflage cap, a wispy moustache and slitty eyes, who looked Vietnamese. They looked intelligent. There was a silence.

'So these are the leaders of the FARC,' I thought. 'A serious bunch of rebels!' My heart fell and I felt fear at being in front of hardened criminals.

PART 2

Sumapaz

CHAPTER 9

Day 12: the first camp

THERE WAS A SILENCE, a lot of looks and the tallest of the bearded men stepped down and introduced himself. 'I am Roberto. This is Epimaco.' He pointed at the stocky man with a thick black beard. 'This is Grandpa.'

'I am Fredy,' said the youngest one, with the slit eyes and the Cuban cap.

'Daveed and Laureano,' we replied.

'We saw you coming earlier. Come and sit here,' Roberto pointed at the top *caleta*. It had a good edge to the bed, which was raised, and a view down the slope. There was a patio in the middle, and trees around it all. It was the edge of the forest crown, round a high hill behind, bare at the top.

So these were fellow captives. Our nerves calmed down. I felt like laughing. How had I really seen them as guerrilla chiefs? We were among friends.

'How long have you been here?'

'Three months, Fredy two and a half, Grandpa less than two months.' Grandpa was eighty years old, with white hair, beard and moustache. He shared the top *caleta* with Epimaco, who was short, strong and calm. Roberto had a single *caleta*, next down. It was wrapped around by black plastic sheeting, and snug. Next was Fredy in a single *caleta*, also wrapped around with plastic. Everyone's hair was long and bushy and they all had beards and moustaches. Well, I had twelve days of hair. We would all end up as scruffy tramps.

A *guerrillero* came walking up, middle-aged, thin, with light-brown hair and a cheeky smile. This was 'Hanibal'. He had a camouflage tent roof with him. He looked around and decided to put it up at the bottom, slinging it between two trees and tying the ends to the trees with bits of twine. This is a process known in guerrilla Spanish as *guindando*, a country word that few Colombians have ever heard before. He put a square of black plastic sheet on the ground.

'Do you have sleeping bags?' he asked.

'Yes.'

'Right, bung them on the plastic. You sleep here tonight, and we'll see what we do tomorrow.'

Another night on the ground. But the old hands had been given raised beds, made of vertical poles and horizontal bamboos lashed to them by lianas. I could see that the guerrilla used no nails nor screws nor wire nor twine. The only tool was a machete. Everything was built of poles and bamboo and lianas – very rustic and primeval.

The camp looked down across a river valley and across at a steep hillside. The river ran east and joined another stream and disappeared north-east. Clouds rolled up the valley, moving fast. A path, up which we had come, led back to the hut where we had arrived. On the way was a lot of boggy land.

'We came here a few days ago from another camp, just there along the hillside. It got so muddy that we sank up to our ankles right outside the *caletas*. Dreadful. It rains all the time. We'll show you the *chontos*.'

'The what?'

The *chontos* are the latrines. Hygiene about excrement is important and enforced by the *comandantes*. We marched across the hillside a certain distance with Fredy and gazed at a long slit trench. The hillside was thick with *frailejon* plants with their silver, silky leaves.

'And these are the toilet paper. We ran out of bog paper ages ago.'

'Oh yes?'

'When you want to go, ask the guard if you can go to the *chontos*, eh?'

When we walked back to the *caletas*, there was the *comandante* on a visit. His name was Pedro. He looked at the *caleta* and us and smiled and asked if we were all right. The older inhabitants joshed him and were friendly, but one could detect wariness. Grandpa started to complain that he was all bruised and could not stand up well. He had fallen off his horse several times and was hurt.

'You have to walk out of here, Grandpa,' warned Pedro. 'Just get better.'

'Lend us the chess set,' asked Fredy.

'OK.'

He went off. The *caletas* of the guerrilla were very close, down the path, inside the trees. We could hear the camp radio set, when it was transmitting. I learned that this was a time of utter silence for us, with our ears straining to pick up some words. The nearness also meant that we had to keep our voices down, if not whisper, and have a look out. If a *guerrillero* approached, whoever saw him had to cough or whistle.

At about half past four, a figure staggered up from the hut, carrying a blackened pot. From the hut rose a wisp of woodsmoke. Ten minutes later round the corner came a girl bringing us supper while it was still daylight. We were introduced to the culinary delight called *arroz guerrillero*. This is boiled rice mixed with little bits of brown pasta. It has no taste at all. It was accompanied by a damper – a pancake of wheat flour – called a *cancharina*. To drink there was hot chocolate, which came later. My chocolate had a dead mosquito floating on the surface. I remarked in a jovial way about the drowned guest.

'You should complain,' joked Roberto.' You should insist on at least four. You need the protein.'

The young woman was 'La Cancharina' by nickname – 'Pancake', a friendly girl of some sixteen years. She worked hard and well and was not dirty. Laureano and I had not come furnished with anything to eat out of, so we were issued with a saucepan each and a spoon. This pan and this spoon become closer to one than one's mother. Guard them with your life. Carry the pan with you on the march. Wash it yourself. Don't lose the spoon. Remember where it is at all hours of the night, let alone the day.

After supper, we took the pans to the washing place, in this case a little stream running out of the trees. It has to be downstream of the cooking place, where the water is used for cooking and drinking. We took our toothbrushes and brushed our teeth, ready for bed. Night was coming and in the tropics it falls between 6.15 and 6.30, fast. It gets cold. The sentry changed on the hour, and maybe the senior *guerrilleros* came to have a look and a chat. Pedro liked to do that.

Who were the rebels here? There was Pedro, and there was Hanibal, the oldest. There was Hernan, a solid, strong, quiet young man. There were two, almost identical, repellent teenagers, Juan Carlos and Vladimir. There was Ismael, a very simple-minded, very strong 16-year-old, who understood little and laughed loudly. And there were the girls: Pedro's 'wife', Janeth, the Witch (*la bruja*), a good-looking woman with long dark hair and an unpleasant hectoring manner. Then Pancake, the pleasant 16-year-old and a sullen, illiterate, black waif, La Negra. There were nine *guerrilleros*, all fit. Nine is below strength for an *escuadra* – a squad – which should be twelve, but this was a *comision*, or special squad, just to look after us. We were in the back lines, with the fighting forces around us.

The first night I was on the ground, under the single tent roof, with Laureano. After dark, we fell asleep, tired after the hard walk. It started to rain. I felt something touch my nose. I put my hand up and touched the roof, which was the thing that was touching my nose. The roof had been badly strung up and had collected water, lots of it. I pushed and it cascaded off. It filled again. I pushed. It cascaded. I pushed . . . you get the idea? It rained non-stop. Sleep was not possible. The morning slithered in over the hills, from the east, as it usually does. Juan Carlos came up with a wake-up grunt and gave us coffee, from a pot, already cooling fast after the climb from the hut. He was coughing up his lungs, disgustingly, as he poured the coffee. When he came with the breakfast of potato soup, he coughed over the pot. A stream of microbes was transferred to the watery soup.

'Oh Christ, please cough away from the soup,' exclaimed Roberto, disgusted.

We all went to the *chontos* and brushed our teeth. The ground was sodden. I was pooped. Fredy kindly offered me his bed and I leaned back and awoke two hours later.

We got to know each other. I was the only foreigner. Roberto and Epimaco seemed to think that they were on the way out soon. They had been in for over two months. Fredy was more desperate. Grandpa had come in with Fredy. They had met somewhere up in the hills, at the *casa de tablas* – the plank hut. There

Fredy had found the abandoned black plastic sheets, which he had stuffed into the cracks of this well-known hut, to stop the cold wind. He had brought them with him and they were used around the *caletas* here. We spoke in whispers, and before going to bed, there was a custom of a 'prayer meeting', heads together like a football squad and a morale boosting talk. How to cope with fear? Roberto and Epimaco were small businessmen in the building trades. Fredy was a young scamp. He had a small Sony radio, AM/SW. It had been handed down from other victims and was in a terrible state. To turn the dial, one had to insert an old doorkey and twiddle. It was impossible to get batteries, so it was reserved for a once a week Saturday night kidnap victims broadcast, in the hope of hearing family messages, while the batteries lasted. An aerial of wire ran from his tent along a branch.

Playing chess was to be the only pastime, if Pedro lent the chess set. I could play with Roberto, an educated man, or Fredy. I learned that the FARC was a strict, if not puritanical, organisation. The only game allowed was chess, because Tirofijo believed that it developed thinking ability. No cards, no drinking of alcohol and no drugs were allowed at all. Cigarettes, yes. Did the *guerrilleros* play chess? Yes. The big challenge was to play Pedro, a good and dangerous player. I had only played chess as a boy, to learn it, but never since. I could move the pieces, but did the king go on its own colour or the queen? How did one castle? I knew no opening moves. So by trial and error, I restarted.

Roberto joked that, when he went home, he would open a restaurant called La Caleta. Customers would have to sit on the floor in the dark and be given a candle and a spoon. The menu would be rice and beans, with *agua-panela*. All profits wold be given to the families of kidnapped people. How could ordinary Colombians understand what was happening to us?

We could move around a little, in the bushes above the *caletas*, without annoying the sentries. Was there any confidence between the captors and the prisoners? It was out of the question to escape over the huge hillsides, with their open spaces. Where were we? We could tell where the sun rose and set. We looked north. A few aeroplanes flew over, to the north, on west/east/west trajectories. They must have been Bogotá to Villavicencio routes. Villavicencio, or 'Villavo' is the largest town in the llanos, or plains, to the east of the Andes. You drive from Bogotá down the mountainside and you round a corner after a couple of hours and see the town under you and an immense flat hot 'savannah' plain stretching far into the east. This is the llanos. The rivers flow down to the east, to the Amazon/Orinoco rain forests and to Venezuela or Brazil in the south. Almost nobody lives out there in the distance. There are no major air traffic routes. When the *guerrilleros* brought their AM/FM radios to accompany them on their sentry duties, the music they picked up was *llanera*, harp and guitar music from the llanos, the cowboys of the plains, *Joropos* songs. We looked north-west and sighed, 'That is the way home?'

There were cattle being farmed up here and the young curious bullocks would wander into our camp, especially in the evening. They were a nuisance and would blunder into the guy-ropes and pull down the *caleta* roofs. Fredy was the most active in chasing them off and hurling stones at them. We usually woke in the dark to hear a snuffling noise as a bullock thrust its muzzle into our space, looking for clumps of grass.

Four days after my arrival, we were sitting on rocks, in a moment of sunshine, when a figure came into sight, down the hill and into the hut. After a time, he was led up the path to us. He wore a white woollen poncho or *ruana*, over a shirt. He was stocky, and strong, with a bull neck. He looked rough. He came in to the patio and greeted us curtly with a *paisa* accent from Medellin. He was unfriendly, a loner, and went to sit on a rock and gaze over the river.

'That is a dangerous man – *peligroso*,' murmured Roberto. He went on, 'You are *ingles* and used to telling the truth. Let me warn you. Here it is the reverse. Never tell the truth. We and they live with lies. Shut up and don't talk. It is dangerous. You don't want them to know that you have been abroad, or play golf, or live in a house, or what your job is. Don't tell them and don't even trust any of us. Get it?

'What can I do for you when I get out?' he continued.

'Er, tell my people. I can't give you a telephone number because we have no pen and you won't remember it. Why don't you just contact my embassy and they will know about me.'

In fact, Roberto and Epimaco were right about their own negotiations. The same day, they were called to the hut below and came back with smiles. They gave us their blankets, clothes, a comb, toothpaste. Roberto gave me an elastic bandage, which was perfect for my wrist and which I wore from then on. Thank you! And one walked up the hill in front, north, and the other went right and back on the trail that I had taken to arrive.

Was that a good sign? The turnover was two to three months? But they were Colombians and not famous or rich. We were near Bogotá. It was easy to get out? Was it?

So Pedro let me have Roberto's single *caleta* and the newcomer moved in to share with Laureano, where I had been. Grandpa was on his own. We were five of us now. The next day Laureano whispered to me that he had quarrelled with the newcomer, who was very rough. But the day after, Laureano himself was sent away, on a mare, which he did not enjoy. Up the hill he went. Was he going home? He looked happy. So quickly? Odd.

We were four. The two best chaps had gone, which was a pity but wonderful for the morale. The kidnap business was working. When would I go home?

CHAPTER 10

The story of Pedro

THE *comandante* of the *comision* at the first camp, behind the front line, was Pedro, a tall, fit Indian-looking man, with slanting eyes, straight black hair and brown skin, a man of few words, as the Indians are. He seemed born to the country life but in fact he had been born in La Mesa, a little coffee town, in the hills above the Magdalena river, very near Bogotá. So he said. Then he had been moved when very young and brought up in the llanos. He was a *mestizo*, indigenous with Spanish mixed blood. Colombia is a country of *mestizo* people and there is a smaller proportion of pure blood indians than in Ecuador, Bolivia, Peru. As a child Pedro had learned to ride and to herd cattle. He explained how to choose a horse. You have to ride in bare feet with your big toe in a rawhide loop as a stirrup. And you have to mount, when the horse is in movement. You want a horse that is fast and sure on its feet to race across the llano and head off the cattle.

Pedro had worked on five cattle *fincas* and ended as the *capataz*, or boss, of the cowboys, when he was scarcely twenty. He was happy with the last farmer, Don Roberto, who was a good boss. He owned the land and the cattle. When they had cattle to sell in the *feria*, or fair, of the local town, they loaded the animals into trucks and followed in a pick-up, with cases of beer. Don Roberto drank with them. They stayed late and danced to the *llanero* bands, of harp and guitar and accordeon.

Pedro was picked up in Villavicencio by the Army one day and taken to the barracks. A major said, 'You are a *guerrillero*. I know it.' He was kept in a tiny cell, with no water, so that he had to drink his own urine. After five days, the major let him out. 'We can't find anything against you. But I know. Bugger off and don't let me see you again.' Pedro had heard the major saying that he was going to a local town to see his family that weekend, by bus. He made a plot. He got on the bus and waited. The major appeared. Pedro shot him five times with a pistol, jumped off the bus and got on the pillion of a motorcycle which was waiting for him.

How had he got to that moment in his life? He did not explain. Obviously he had the contacts already. He went into the guerrilla. We found out later that he had been captured and sentenced and had been released in the last big exchange of prisoners. He was working his way up again in the *Frente Oriental*, and had landed this duty with prisoners.

44

He played an excellent game of chess, and you had to be careful as he advanced his knights and bishops. Counter-attack up the middle to get behind him and see if you could be ahead of him by one move was the way to hold him back. He would have sneaked a knight and a bishop up one side, and his queen roved around early in the game.

'Pedro, I have broken the zip of my sleeping bag,' I said. It was cold in these hills and the sleeping bag was our protection. It takes time to get used to sleeping in a bag and not thrashing about and breaking the zip.

'Give it to me,' he said. 'I can fix it.' And he cut the thread, opened the bottom end, rezipped the zip and sewed it up. He also gave me batteries for the radio and took it away and mended the dialling knob, so we did not have to use the old key. A practical man.

There were cattle roaming on the hillside. The hut belonged to some men and these were their cattle behind the guerrilla lines. The men came to look at their stock and we saw them in the distance. Pedro negotiated the purchase of a bullock and it was killed and he did the butchering. We ate meat.

Was it his Indian blood, his *mestizo* status in society that had led him here? Was it a problem with the law? Was it poverty? Surely not an intellectual curiosity?

'When will there be peace?' I asked him.

'When we march up the main street of Bogotá,' he replied.

People always ask whether the FARC 'has a political programme' and there are many who say that they are just brigands or narcoterrorists. They are certainly one of the most difficult groups in the world to negotiate with. 'They never agree to anything,' complained my neighbour, a professor of politics, whom I see when I take my dog for a walk.

But I do have in my study a copy of the famous photograph of the Cuban rebels, Castro, Dorticos, 'Che' Guevara, walking up the main street of La Habana. They had won power by the gun, and never permitted a free election ever since. Would the oligarchy, or even the lower middle classes, of Colombia run away and let the FARC march up the main street of Bogotá, La Septima, and take over the country? Not likely! But the idea beguiled Pedro. Would the FARC not have to defeat the whole Colombian Army first? Aye, there's the rub!

But where did all this start? Whence did it come, this violence, so that we, foreigner and Colombian, ended up as prisoners of other Colombians, rather than having an argument in the pub, or supporting different football teams? This is not how life is in other countries, is it? Half the kidnaps in the world happen in Colombia. Is the country socially divided or do the criminals just get away with it? Are the police and the law courts ineffective or corrupt or both? Was Pedro going to get away with it? Would we all die?

Who best to tell me but my Colombian friends? They had seen it, perhaps not from the start. The start was a long way back, oh yes.

★ ★ ★

I asked them once when I was in the free world. We had taken our orchids to a show in the city of Pereira. If you want to know Colombia, travel by road down into the valley of the Magdalena river and up into the Cordillera Central, over the mountain pass of La Linea, and into the Cauca Valley, which is the most fertile, warm, well-watered land in the world, in the best coffee-growing country in the world and one of the only areas where sugar cane grows all year round, not in seasons. The *guayacan* tree blooms yellow along the road sides. All the land is cultivated, growing coffee, avocados, asparagus, bananas, oranges, maize, tomatoes.

'Do you know who the first kidnap victim (*secuestrado*) was?' asked Margarita, with a cigarette in her hand. We were sitting on a terrace, with a new moon and the sound of a million insects scraping their violins. She was in her element, far away from cold Bogotá in the mountains. She had been born in Cali, the capital city of the Cauca valley, the centre of the sugar cane fields, a hot city.

'No, I don't. Tell me.'

'It was Elisa, the daughter of Harold Eder.'

In Cali, and in most of Colombia, people know who the Eder family are. Immigrants from the eastern frontiers of Germany – East Prussia or Lithuania – in the early nineteenth century, they were among the first to set up sugar mills and railways to the port of Buenaventura on the Pacific. They were hard-working entrepreneurs.

'No, it was not,' interjected Jose Fernando, our host. 'It was a man called Giraldo in Manizales.'

Manizales is a town high in the middle Cordillera, above the coffee fields, a high cold town, whose people are closely related to the *paisas* of Medellin. From where we were sitting we could almost see the lights of Manizales above us, only forty minutes drive away.

'No,' retorted Margarita firmly. 'He was after Harold, who was himself kidnapped in 1963. He was taken in a sugar farm and found dead in the Manuelita sugar mill.'

'And then Oliverio Lara,' replied Jose Fernando, 'in the Huila. They never found his body. They did find Harold's body.'

'And did the families pay?' I asked.

'No,' said Margarita, drawing on her cigarette. 'People say that money was not asked for. Those were cruel vengeance kidnappings. For hatred? For politics?'

'Oliverio was not a very Christian man in the way he increased the size of his land,' came the voice of Hans, from the darkness.

'But Harold was a good man,' insisted Margarita. 'He probably found out about a theft in the mill and the workers killed him.'

'Ah, it was money,' I murmured. 'So kidnapping is nothing to do with politics or social problems? At the start?'

In fact it is not so easy. I was on the wrong track.

'Well, you have to look back to the *Violencia*. For example, in 1946, there was a massacre in the Liberal party office in Cali. The general in Cali was Rojas Pinilla.'

This caused a pause for thought. Was it not later than 1946? Margarita thought not.

Rojas Pinilla was the military dictator a decade later, who was asked to take power in 1953 to stamp out the violence, the only interruption to the strong democratic electoral tradition of Colombia. It is violence itself that snaps the democracy of the country. Strong men are *caudillos* or heads, leaders who are needed to sort out unbearable situations such as violence. By 2002, we had got into such an unbearable situation. History was repeating itself.

'In our house in Cali, we could not sleep in the bedrooms with windows that opened on to the street. In the night, the *chulos* or *pajaritos* would ride the streets and there would be shooting.'

'I remember the massacre in Genoa, in the Quindio (province) when I was in school,' added Jose Fernando. '*The bandoleros*, led by 'Chispas' (Sparks) and 'Aljure', went in to the town and killed the men and tossed the children on to their bayonets. They did the *corte de corbata* (the necktie cut) where the throat is cut and the tongue pulled through it, and the *corte de franela* (the flannel cut) which is worse.'

I thought of the savagery in the Spanish civil war, the hatred of the priests, and of the Nazi cruelty. We were not much better in Europe, were we? But we have learned our lessons and set up the European Union to learn to live together and stop fighting. That has not stopped the violence of the Irish and the Basque ETA.

'President Guillermo Leon Valencia finished with that,' said Margarita. 'In 1962 to 1966, with Capitan Matallana, who was in charge of the Marquetalia area. He said, "Bring them in – dead or alive – better dead."'

'Yes, it got safer,' said Jose Fernando. 'I remember. We travelled in . . . what was the word? Convoys. Yes. With the army in front and behind.'

'There were two independent "republics",' said Margarita. 'One in Sumapaz with its headquarters in Viota, under Juan de la Cruz Varela, and one in Marquetalia, in Tolima.

'No, no,' interrupted Margarita, with the excitement of memory. 'Anyway, it started in the 1930s. Or 1926, when the *chulavitos* started and the massacre of the banana workers. In 1938 my mother was in Caicedonia one day and saw a boy of nine years old walk up to a policeman and spill his guts with a machete. She said that it was the strongest memory of her life. But it was normal for the times. Oh yes, normal!'

We grew silent and there were only the insect sounds of the night. Have we got out of these cycles of violence and its repression under the 'strong men'? It looks as if we have not. But the new factor, I realised, is drugs. In the 1980s Colombia added to its woes when it became the supplier to the drug consumption culture of the USA and Europe. The all-corrupting billions-of-dollars bonanza.

CHAPTER 11

The family plans

O N SATURDAY 11 MAY, the guerrilla finally spoke to my lawyer, on his home number, after that initial call up the mountain. There had been three calls on 9 May but he had come home late and they had stopped trying. They tried to confuse the situation by saying that they were the 'paramilitary', the AUC – *Autodefensas Unidas de Colombia*. They had me and wanted two million dollars. I learned all this later. Nanette and John were at the farm. On the Monday, the lawyer came and relayed the message. He was told that a committee was being formed and a negotiator had to be found and that he had done his part, so 'sorry for the inconvenience and thanks'.

On 18 May, a telephone call had been received by the maid. A man asked for Señora Cecilia (Nanette's christened name).

'She is out,' answered that maid. It was a Saturday, and so John and Nanette were on the farm, paying the *mayordomo*, checking the coffee and fruit for sale, and giving water and fertiliser to the orchids. The dogs had gone down and were happily jumping into the pond and chasing the cat.

'Then I shall call later,' said the voice and rang off.

When the family came back home, Ana described the voice as 'a policeman's voice'. I now wonder about that remark, not idly said.

At five past three, the telephone rang in the flat in Bogotá. John picked it up.

'Alo?' he said.

A voice said, 'Señora Cecilia?'

'Who is it?'

'La señora Cecilia?' the voice repeated the question.

'*Quien es?* Who is it?' asked John.

'Señora Cecilia?' the question came again.

'My name is John Hutchinson, the son of David Hutchinson. Do you have anything to say to me?'

'Ah! Ah!' The voice took a different tack. 'We have Señor Hutchinson. We demand two million dollars. It is a financial kidnap (*una retencion economica*).'

Although John had rehearsed this moment and knew the line to take, it was a dramatic moment for him. He had to gain time.

'We are very worried about el señor,' he said firmly. 'We shall do what we can to have him back home. But we are not ready to talk. We are not Colombian and need help. Can you give us time? Can you ring again in a week?'

48

'Very well,' was the answer, to John's relief. 'You know that he is in our hands,' said the voice. 'It is up to you. We shall ring in a week'

The voice had not said who he was nor to which organisation he belonged. But the contact had been made, and it was quicker than it might have been. This was the first mention of money. John and Nanette looked at each other and he related what had been said. They both knew that the demand would be huge. But this was outrageous. No such money existed.

'Where do we get the money? We don't have it.' The family was on its own, facing an extortion in a country that was not their own. Who was going to help them? John went to see the Embassy. They could see that there were going to be calls, and lent him a recording machine to attach to the telephone. The analysis of the calls was going to be important. It was the only evidence that the family would have.

A Colombian friend emailed from Paris. 'Nanette, I am thinking hard about you and David, and hoping that the nightmare comes to an end quickly. You know that we Colombians are fond of David and the pride we feel that he decided to live in Colombia. I feel so ashamed that the country returns his love with such cruelty. I pray to God that he returns safe and sound. I send a big hug to you and the family.'

It is a constant embarrassment to Colombians of all sorts that foreigners get caught up in this dreadful harsh treatment. Colombians are sentimental and are very good and generous friends.

John's boss in the English engineering company where he worked sent a message that he was glad that there was hard news, rather than uncertainty. The time taken so far was paid holiday and, if John wanted unpaid leave of absence, he could ask for it. How much time could John devote to the negotiations, when he had a job to do?

As the time passed, fear was increasing not diminishing. Danger lurked everywhere, for everyone. It was decided that nothing could be said over the open telephone lines. The police were listening. Victoria said to her cousin in Argentina, 'You can call but you can't say anything about the negotiation or movements or anything. The fact is that these days have become very hard for us. The impact and the fear are great, thinking of what Papa is suffering. We are far away and our days are full of stress and fear. I can't communicate freely and the decisions are tough. I can't wait for the end to come and have Papa with us with his bad jokes and his big tummy.'

15 May had been Nanette's birthday. Our friend Tony had written, 'I should like to wish you happy birthday at this unhappy time. I can only say to you HAVE FAITH. It does not really matter that David does not believe in God . . . because God loves us all. We all have failings and commit errors. God forgives all errors. For God, it is sad that many of us do not believe in Him, but maybe it makes Him much sadder that those who do state to believe in Him conduct their lives

in the most unchristian manner. I believe that He holds in much greater regard those who do unto others as they would have them do to themselves, as is the case of David. So having said that, take FAITH, as I don't believe that God will abandon you, David or the many friends around the world who are praying for you.'

Nanette is a Catholic and churchgoer, but married to an atheist. When in trouble, and feeling helpless in the face of danger, mortals have always called to their God to help them. Otherwise the fear and sense of powerlessness might drive one mad. Or is it that praying is another facet of 'fatalism'. I myself understand the calm that fatalism brings, when you say 'If I live or die, I shall do my best and keep my chin up.'

My sister-in-law, Graciela, in Buenos Aires, decided to consult a clairvoyante. 'Vic, yesterday I consulted a highly recommended clairvoyante because I wanted to ask her about David. I showed her some photos that I had in the office (she came to the office) to see if she could 'see' him and of course she asked for his date of birth. I never remember dates and told her that it was the twentysomethingth of February and he was 59. She said that she could see him, he was well and surrounded by people and in a place full of plants and vegetation and earth. Eating little, either because he did not want to eat or because there was little to eat. He had not been hurt and it would go on for five months. If I gave her the exact birth date, she could see more.

I don't know what you think about clairvoyants. I don't really believe in seeing the future but I do believe that they have a special mental energy which lets them see what is happening. When the aeroplane crashed in the Andes (Vic knew that this was a reference to the event which the English writer Piers Paul Read had written about in his book *Alive*, when the Uruguayan rugby players had had to eat each other to stay alive) they were not found and nobody knew what had happened to them, but the parents, especially Carlos Paez Vilaro, who is a well-known painter in Uruguay, consulted lots of mediums and all said that they should go on looking as there were lots of survivors. And that is what happened because the parents went on and on looking, after the governments of Argentina, Chile and Uruguay had given up in disbelief. Then two of the boys walked out of the snow and came across a muleteer and told him that they were from the crashed aeroplane. Their parents were told and the rest were taken out in a helicopter.

I think that it is worth trying anything. I tell you, that I felt much more positive, without actually jumping in the air.'

She ended her story.

Now I am writing this down, I think that perhaps she should have jumped in the air a few inches. The clairvoyante, by the name of Noemi, sitting in a chair in an office in Buenos Aires, had a pretty good vision of me, two thousand kilometres away. Amazing.

CHAPTER 12

The mountains and an air attack

WAS I IN A PLACE OF PLANTS and vegetation, surrounded by people and eating very little? Yes, I was. The clairvoyante in Buenos Aires could see me, but my family could not. No second sight in the Hutchinsons.

We four captives were getting used to the camp above the hut. Fredy was nervous and depressed about getting out. He had heard no messages. He used to cry. Grandpa was a wreck and confused. The dangerous chap glowered and sat alone on a rock. I had a decent *caleta*, and another three blankets, inherited from the leavers.

The horrible Juan Carlos and Vladimir had worse coughs, and the girls caught them. The boys coughed disgustingly above the pots. It had to happen. I got a feverish cold from them and became delirious and hot. I went to bed.

'Ask for antibiotics,' said Fredy.

'No. I know myself. I shall put on all my clothes and all the blankets and go to bed and sweat.'

So I did and the fever went in a day and I got up, sweat-soaked and shaky. We could bathe in the stream that flowed to the river, which is below the hut, where the water was used for cooking. It was freezing. Since it rained a lot, the clothes that I had arrived in, my nice clothes, were not drying. Pedro decided to heat up water over the fire and let me and grandpa bathe in warm water. Nice of him. An attention to the oldies. We stood outside the hut and exposed our withered flanks to all and sundry and poured the warm water with pans over us. Then we went into the hut and sat on stones or logs by the fire to keep warm. The earth floor and plank walls with gaps in them and corrugated iron roof made a primitive room. The girls had large blackened pots on the boil. Next door was a store of rice, sugar, coffee, pasta, dried beans, staple for the guerrilla. And that is where the radio of this *comision* was set up. This is how they reported and received orders.

We learned how to make *cancharinas*, flat wheat pancakes, fried, and *sapos*, rounder flour dampers, twirled around a stick and fried too. Rice and beans were the staple food, every meal, or lentils, or dried peas.

Two days after Laureano had ridden off, we saw a strange figure, with a mass of white hair and white beard and mounted on a mare, coming down the hill behind the hut. 'The Witch', who had gone with Laureano, walked in front. The new arrival went into the hut and, after a while, we saw him walking towards us.

'It's Papa Noel (Father Christmas),' I said to Fredy.

When you are a child, you believe in Papa Noel. When you are grown up, you are Papa Noel. When you get old, you just look like Papa Noel.

A genial figure came into the patio and greeted us. He was dog-tired and had a bloody scab on his head. Pedro came behind and said that the newcomer should share with Grandpa, as Epimaco had before. We were five now and full up. This was an old man. He told us that he was 74. He had fallen off the mare several times and was in pain and tired and frightened. We made him rest and gave him Laureano's sleeping bag.

Papa Noel was very frightened. He explained that he had been kidnapped in his car after lunch with a friend in a restaurant, at a police roadblock near the airport, in the middle of the city. He was pulled to the side of the road by traffic police and made to get out.

'We have been looking for you for ages,' the supposed cops called out. They made him get into a jeep and drove him to a suburb in the south. He had been kept in a room in a house for several weeks (he said it was three months but he was confused and shocked). He had been told to summon his captors by whistling and could not talk aloud. They had always had masks over their faces. They gave him fruit and more or less good food – chicken, meat. He never left the room and slept on a mattress on the floor, and washed with a bucket. He was terrified, poor old man. He cried like a baby, the tears pouring down his red cheeks.

Fredy remarked that he was taken by traffic cops too. 'I had an imported Fiat car from Italy. I loved it. Maybe it was the only one in Colombia. It was stolen one night. I reported the theft to the traffic police. One day, they rang me and said that they had found it and wanted to see me, about the papers. They arranged a meeting place and I went. They made me get into a car and drove me away into the hills. I walked alone for days and then met Grandpa, in the plank hut.'

'My wife had cancer,' sobbed Papa Noel. 'I was told that she has died, while I was in the house. I could be at her funeral and I am alone now.' It was awful.

We looked north at the river and the hill opposite. If it rained hard, the river boiled and crashed rocks downstream. If it had not rained, the water level fell. We were not allowed down there. The rivers in the hills had trout in them. Rainbows. There was little food in the water. It was cold enough for the trout to breed well, but not enough grub for them to grow large. They were abundant and like sardines. They are not native and some Scotsman must have brought them a century before. In fact they are carnivores and damage the local fauna in the rivers. The guerrilla fished them with a cane and three-metre line and hook and worms. It was more difficult to find worms than catch the trout. On a good expedition, the catch could be a hundred and they were a welcome supplement to the rice and beans. They could be fried crisp or made into soup. It was like eating little sardines in Spain or Greece. No white wine, however! The bones were tossed into the bushes, along with any left-over rice or beans.

I sat on Grandpa's bed, talking, and looking at a clump of bamboo in front, where we parked our walking sticks and pans to dry.

'Look at that. Something is moving.' It was a mouse.

The space between the *caletas* had turned into a muddy bog, slippery and dirty. I said to Fredy that we could pave it with rocks, of which there was no shortage on the hillside, on the way to the *chontos*.

'I can't carry big ones, with my broken arm. Can you help?' It was a good way of getting Fredy to have a task, and not mope. The other two were not going to help. Fredy liked the idea and we laboured away for several days until there was a stone patio. The guerrilla watched us. Hanibal remarked that we should not do anything that could be seen from the air. Hum.

We actually had a clear sunny dawn one day and blue sky. There was a noise in the north and we saw aircraft. Two. Circling. Little jets. Were they Israeli KFIRs? They came back and plunged down. Bang, bang. We could hear the noise of firing. Rockets left their wings and shot down, with white smoke trails. It was the other side of the hill. Not so far, as then we heard machine-gun fire as the FARC fired up at them. The FARC did not have anti-aircraft missiles here.

'Are those missiles or rockets?' we asked Hanibal who was watching.

'Rockets. *Cohetes*. They are not guided.'

'They are aimed by eye?'

'Yes. They never kill any one.' This was a typical example of FARC scorn for the Air Force, which we heard any number of times afterwards. At least they were not aiming at us. I remembered the *comandantes* at the camp on the way, who had said that we had better move on as it was dangerous to be with them. The FARC was very near Bogotá and the government was on their trail.

'You know, we have rockets too,' confided Hanibal. This was to be proved later in an interesting way.

Before lunch all the *guerrilleros* arrived and covered our patio and the *caletas* with bamboo branches, as Pedro thought we could be seen from above.

How were we going to get on with the rough character? Even if he was dangerous as Roberto had perceived, we were all in the same boat. I decided, privately, to call him Brutus, the big hulk in the Popeye cartoon.

'Can you play chess?' I asked him.

'No.'

'Do you want to learn?'

'No.'

I left it for a few days. He was not a collaborator and would not help us with the laying of stones in the patio. I think he moved in a different world, and did not meet people like us normally.

'Come on. We shall teach you chess.' I brought up the subject a couple of days later. 'Papa Noel, you'll learn too?'

'No, I can't,' replied Papa. 'I can't think straight.' And we did sit down and try and he could not. An intelligent man, but he was too frightened and weepy.

'Grandpa, come and play chess,' I called out.

'No, I can't see the pieces,' the old man replied.

'OK. Teach me,' suddenly interrupted Brutus.

So we begged the board and pieces from Pedro and set it up on a rock and started.

'This is the king and the queen. The object is to capture the king. It is a war game. The pieces move as follows . . .'

Brutus played every day. He was calming down. Every now and then, he reflected, 'I don't know what I am doing here? Who was it that betrayed me? When I get out, I shall kill them.'

Papa Noel found out that Laureano had been with us, and told us that he had met Laureano, in the house of the planks, a day before reaching us. Laureano had fallen off the mare and hurt his leg badly. He was limping and in pain. He thought that he was off to the camp of Romaña, the bandit chief. We hoped that Laureano would go home soon.

'Sod that *hijo de puta*,' said Brutus. They had had an argument about blankets and Brutus was an angry and unforgiving man. Nasty.

CHAPTER 13

Looking after Grandpa

PAPA NOEL WAS SLEEPING WITH GRANDPA, and he did not enjoy it. Grandpa was a wreck, mentally and physically. It was terrible of the guerrilla to kidnap an 80-year-old. He was deaf. He used glasses and did not have them with him. He had fallen off his mare on the way in and was bruised. In order to put him to bed, we had to take him by the arm up to the bushes to pee and back again. We had to make up the blanket underneath the sleeping bag (which was pronounced *esleeping* in the Spanish way), open the sleeping bag, tip him up on the bag and roll him over, put a blanket in with him and roll it round him, zip up the sleeping bag and put a blanket on top. Grandpa's dinky tweed hat had to be hung up where he could get it the next day. His walking stick had to be leaned on a bush within sight.

In the night, he peed in his bed and wet his trousers. At dawn, we called to him. If he was awake, we had to get him up, and change his wet trousers and walk him for a pee, then take out the bag and blankets and hang them out to dry on a branch, if it was not raining. He could not stand up without falling forward on his face. If we were not quick, he would crash into the mud and cut his face on a stone. This happened more than once, poor old man.

'I can't stand up straight,' he lamented.

'Look, Grandpa, you will have to. You must get out alive. We'll help.'

'All right.'

'What's that lump on your neck?'

Grandpa had a swelling on the left side of his neck, like a goitre.

'It is a tumour (*un turupe*).'

'Is it benign? What are you taking for it, Grandpa?'

'The doctor said it is a cancer. At my age there is nothing worth doing about it.'

'You are going to live another twenty years, Grandpa, and we are going to help you walk out of here. All right?'

'I can't walk all that way again. I am a mass of bruises, and I have lost my sense of balance.'

When you are in a bad situation, it helps to have someone to look after. You can concentrate on the other person. And it made me feel humble to see this old man coping. What was my problem, a mere babe at only sixty years old? No, it was Grandpa who had to survive.

The area around our *caletas* was either bushes and trees behind, or huge jumbled rocks in front. Below, it flattened out. We were allowed down there because that

55

was where we met the stream for our washing of dishes and bodies and tooth-brushing. I decided to make a walking circuit, and when I could I walked in circles around it. Of course it got muddy quickly. I walked singing marching songs.

'Pack up your troubles in your old kitbag, and smile, smile, smile. What's the use of worrying, it never was worthwhile . . .'

Papa Noel joined in the walking and he cheered up. He chatted away and even sang a song of his own.

The thing was to get Grandpa down. He was a defeated man, so he had to be bullied. Papa Noel or Fredy and I took him under each armpit and walked him, with wobbly knees, down to the track. He sat on a rock for the first few times. Then I made him walk with us, using his stout stick. He shuffled along, but it was a huge improvement. We dragged him back up the hillside, and sat him on his *caleta* edge.

'I am so tired. I don't want to walk any more. They will have to get me out on a stretcher.'

Sometimes Pedro would be there. He had no patience with the old man.

'Old man, you have to walk out of here. You came in and you will go out.'

Or what?

'Can't you give me a mare?'

'Maybe some of the way. But not all the way. Stop complaining and get yourself going.'

'Pedro,' I asked. 'Can we have a hot bath? Grandpa pees in the night and is filthy. Come on. And I am an oldie too. Buggered if I am going to wash in the river. I'd die of pneumonia.'

I was lucky once and Pedro gave orders to heat up water. Only we two oldies could have a hot bath. Next to the hut was a plastic sheet draped from the side over some poles. Under that lean-to it was dry, but muddy. Clothes could be hung to dry. The water was put into bowls there and we stripped off and poured pans of water over us and soaped up. It was cold and usually raining and our feet ended up muddy, but all in all it was a triumph. I think it did Grandpa good to clean up. His white locks and bristly moustache and beard all perked up. We could then sit inside the hut and watch the girls cook. We did that several times, even when it was not bath day. We might get a coffee or some *panela* to eat. It was as close as we could get to going to the pub. And next door, for the hut was split into two rooms, were a food deposit and a bed and the radio transmitter. Perhaps we could overhear some talk? Fredy said that, when they arrived, they offered to tidy up the hut, and were allowed to do so. There were split bags of rice and sugar, wasting their contents, and squashed potatoes, and this attracted the mice, who ruined more of the food.

The corral that surrounded the hut had been trampled by mules and rained on, so it was a knee-deep bog. It was very difficult to cross to the grass leading to the path up to our *caleta*s. One nightfall, almost dark, I saw a giant snipe swoosh in to the reeds not ten metres from me. It is not a common bird but the place and the hour and the size are right for this interesting bird. What was a paradise for the giant snipe was hell for Grandpa, who would often fall on his face into the mud, even if we were trying to hold him up. Then we had to change his clothes again and ask Pedro to get them washed and, what was more important, dried over the fire.

'Grandpa, play chess with us.'

'I can't see the pieces. No thanks.'

But he, with his pure long sight, could see a cow on the hillside across the river, so the best thing for him was to take him to the walking track and make him stagger round a few times. It was working and he could keep his balance better and move a bit, albeit with his stick. It was the result of a relentless application of 'You can do it.'

Chapter 14

The family find a negotiator

M AY IS A BUSY MONTH IN BOGOTÁ. It is before the summer holidays, and after Holy Week, so there is a rush to get everything done, and a conflict of dates for all the events. It rains a lot, as the dry July-August period is still far off. Of course, with global warming, the seasons are not as clearly demarcated as in the past. Indeed Bogotá is a less cold city than it was once. The fireplaces (*chimeneas*) that had been built in all the old houses and still are built into the new apartments are not lit as often as before. The caricature of a traditional Bogotá gentleman – a *rolo* or *cachaco*, with his raincoat, scarf, umbrella and hat – has become a myth (except for the late and much-loved Jaime Recaman). In May the amateur theatre groups usually put on their first show of the year. I had been in the middle of organising mine, a concert show. My disappearance threw a spanner in the works, for I was the only one to know where the sausages were to be bought and the marquee was to be hired, essential in case of Bogotá's unpredictable rains. We were going to use a school with a garden. I thought a lot about this show, as I lay in my *caleta* in the mountains. I did not know, but it was cancelled. The songs ran through my head.

'Oh Danny Boy, the hills are ca – alling
From glen to glen and from the mountain top . . .'

It was *Pais Libre* who had said that the family needed a committee, to advise them, in Bogotá. There was the Embassy, the police, the security company. But who was going to negotiate? Any security company would cost US$2,000 a day, plus out-of-pocket expenses. Only a large business could afford that. We had no kidnap insurance. And these experts do not negotiate, only advise, despite what Hollywood films may portray. In the absence of a Russell Crowe, let alone a James Bond, who would help? Who would talk to the kidnapper, a brave and horrid responsibility? Nanette and her friends formed a committee. There was an expert banker, and there was Pepe, the brother of a close friend, who had had to negotiate a kidnap in Medellin, some years before, for a relative. Would he be prepared to negotiate? He said that he would think about it, of course.

John and Nanette were elated. The anxiety was so great and a solution was at hand. But the next day he had spoken with his family and called up.

'Sorry, but no,' he said. 'After I got my uncle out, I had a bomb thrown at my house in Medellin, and we had to leave and set up house in Bogotá. It is too dangerous for the family.'

John and Nanette were plunged into depression. No advance had been made. Who could help?

'Would so-and-so do?'

'No, he would be wonderful, but he lives in Cali.'

'What about whojamacallit?'

'He is too emotional and a bit wild.'

'The negotiator must be Colombian?'

'God, I think so. The foreigners can help on the committee, but it must be someone neutral, who can talk to them in their own language.'

What would negotiation involve? The brother of our friend had done it and could tell us. 'They telephone and you negotiate them down. You might have to go to meetings.'

The international security companies had to find their own negotiators too. It was the same difficulty of finding a person who can be accepted as a neutral channel of communication with the FARC, and someone whose life would be respected.

Nanette went to dinner at the house of friends, who were anxious to be of help and comfort.

'Who can we find to help us? And it must be right away. I cannot stay here, I am told.'

Her friend Maria Elvira spoke up. 'I go to mass at a church, where the priest has, I think, done this type of thing. He is a young Spaniard. I can talk to him.'

'Oh, please do.' There was no other option. Time seemed to be important. The process of getting me back had to start. How? Any family in this situation is caught unprepared. Emotions run raw. Death is not far away.

So the next day, Nanette went to the church to see the priest. It was her birthday. The church was really a chapel, attached to a mission, where there was a small school for orphans and the children of abandoned mothers. The chapel was a thing of beauty, with high white walls and gilt wooden statues in the altar screen and in the stations of the cross. The priest was finishing mass, and when the children trooped out, he came down and introduced himself. Padré Rodrigo was young, tall, and extrovert. He sang well and told risqué jokes. He was popular with the lady volunteers who came to help in the school and the library and the fund-raising. In a poor country, voluntary work is endless and satisfying. The state cannot reach everywhere. There is no money for unemployment insurance.

Padré Rodrigo listened to the anguished young wife. He had heard these stories before. His vocation to serve God was clear and strong.

'Don't worry. I shall help you,' he smiled. There it was. Quick and sure. So we started to know this remarkable and fearless man. He did not know us at all. But he would put his life on the line to help us, without hesitation.

'If I have to go into the mountains to meet these people, I shall do that. I shall talk to them. We have to organise mobile telephones. You and I shall be in touch all the time.'

Nanette went straight before midnight to the house of a committee member and recounted the meeting. This was the way ahead. She was confident of the priest. All the members of the committee were pleased and the Padré was asked to come and meet the committee as soon as he could. The committee members met after work next day at the flat of one of them. The whisky was opened and the ice taken out of the fridge. The Padré came and accepted a glass, and looked at these friends of a man he did not know.

'I have done this before,' he said. He told a tale of one previous kidnap of a foreigner. 'You have to get me a mobile telephone, and they can ring me on that. You give them the number. They will call. Be patient.'

He was a busy man with his church duties and left after a while. The committee looked at each other, after the door was closed. They had no other choice. None of the organisations had been able to offer a negotiator. This was a gift horse and it was not possible to 'look in his mouth' as the saying goes. But they liked him and his style.

'What do you think?' said Bill.

'I like him,' answered Gustavo.

'Maria Elvira knows him.'

'So we go with him?'

'Yes.' Some of the anguish was dissipated. They were on the track of a solution. Nanette's tears would dry up and she could sleep.

On 22 May, the rain had started to fall, making the coffee farmers and the ducks happy. John was looking out of the window and the telephone rang.

'It's them,' called Ana nervously, and handed the telephone to John, whose heart thumped too.

'Ola, John Hutchinson,' he announced.

'Alo?' a strange voice.

'Ola, John Hutchinson, si?'

'Si, right, OK. Look. It is the same person who rang the other day.'

'Oh yes. Good. Yes,' mumbled John and collected his thoughts. 'First, thank you for giving me a few days to get myself organised. I am not from here, so it is a bit difficult to manage things, but . . .'

'Aha?'

'I did have some questions. I don't know whether I can ask you. What group are you from?'

'Look. No, that is not so important,' replied the *guerrillero*. 'The important thing is that Señor David is held by us and that the demand is purely economic. The rest is just bla bla (*puro cuento*), no?'

'Ah, si. How is Papa?' asked John. 'Is he there? Or perhaps I can talk to him? Or how is it?'

'Well, that is very difficult (*supremamente dificil*),' demurred the voice. 'That is something that I cannot guarantee.'

'Ah, well,' said John, disappointed.

'Let's get to the purpose. We shall make the suggestion that you can speak to him,' offered the *guerrillero*.

'Si?' asked John, his hopes revived.

'We shall do everything possible, but I cannot guarantee which day. Look. When we get to the point of agreement. Eh? Then, like that, surely we can.'

'Eh, *bueno*. That would be fantastic,' said John, with enthusiasm. 'Very grateful. Can I ask you? You have a name? Or you call yourself something?'

'I think that is not necessary,' replied the *guerrillero*, coldly.

'*Bueno.*'

'I think that is not necessary. The important is what I have just told you. It is that he is held by us. And in our hands.'

'Is he in good health?' queried John. As much information as he could get was what was needed.

'*Y que tal?*' said the voice, sarcastically. 'I can't say he is very well. Because the truth is that it is not easy to stand up to the conditions, no?'

'Si, si, OK, *bueno*,' said John. This was a bit discouraging.

'I think you understand that well enough?' asked the voice, with a hint of malice and a threat.

'Si, si. Something important I wanted to say,' remembered John. 'The amount. That worried me a lot. I have to tell you that that much money we do not have. It is pretty crazy figure. It is a fantasy. But . . .'

He was cut off by the voice, who said firmly, 'No, look here. We manage our information accurately, accounts, the capital he has, and the children, the family.'

'Oh, yes, well (ha ha ha), you see the truth is . . .' said John.

'Because we do not plough the desert (*nosotros no aramos el desierto*),' warned the voice, using the famous phrase of Simon Bolivar, the Liberator.

'Ah, si, ah.' John ploughed on. 'We are just middle class, so . . . you should know, the old man is a pensioner. In fact he lives in Colombia . . .

'Ah . . .'

'. . . because his pension is not enough to live on in England. But, well, that is the way it is. Obviously we want to resolve this situation well, with honour, as quickly as possible, calmly. I suppose that you are in agreement?'

'Si, we are perfectly agreed on that,' said the voice with satisfaction. 'The faster you resolve the situation, the better for you.'

'Si, si'

'And for him, eh?'

'Si, si,' John went on. 'We have to talk about the amount, something more realistic. What I wanted to say, as I said before, is that I am not in a good position to negotiate. My Spanish is not perfect. The other thing is that I have to go back to work, or they will fire me. So I am going to travel, I thought on Friday. And with his wife, because she is finding it a bit difficult to manage the situation. But we have found a friend, who has our full confidence, and, luckily, he is ready to help us here, and he has authority to speak for the family, and he is Colombian, so his Spanish is perfect, right, see? I had planned to give you his mobile phone number, and you can ring him whenever you like. He will carry the mobile and can answer at any time, so can you take note of the number now, please?'

'Si, wait a minute, go on talking,' agreed the voice, and asked, 'This friend has full authority to negotiate?'

'Si, exactly, he has the full support of the family, and, well, yes.'

'He is not, perhaps, someone from the Gaula (the anti-kidnap special police), or the Army?' asked the *guerrillero*.

'No,' said John firmly.

'It's that they, possibly more than you, are waiting . . . waiting for the call.'

'No. I tell you . . .'

'Well, it is that I am getting at the following,' warned the voice again. 'We are not scared of that, eh.'

'Si, si.'

'Believe me, that does not scare us at all.'

'No, we . . .' interjected John, before being brusquely interrupted.

'This is the way it is,' said the voice. 'The way it is, is like this. Two things. If you are thinking of doing a rescue operation by force, let me tell you.'

'Si, si.'

'It is not possible. It is not possible. I tell you with total confidence and I know what I am saying.'

'Si, si,' agreed John.

'Right. Secondly,' went on the voice, 'they are aware, so, that is, some of you choose those confidential friends . . .'

'Ah ha.'

'If one of them, someone from the Gaula, they offer to deal in this kind of business.'

'Si, si.'

'If it is one of them, from the Gaula, it is a problem, because they get involved with you and not with us. That delays and messes up the operation.' This was a significant warning to us.

'Absolutely. I am going to say something to you to make you feel better,' interrupted John. 'The man concerned is from the Church. He is a priest, known to us. A good friend of the family. So we prefer for your safety and our own to work away outside the authorities and manage it so that we are happy about the route we are taking.'

'Aha. Right. He is a priest, you are telling me?' asked the voice, to be sure.

'Yes, exactly, correct.'

'Aha.'

'And he wants to work independently from the authorities and they don't have the number of this mobile that I am giving you. That is, they would not be listening to what is said. Not at all.'

'*Bueno*, that's . . . it's this,' apologised the voice. 'Because I can't er . . . Because I am in a great mountain. I don't have a pen with me.

'Si?'

'If you'd be so kind, if I ring tomorrow, if I can,' asked the *guerrillero*. 'Leave the number with your secretary, someone, the maid, I don't know.'

'Si, rest assured, ring tomorrow,' agreed John, happily. 'I shall be here. At what time can you call? Maybe the same time in the afternoon?'

'I don't know,' confessed the voice, with hesitation. 'It has got difficult to make calls. I don't know what time.'

'Don't worry. If I am not in, the maid will answer.'

'*Bueno*, if I try to call before midday, if I can,' wrapped up the *guerrillero*.

'OK. I shall try to be here . . .'

The telephone was cut off. John looked at Nanette. The call had been recorded. They were both nervous. They replayed the call several times. This was the voice of the man who held me prisoner, God knows where. Was I in fact alive? It was frightening.

Nanette rang the committee for a meeting and everyone listened to the conversation, and gave their reaction. They knew that the next stage was to give the number of the Padré to this kidnapper, and start the negotiation.

Pepe thought that the voice came and went, and that he was speaking from the mountains, in difficult radio conditions. He was the one with experience.

I had been carrying my mobile telephone, when I had disappeared. This had been reported to the Gaula. They had asked John not to block it, so that they could track it. Even if a handset is switched on, not even being used, it can be traced. They had traced it to Ibague, the biggest town in the department of Tolima, down in the hot Magdalena river valley.

'I think they took him to Ibague,'said Pepe. 'That's where he is. In the hills above Ibague.'

John developed the theory that I had hidden the phone under the car seat, switched on, so that I could be tracked. This is an example of the 'James Bond' school of thought. Fiendishly clever David lays an electronic trail and the SAS parachute down and rescue him. Of course I was a million miles away and the phone had been taken off me by nine o'clock on the night of the first of May and given to other rascals. And my shoes with the secret transmitter were thrown under a bush in the south of Bogotá. Ha ha. Just a joke.

The tape was played to a couple of policemen from London, marvellous men, in a hotel in Bogotá. They opened the door and looked down the corridor, in case Rosa Klebb were there, dressed as a cleaning lady. The tape was played several times and analysed, after translation by John.

'This is the guerrilla and they want money. It will take a long time. He will come out. You need patience. They have to realise that he is a retired employee and not rich.'

'Too bloody right,' confirmed John.

'Sorry that we can't help more. This is not our terrain. If it were London, we would get them.'

The game was afoot, Watson. But they had not got Jack the Ripper in his time. Because he did not use a mobile phone?

CHAPTER 15

Girls and guns

PANCAKE WAS NOT STUPID and had had some education. She would talk when
on sentry duty.

'Say something in English, meester,' she asked. I did.

'*No entiendo*. But I do know some. I learned it at school.'

'Well, I could teach you,' I offered.

'All right.'

So we started. In fact she had some knowledge and remembered a few words.

'My name is Rosa.' (That was her real alias – she was forbidden to use her real
birth name.)

'Good. How many brothers and sisters have you?'

'Eh?'

'Brother, *hermano*. Sister, *hermana*.'

'Ah si. I have one, two, shree, four, fife, six, seven brother and sisters.'

'Your mother and father have eight children?'

'No, my muzzer and fazzer, they have seven children.'

'Then you have six bruzzer and sister?'

'I have seven bruzzer and sister.'

'Then your father and mother have eight children.'

'My fazzer and muzzer have seven children.'

'You have six brothers and sisters?'

'No. I have seven . . .

'OK, OK, we have a problem. You learn quickly. We have another lesson
tomorrow?'

'Yes, please.'

And off she wandered, muttering, 'I have seven bruzzer and sister.' We
managed two more lessons. But I discovered that these people have neither
patience nor consistency. Their commitment is nil. They have given up on
educated life.

She was born in a country family in Tolima of seven (eight?) children. A happy
family, perhaps, but poor. She left school young, and seemed to have a hankering
to learn more. She went to work as a maid in a local town, for a low wage. She
was a good maid, good with children, she said. One day she met someone who
talked of the life of the guerrilla. Before she was fifteen, she had gone to try it,
and was good at it. She did not talk of political theory at all.

She was the 'wife' of Juan Carlos, one of the crazy teenagers. 'I admire him so much,' she said once. 'When he goes in to battle, he runs straight at the enemy, shouting and firing. He is so brave.' She was a fighter too. She had spent time with the flying column *Manuela Beltran*, or so I understood. She had not seen her family for several years. Perhaps if she had finished studying, she could have got a good job. But she was born poor in the remote countryside. Was she an example of the lack of reach of the State to remote parts of the country?

La Negra was a less promising girl, with everything stacked up against her. She had been recruited by the FARC while begging money at traffic lights in Bogotá. She was very black. Her fingers were small, on podgy hands, and her mind was not up to scratch. She looked genetically below par. Her mother had been a prostitute, so she had grown up with no real family, no money, no education – a street waif, with a uniform and rifle.

She came to see us to borrow a needle, which Fredy had managed to scrounge. We had to repair our own clothes, and the needle was a valuable asset. It was not a good idea to lend it to her, but she had a gun and was our captor. The next day I asked for it back.

'Ah, si, I'll bring it,' she said. It never appeared, and later she confessed, 'I lost it.' She was fifteen years old. She and Pancake fought, and both got sanctions. Sanctions are an important part of the rules and discipline of the FARC, as well as a way of getting jobs done. One task is 'loads of wood' (*cargas de leña*). It is an endless drudgery to carry dry branches to the fire-place, for cooking. By the time we had been several months in captivity, each had over 150 loads to do as sanctions.

In battle and in carrying loads and in doing their turns of duty, the boys and girls were equals. Everyone cooked, everyone washed clothes, everyone fought in the front line. The girls had sexual partners, and if two people agreed to get together, they asked the *comandante* and their union was recognised. Each girl had several men sniffing at her.

The FARC's weapons were rifles, and some pistols. These were not always enough to go around, so that the sentry had to find one and hand it back. The top of the range was the Galil, with a folding stock, the rifle used by the Army, and presumably captured from the Army in combat. It was the one that the *comandantes* carried. Then there was the AK-47, with a plastic stock. Its markings read IMI, so I wondered if it was assembled in Italy. The bottom of the range was an old rifle with a wooden stock, inscribed Northern Industries USA. Was this a M-16? It looked more like a sporting rifle. The troops wore a chest harness (a *pechera*) with loops and pockets for grenades, which did exist, and knives. They had rubber boots on their feet, never leather boots.

Gradually a story leaked out that in 2001 ten thousand Russian rifles, the AK-47s I suppose, were traded to the FARC in exchange for forty tons of cocaine. The deal was set up by Peruvian government officials and Jordanians, to get the documents plausible and the shipment going. The rifles were taken or dropped by parachute into Pastrana's distension zone.

After my march into this first camp, using smaller rubber boots than I needed, I noticed that the nails of my big toes had turned black. They became loose and were clearly going to fall off. And my heels were rubbed raw and bleeding. Pedro noticed that and brought me some sticking plaster.

One day, two of the *guerrilleros* walked through our *caleta*s and along the hillside, to the east. We saw them at the end of the day, below us, by the river, carrying cardboard boxes back to the hut. They were full of rubber boots – the Venus brand from Ecuador – as we saw when we went down to the hut another day. So the hills had their hiding places for equipment, caves or pits to bury stuff, the logistics of the war. But very few of the boots were of a size above 43, which was too small for me. So my toenails had no chance.

CHAPTER 16

Brutus and Hanibal

ONE EVENING, BEFORE NIGHTFALL, that is about half-past five, after supper, Hanibal walked up to our *caleta*s, and greeted us. It was getting cold. Grandpa had peed nearby and been helped back and his boots taken off. Now he was zipped up in his *esleeping* and only a tuft of white hair and bushy white moustache protruded. (When Grandpa could not remember the word *esleeping* (bag), he used to call it a 'yuppie' (pronounced 'joopi').

Hanibal watched.

'*Bien*,' I said. 'Now we stick a stamp on him, take him to the post office and post him off to his family'.

'*Que?*' guffawed Hanibal. 'What did you say?'

I repeated this feeble joke.

'Mister, you are a loco. Post him? Ha, ha.'

I thought that Hanibal had never posted a letter, indeed never written a letter (he was illiterate), and never received a letter. He did not know what a post office was. In fact the inheritance of the Spanish empire does not usually include an efficient postal system. Letters take for ever, and no one pays a bill by post. People do not trust the postman. All bills are paid in the banks. The result is that the banks have enormous queues of messengers and maids paying minuscule telephone or electricity bills, which is a huge cost to the poor old banks.

Hanibal was still chuckling. The guerrilla are great jokers and laughers, and practical jokers too. It is the old country way of life. They are not as solitary or tense as city dwellers.

'Good night. *Buenas noches*,' from the *caleta*s. At the bottom was the lair of Brutus. As Hanibal passed, Brutus called him 'Hey you, come here.' He sounded harsh. Hanibal ducked under the branches and crouched by the entrance.

'*Que?* What do you want, man?'

'Look! What am I doing here? You think I am rich? Ha? I am a poor man. I was poorer than you when I was a nipper. You made a mistake. I know what it is to sleep on the floor, to have one pair of trousers, to go without food. *Hijo de puta*, what I have is what I have earned by the sweat of my brow. Why do you think you *hijos de puta* can take it away from me? *Puta*! Do you think you can become popular with the Colombians by robbing the poor? Why don't you rob the rich *hijos de puta*?'

'Look,' interrupted Hanibal, 'I don't know anything about this. I am just here to guard you. You pay and you go.'

68

'*Hijo de puta*, I want to speak to the *comandante*s. I don't have any money. What I earn I spend. OK, I like to party and bonk *las putas*, what's wrong with that. Everything I earn I spend. You think I am rich. Let me tell you that if I live well, it is by working my butt off. I know what it is to be poor. What I have I have earned. It is mine. OK, I live in a house. What is wrong with that? I have a business, which does not make me much, enough to live well enough. Why do you *hijos de puta* want to take away from us poor Colombians the little that we have. Why don't you work? Ha? Instead of stealing from people who are just like yourself. I know lots of rich people. Why don't you go and screw them?'

Brutus was getting really worked up. Righteous anger, and in fact impressive. He went on, and on, as the tropical night fell quickly. Was he pushing his luck by shouting a tirade of gross language at his captor? But he must have felt the equal of Hanibal, although he despised him for being an unsuccessful and useless bum.

'I had nothing. I ran away from home when I was ten and slept on the streets. I worked and came to Bogotá and started in business. I never had any money. Now you want to take it all away from me. Why? If all Colombians were like me, the country would be all right. Why don't you leave me alone? It is a mistake. Your information is wrong. Who told you about me? It is lies. It is the oligarchy, the land-owners who have the money. Me? I just have enough to live. And you *hijos de puta* are going to put me back on the streets.'

He was prickly and not happy in our society. He had come from a different level and knew it. But we had to get on. I had finished a game of chess with him once, when he muttered, with his head down, 'If Bogotá is that way, then I am going to escape over that hill. Come with me.'

'Don't be crazy. They will track you down in a flash. These hillsides are impossible to hide in. And you don't know which way to take.'

'I can't stand it here. Come on. We can get away one night and make it home.'

'I don't think so. They know these hills. It is their *tierra*.'

'Well, I am thinking of it.'

Hanibal was born in Antioquia, in the *Oriente* (the East). He was a *paisa* from near Medellin, a country boy, good with his hands, but illiterate.

'My father was poor and we were many brothers. No, I don't see them. My father had a little land and worked hard. He bought some more land, and put cattle on it. We planted beans and potatoes and carrots. He did well.'

'So, why are you a *guerrillero*? If you can see that your father was a good man, who had success, because he worked?' I said once.

'Eh, Meester, it is more complicated. We have to fight the oligarchy.' So he had picked up the claptrap of politics. I shut up.

'I worked in a flower farm once. I am good at that.'

'Why did you leave?'

'I got fed up. It was always the same. I did want to stay.' He was a restless man, a bad worker?

'I have been in the guerrilla for over thirty years. They sent me to Cuba for training in aircraft. I can fly.'

'What a bloody liar,' said Pati, whom you will meet later. 'He can't even read. They never sent him anywhere.'

'I am 51. But tell me I don't look it.' He smiled. His figure was certainly trim. He dyed his hair, and did not deny it. He was a good walker. He knew the names of many birds and trees; indeed he would answer any question, even if he did not really know. He was the best and keenest fisherman. He made the best *caletas*.

'Who are the best *guerrilleros*,' we asked once.

'*Los indios*. Then the *paisas*. Then the people of Tolima.'

'*Los negros?* The people from the coast?'

'No. They are useless.' He did not talk of city people. The skills of Robin Hood and his merry men are forest skills.

When the aeroplane carrying the Minister of Social Services and Pensions, the clever and nice Juan Luis Londoño, a favourite student at Harvard, hit a mountainside going to Cali at the year end, the Army rushed out to find him. It would have been awful if a cabinet minister were to be captured by the FARC.

'I know all that land,' said Hanibal. 'I was there in a camp and have walked all the paths. The FARC will be there first.'

In fact, the passengers all died in the crash, and the government had to reconsider letting its ministers hire cheap private aircraft for work trips to save cash.

Later, however, we learned that Hanibal had been in the guerrilla for less than five years. So he was 51 years old, had fewer than five years in the forest, and a heap of missing years. The usual explanation is that these lost years are prison years. Maybe twenty years? A stiff sentence, for aggravated homicide?

'I won't go back to Antioquia,' he confided one day. 'I have asked for *licencia*. I am old enough to be released. I am thinking of other places, where they don't know me. I want a bit of land. But I have no money. Meester, can I visit you? You give me a job as a bodyguard? Pay me three million pesos. I know the business. No one would mess with you. I know where your farm is. I visit you? You give me a coffee and we talk?'

'Look, man. I am a retired *viejito*. I don't work and I don't have a bodyguard or employ anyone. I don't have the money.'

'Ha, ha, Meester, you are rich. I am a good worker. I know about coffee and flowers. I visit you.'

Christ, what a nightmare – this criminal trying to be a friend or an employee. And knowing me. But then how do you rehabilitate the drop-outs in society?

'You know,' he said one day, 'the *zona de distension* was bad for the guerrilla. The chaps got sloppy and used to driving in trucks and drinking and sleeping in beds. It is better now that we are back in the forest. No booze; sleeping outside and on the march; discipline. We are fighting a war. This is better.'

Perhaps he had become an ascetic. Managing in the forest made him feel a better man than living badly without money in semi-comfort. He also was far away from the competitive outside world which laughed at him for an illiterate ex-convict and paid him bottom wages. Not that he fitted in well with the youngsters. He was a loner. He talked to us a lot, more than any of the others.

I remember him saying once, 'Meester, let me tell you. If you see me when you are back home, in the street or somewhere, you don't tell the police. Once there was a *retenido* who recognised some *compañeros* and went and told the police. They were caught and are in prison now. Of course we had to go and see him in his home. He was killed in front of his family.'

'So you go and kill people?'

'I am just telling you. Don't talk to the police.'

CHAPTER 17

They call back

O N 23 MAY, THE TELEPHONE RANG and Ana picked it up.
'Alo?'

'*Muy buenos dias.* The Hutchinson family?'

'Who do you want to . . .?'

'With any one of them.'

'One minute.' And she whispered to John, who took the telephone, with some trepidation and accelerated heartbeat. The recording machine was on, as it had been for the earlier call.

'John Hutchinson here.'

'*Si, que hubo?* How are you? *Buenos dias.*'

'Si. Have you rung about the telephone number?'

'What, what?'

'Have you rung for the number?'

'Si.'

'Right, a second, I don't have it with me.' He went to look for the piece of paper with the number and came back. 'Alo?'

'Si?'

'It is a mobile. 033 and then 77385. I repeat . . .'

'Very good. Whom do I talk to there?'

'To Padré Rodrigo. As I said, he is a priest. He is available at any time on this mobile, as I told you yesterday. He has all the support and the authority of the family, no?'

'Aha?'

'Well, perfect.'

'The other question is whether you can do us a favour and help with prepaid cards so we can ring up.'

'Eh? Help, so you can ring up? Well, yes, we can do that.'

'All right.'

'How do we deliver them?' asked John.

'No, no, that's all right. Do me a favour and give them to the Padré. You don't get mixed up in that.'

'Ah, OK. We can help with that.'

'All right. That will be as soon as possible?'

'Yes.'

72

'Or you are not in a hurry?' asked the caller, sarcastically.

'We are in quite a hurry. Myself, as I said, I have job. I have to get back to it. And, well, his wife is a bit upset, so well . . . I think we are going away this weekend. When we can get a flight and arrange . . .'

'Well, perfect, very kind of you, then . . .'

'No, it's nothing. With luck, this will all turn out well.'

'*Si, si, perfecto. Bueno, muy amable.*'

'Fine, right, goodbye.' So the call ended, with all the routine polite noises of Colombian conversation. The handover of the negotiation to the Padré had been done. Would it work?

Roberto had got home. Wonderful man, he did find the telephone number of the Embassy and telephoned them. The Embassy rang the house and said, 'Nanette, there is a man who rang and says that he was a prisoner with David and would like to see you.'

On 25 May, John and Nanette met Roberto in a neutral place. This was the first solid news. A real kidnap victim, as I was, and who had been where I was and had seen me. I had been taken by the flying column *Teofilo Forero* and passed on to the *Frente 53*. We were in the *paramo* about three hours from Bogotá. I had bust my wrist but nothing serious. We passed our time playing chess and looking at insects and birds. I had been taken from the garage of the flat. That worried the family greatly and a bodyguard was arranged for a while. Roberto had been handed over against payment. This *frente* acts honestly (ha ha). Roberto was very nervous. Poor chap, he had just got out and had not recovered his nerve.

'He must be cold,' worried Nanette,

'Don't worry,' Roberto comforted her. 'I left him all my blankets.'

The committee of friends were taken by surprise by the news that I had been taken in the garage of my building. Now that they knew, it produced in them a frenzy of suspicious thinking. Ana, the maid, became the chief suspect. Did she tell them that I had murmured that I would be back about eight at night? How could I have? I did not know that I would have an early supper with Raimundo. So where did the time of eight o'clock come from? It must be the time fixed for the kidnap. Or invented afterwards? Their minds raced. It was insecure. She must be fired.

'No. You are wrong,' said John, stoutly defending the girl he had known and trusted for years,

Father Rodrigo held up his hand. 'Ah, there is nothing that a woman will not do for her lover.'

Then it was the people at the farm. They had the contact with the FARC. They rang Ana and asked at what time el señor would come home. She told them 'eight' or 'in an hour'. The farm people then rang the guerrilla and told them to move at that time. They must be fired or reported to the police. Or they were faithful and honest and the porter had let the gang in? But not on his own. It must have been Ana again.

The family left the country and installed themselves in London but only after Nanette had put up a big fight. She was strong and determined to stay and be at hand if things broke. She loves Colombia and has so many friends to support her. But she went, as the committee insisted. That made the Foreign Office and the family and friends happier. The FARC had our home telephone number and it was what the Padré advised. Let the guerrilla just have one point of contact – him. But the negotiation was now at a distance. Would it be well handled? What if I called?

CHAPTER 18

On the run in the mountains

I T WAS NOT LONG UNTIL Papa Noel left us. He was given a mare and put on it and led up the path the other side of the hut, going north-west. I had asked him to contact the Embassy. Was he going home? Why otherwise were they sending him away from us? It was a mystery. His white head disappeared over the crest of the hill and we were now four: Grandpa, Fredy, Brutus and I. Fredy was the one who most felt that he was due to go home. He spoke to Pedro often and asked him anxiously what was going on with his negotiation. At least each of us had a *caleta* of our own. We had to put Grandpa to bed and get him up in the morning and take him to pee in the bushes. Fredy had been the one to do it when I came and Epimaco had left, but he was getting nervous and irritable and lost his patience with the old man. It was not in the nature of Brutus to help anyone.

After the rocket attack and the covering of our *caletas* with bamboo fronds, I suppose that Pedro felt the need to move camp. Maybe we had been seen from the air. Maybe the constant walking up and down to the hut had left a trail that could be seen from the air. It was not safe to stay. He had to keep his prisoners alive. So one morning he sent his boys, accompanied by Fredy, along the hillside, eastwards, to scout a new site, or so Fredy said. They cut poles and lugged roofing canvas and cooking pots. It was not far away. With precision bombing, it was not necessary to go too far.

Fredy came back that night and kept quiet. But early next morning, he was called to the hut below and came back, elated to pack his things. He was off home. 'I was told last night, but could not tell you. I am so happy.' Tears ran down his cheeks. He had been frightened and was very excited. He gave me the little SONY radio and a pair of scissors and went off up the hillside, in the same direction that Papa Noel had taken. Later Hanibal said that he had walked at speed all day, faster than the guerrilla could, in an excess of energy, and was home on the second day.

We completed the move. The new site was only an hour away, with the same view, on the same hillside. There was a stream for cooking and another stream for bathing. We were lower than the guerrilla in some trees on the edge of the open rocky hillside, overlooking the river where the trout were. We could not see the hut any more. The *caletas* were raised, not sleeping on the ground, but it was colder here. Fredy's black plastic strips were needed to close the sides of the *caletas*, particularly for Grandpa. It rained incessantly. At night I lay on my back and the thunder sounded right over us and the lightning blinded my eyeballs,

75

through the closed eyelids. Real mountain weather, but it was a tranquil spot. We were left alone. I made a *tejo* pitch on the path. *Tejo* is a game of throwing a heavy stone at a target. The player with the most hits of the target wins over a series of ten throws. I bullied Grandpa to play, against his will, to keep him busy. Brutus would not. There was a large flame parasite on a bush near us and I could watch the long-tailed Sylph hummingbird feeding on the scarlet flower bunches.

I had the radio, and Pedro gave me batteries which was nice of him. It was in a bad condition, but I could fiddle with it delicately and pick up SW from abroad. Radio Exterior de España, Voice of America, French Radio, and then the dear old BBC World Service *Outlook* programme, with Heather Paton. And a serialised book – *Goodbye To All That* by Robert Graves, which I had read at school, read by John Le Carré himself. At five in the morning, alone in my *caleta* in the rain, I revelled in these voices.

The major need was to wash our clothes and wash ourselves. The clothes were one thing. The guerrilla has bars of blue washing soap (*Jabon Rey*) and there was a stream. We found the way across the wet bog to the stream but then how were we to dry them? It rained so much. In the dry hours, we draped the clothes on the bushes and watched the sky. If the rain came, the clothes were rescued and taken out again later.

But what about us? Who had the courage to strip and stand in the freezing mountain stream? Brutus had the most courage. I splashed water over myself like a cat and towelled hard but Grandpa refused. We had to wear all the clothes we had all the time, especially as night fell, for it was damn cold all the time.

The aeroplanes made Pedro worry about the smoke from the fire. There was a tent over the fire to protect against the rain. If it rained, the smoke was not visible but if it was a fine day, then the plume of smoke could betray us, so sometimes the fire was not lit until after dark, and that meant that the supper came in the darkness and we had to eat blind. Next morning we washed the pan in the stream.

When we sat and watched the valley, we could see how the rainforest water cycle worked. The clouds came up the valley from the llanos, until just below where we were and, instead of crossing to the Bogotá savannah, unloaded their contents on us. The rain soaked the bogs and leaked into the streams. The bogs (*humedales*) kept the rivers running the whole year. The rivers ran into the Amazon/Orinoco plains and out into the Atlantic, but on the way evaporated enough water to form the clouds that came up the valley and soaked us. You could see these masses of cloud racing up and down the slopes and, on the slopes between us at the top and the hot llanos at the bottom, it was 'cloud forest', a damp paradise for vegetation and birds and insects.

Pedro wanted to eat meat again. The cattle belonging to the men of the hut were around. He negotiated to buy a steer (*un novillo*) and selected it and sent

Vladimir to get it and kill it. The steer was not in agreement and escaped, so we had the gratifying sight of Vladimir being pulled across the rocks and wrapping himself around a tree. The steer got away but the next day he met his fate, and we began to eat offal.

'We shall stay here until they finish the meat,' thought Brutus. 'Why don't they give us the good meat before it goes off? We have to eat all this rubbish first. I should like an *hijo de puta* chunk of steak.'

But it was not to be. It was soon that we were told to pack. There is something comfortable about staying and making a routine and hoping that the next move is to go home. Moving is unsettling and unpleasant. The guerrilla hinted that we might move down to the llanos, further from Bogotá. Bad news. So off we went, along the hill and down to the river. It was boiling and splashing, full of the rains. How was Grandpa going to manage the walk? He had to and he did, quite well. He was on the mend, physically and mentally. We marched along the south bank until there was a crossing place. It was difficult. First we had to wade into the water and then hoist ourselves on to a rock and jump to another rock and to a foothold on the opposite bank and up. The guerrilla took our backpacks. Grandpa was carried on Ismael's back. We arrived wet and took off our rubber boots to empty them out. Then we walked across the slope on the north of the river, through bushes, and found a clearing and huts on the other side. This was the 'Patio'. The clearing had been trampled by mules. It was like a large football pitch and must have been visible from the air. We had our *caleta* in the trees on the other side, at the top. It was one *caleta* for all three of us. It looked as if there had been a fighting unit of the FARC there before. It was on a slope and in dark trees with nowhere to walk and it was miserable and cold. The rain was becoming worse, if possible! Water flowed under our *caleta*. Water flowed everywhere.

We saw less of the guerrilla. It was difficult to get them to lend us the chess set. Brutus had found that chess interested him and took his mind off his situation. The Patio was boring and enclosed. We were forbidden to cross a line below our area. What could we see, when the weather allowed us out? On the trees, there were some orchids – an *encyclia* with a long flower spike, and little ones, like pink snowdrops, which may have been *telepogons*, or not orchids at all. Not many, but some. Flocks of blue jays passed through the tops of the trees, feeding. A pair of *curassows*, big quiet dark turkeys, came and stayed for two days. Brutus threw sticks at them, but they paid no attention. There were no stones here to throw.

'Hey, leave them alone,' I remonstrated. 'Don't you like watching them?'

He threw more sticks at them, moodily.

Hummingbirds would come, looking for flowers. I saw a Pygmy Owl, tiny, immobile, turning its head around 360 degrees. It sat for two days.

'They are going to take us down to the llanos,' said Brutus. And after a while, indeed, we packed up and went further down the hillside. We walked in the rain to a steep bank and scrambled down. There were big three-metre vertical slides, difficult with a pack and a broken wrist. Grandpa found it difficult and needed to be manhandled. At the bottom, a raging stream came from the left out of the mountains and joined the river. It was very difficult and dangerous to cross. We formed a chain and the boys hung on to the old prisoners as we waded across. The bottom was of large slippery rocks. The torrent battered us. At the other side we stopped and found a pile of rocks where the fireplace was. Beyond it was a pile of woodshavings. There had been loggers here. Someone had planted eucalyptus trees, not native, and not particularly valuable and there were large pines. We called it *Los Pinos* (The Pines) like some house in Weybridge in England. We put our *caleta* over the shavings, and slept on them. Once again there was a communal *caleta* for all three of us. The rest went on into the trees and pitched camp. We had come down and, at this altitude, we were in the clouds which we had seen from above. It was wet and miserable and there was nowhere to walk at all, but we got the chess set. The *chonto* was the river; drop your trousers and crouch in the water – the original WC.

I would wake up early and get up and pee and brush my teeth. I decided the first day to walk down through the *caletas* of the guerilla to the *rancho* to say '*Buenos dias*' to whoever was there doing the cooking. They could only tell me to go back. It was always Pedro who was up first. He was polite at that hour. He liked a coffee first thing. I could usually succeed in being given a coffee too. The fire would be lit up with lots of fresh wood. Pedro would switch on his AM/FM radio and hear the news. The rain would be pelting down and I could get close to the fire and also bring clothes to dry on the poles on which the cooking pots were hung. This was the year in which Juan Pablo Montoya was getting to the top of the Formula One car racing. He was the best-known Colombian in the world. I asked Pedro whether he had won, after the Sunday race days. It was also the Football World Cup and England had a good chance. Colombia had failed to qualify, a blow to the pride of a country that loved its football. At the end, I could say that England had the best score against Brazil, so were the second best team. Argentina and France had failed miserably. And I missed seeing any of it, lost in the cold forests of the Andes in the hands of rebels. But the radio kept me informed, as long as I could get away with it.

The other two did not manage to come to the *rancho*, feeling it was out of bounds. The other guerrilla came and went. The duty cook was by the fire all day. One day Pancake managed to throw cooking oil on the fire and burn a hole in the roof. This was bad, as camouflage tents were scarce and the rain was fierce. She stomped out and cried by the river. One day Ismael was brought in from cutting wood, with blood pouring down his hand. He had chopped with his machete between his thumb and index finger. It was a bad sight. Pedro sewed his hand together and bandaged it. It swelled up like a melon, but healed.

Juan Pablo and Vladimir reported a family of turkeys roosting on a branch of a big pine tree. They got permission to shoot them. The sound of AK-47 single shots rang around the valley. They came back. No turkeys.

'You incompetents,' laughed Hanibal. 'You should have adjusted the foresight from 200 metres to as close as possible.'

'We did.'

'Then you are lousy shots.'

Hanibal went fishing and caught little trout. It was difficult to get worms, and he had to stop. I was kicking some dead trees and found maggots inside, big white maggots, called *chizas*, which eat wood.

'Let's fish with these,' I said.

'You fish. I am busy.'

So I took his rod and the maggots and went along the river happily. I fished around the rocks where the water swirls round and pulled out a few. It was not the Hope River in Scotland, but it was a fine mountain beck. There were dippers flying from rock to rock. I was being given some free space. But the maggots ran out.

Then we were on the move again further down the valley. We had to cross another stream and enter a wood and camp above a little beach, where the *rancho* was set up. There was less space, and a denser wood. It rained much more, all the time. The *rancho* was washed away in the night and we lost some pans, machetes and food. It was awful. We could not go back as the stream rose and was too dangerous to cross. After Pancake had burned the roof, the spare one was deployed and it was full of holes. As one stood eating (there was nowhere to sit), water cascaded down one's neck. Brutus called it 'The Pit'. But it was safe. The Air Force could not see us under the rainclouds and trees. Were we on the way down to the llanos or just hidden here or what? It was awful. Grandpa could not get down the bank to the *rancho* on his own. Then the bank collapsed and became a mudslide. We were wet and filthy.

Pedro must have seen all this. As soon as we could cross the stream, he said, 'Let's go. Now, now. Hurry.' Before it could rain again and the stream could rise.

We went back to The Pines. It was better but it did not stop raining. We were back on the shavings, playing chess in the semi-darkness and going to the rancho in the morning. The boys said that they were building a bridge of logs to cross the main river and get us to the other side, then we could march down to the llanos. This side was too difficult.

One night there was noise and flashlights. In the morning on the way, I found a new *caleta* and a sleeping bag full of human being inside. The radio had been lent to this new arrival.

'It's a woman,' announced Brutus. 'I saw her.'

The second day I saw her on the way down. I had been listening to John Le Carré, with the famous World Service hisses and buzzes. On the way back, I saw that she had woken up. I stopped and whispered, 'What's your name?'

'Pati.'

'How old are you?' (Not a gentlemanly question.)

'39.'

It was too dangerous to continue, as Pedro's *caleta*, which he shared with the Witch, was five paces away. The Woman had long black hair and a fine face and she was alone. She must have been kidnapped too. She was stuck in her *caleta* by the rain and the dense forest.

A week later, while I was in the *rancho*, drying my wet clothes, she appeared with a toilet roll on her way to her *chonto*, but backed off and disappeared silently. We had to pretend that she did not exist and the guerrilla said not a word about her. That was the rule, apparently.

I would sing a bedtime song normally, before entering the horrid *caleta* and the shavings floor. When she came I sang more lustily in her direction, to let her feel that she was not alone. I thought that I heard her crying at night.

Then we were visited. I was by the river watching the natural camouflage of a small trout, when three *guerrilleros* walked across a fallen tree trunk and sprang confidently over the big rocks in the middle of the river. The first one was a fellow with lots of bandages and one eye and several fingers missing. The second was an Indian girl with a terrible sore throat and the leader was a thin-moustached *comandante* with a beret, who was carrying a pine seedling that he had uprooted. They came and looked around. The *comandante* was called Ferney. He was Pedro's boss. They came and they went, probably to meet the Woman.

The river continued to rise and the rain never stopped. Even the guerrilla had problems with the river. The food stores were still at the hut, the other side of the river. These boys, and the girls, too had to porter great bags of potato or rice or cooking oil over the water. Ismael fell in and nearly drowned, we were told. We oldies were stuck and that went on for ten days. Brutus decided to help.

'I know about radios. When I was a boy in Medellin, I liked to repair radios. Let me have a look and mend the dial.'

Why did I not say no? He opened up the little Sony and borrowed a penknife that miraculously had not been taken away from Grandpa. He turned the capacitors around and broke the connection to the speaker. Then one of the capacitors fell off and he threw the radio on the floor.

'Better throw this rubbish in the river. It can never work, bit of shit.'

A strong desire to beat his head in with a blunt instrument bubbled up in me. No more BBC World Service. A line to the real world outside was snapped. I felt more like Robinson Crusoe, and this fat pig was Man Friday, or Man Saturday Night at the boozer. Grrrrrrrrr!

The day came when Pedro walked up and said that we must move immediately. Grandpa was terrified of climbing the bank on the other side. It was high and vertical and he did not think that he could do it. The crossing was dramatic, with the force of the water pushing us downstream. The climbing was not easy, and the broken wrist required a technique of hooking the elbow over the branches and pulling up. I left my pack at the bottom. When I reached the top, Pancake said 'Where is your pack?'

'You get it. I can't climb with the pack and my arm.'

'You will need it.' She was not going to get it. So I had to go down and get it. Halfway up, she did take pity and come to heave it up to the top. We walked on and arrived back at the Patio. Ferney the *comandante* had his *caleta* there, with One Eye and the hoarse squaw. We were back at the horrid Patio. Our *caleta* had no roof and the grass on the floor was wet. No one came to help put up the roof. Brutus was angry and unwilling to help. Pedro came up and looked and warned us not to come down lower than a line across a tree below the *caleta*. He looked at me, with a straight look.

'Especially you, Meester. No coming to the *rancho!*'

My special tolerance from The Pines was over. We had wasted a month, the whole of June, down in The Pines and The Pit for nothing. We were getting nowhere.

CHAPTER 19

June: the family

THE THIRTY-FIRST OF MAY was a bad day. The FARC had not contacted the Padré as agreed, but they did ring that day. He said that the money did not exist and he needed to speak to me and see if I had agreed to the amount. They said that 1.3 billion pesos was not enough and they had to have one million dollars. They would ring the next day to see if the Padré would pay 'or they would know what to do with the old man.'

The committee had had advice from experts and was ready to face the escalation of threats. They recommended that the Padré say that there was some money available, that when the FARC were reasonable, the discussion could advance, that if they killed the 'old man', they would get nothing. Then they were to ring off. A silence could develop. It was going to be important to stick at the available money and not be soft or hint at a bigger figure that does not exist. The family is neither large nor tight and the children do not live with their father, after his remarriage, and the English are a cold-hearted race.

Have the captors realised that they are holding a retired man, not a rich businessman? Roberto had told the family that the guerrilla was excited before I arrived, saying, 'We are getting a rich foreigner.'

The FARC negotiator was asking for gifts. He wanted pre-paid telephone cards. He could have them.

They rang back again the same day, and were given the agreed hard line. They got angry. 'We shall chop him up and return him in a rubbish bag,' they said.

'Go ahead,' was the reply. 'Why should I care? I am not a member of the family, and you will get nothing. You don't impress me with your threats.'

They rang back on Saturday, 1 June. This time they were calmer and asked what the Padré was going to do. He improvised that he was going to speak to a bank. But it was a Saturday. He had to gulp and say that it was a special meeting. They rang off. Now that he was on this track, the committee suggested that he go on, next time, to say that it is difficult to arrange a loan in England and bring the money over.

'Can I offer more money?' he asked.

'No, not a cent more,' was the answer. 'Stick.'

The next time the *guerrillero* rang, this line was taken. This man then said that he was going to travel for five weeks, so the Padré said that we would expect no calls for five weeks. The caller backtracked and said that he could call from wherever he was. But he introduced a worrying theme, that I had offered more money. The Padré said that, if this were true, he would have to talk to me. The *guerrillero* said that that would only happen after a deal was made and a proof of survival was required. So the idea of 'my offer' could be a bluff. The deal was on track and could be all tied up in a few weeks.

Another call was made to the Padré the same day. When the game is afoot, it moves fast. This time the Padré was able to spin out the discussion, developing a long tale of how difficult it is to make money growing potatoes. How many hectares, how much work, how much wages paid, what lousy prices in the *Mercado de Abastos*, so that the farmer ends up with so little money?

'*Entiendes*? Do you understand?'

'*Bueno*, but there are *los ricos*. The rich can pay.'

'Forget it, honeybun. There are no rich. You have chased them all away. They have left for Miami, those that you have not kidnapped or killed. The ones who are left are the poor. Take it or leave it. Our offer stands. Get it?'

'OK. I shall be away for a week, I shall ring you.'

So, was I alive? Probably? They could ask for the money, and I could be dead already. It has been known. They were ringing up a lot.

They rang again on 6 June. They hinted that they could come down. But for what had been offered, 'We won't even tell you where the body is.'

In London, they had to think where to find money. The amount demanded did not exist, let alone more. Which bank would help? Ha! Sell the furniture and mortgage granny. The *El Tiempo* newspaper ran an article about people who had had to pay several times. And how Sumapaz was a nest of kidnappers, where the Army never entered.

It is easy to dream that the FARC 'need the money' and will settle for less. How likely is that? One reads too much meaning into the slightest thing. They ring a lot? Ergo, they are desperate for money.

Contacts were made for a broadcast message on Caracol radio in the *secuestrados* (kidnapped victims) programme. It would be a 'chin up, old man' message. But the English policemen thought that that was inconsistent with the 'keep it quiet' policy. A better idea would be a letter through the Padré or the Red Cross. However, Nanette decided that she wanted to do it, in Spanish, and low key. The press would not pick it up.

The bill for my mobile telephone arrived and was large. It had been on me on 1 May, and reported to the Gaula. They had wanted it kept alive. Who had to pay these calls? We did. It was forthwith blocked.

On 12 June, the FARC rang on the mobile which the Padré used for this. He had been on a trip and had forgotten it for some days. They were upset because they knew that the Gaula were on the case. Oh, yes? How do they know that? They accused the British Embassy of sticking the fuzz on them.

'What, what? Drivel. We have not spoken to the Embassy. You know that we are only talking to you and not to the cops. We would not do that.'

'Anyway, the money you have offered is too little. Do you want the corpse of this *hijo de puta*, or what?'

'We are trying to sell the garden furniture, but it is raining in England.'

'We are fed up with you. You are taking the mickey.'

'Great, can I resign? You are not prepared to deal and I have other things to do.'

'No, no, we had better carry on with you.'

'Then climb down and talk sense.'

The cat biffs the mouse and the mouse nips the tail of the cat. When would they ask him to travel to see them? And where? In the hills above the town of Fusagasuga? The Padré had a great style in giving as good as he got from these people and saying, 'We don't care a fig for your threats.'

On 21 June the Padré said that on another case he had had to speak to another *Frente*, the 22. Hugo, the *comandante*, was a superboss in the kidnapping line, and although he did not have me (I knew that, and Roberto had said the same), he would listen. The two million dollar demand is crap. The Padré could ask for the Mercedes back so that it could be sold, to raise money.

But the Army found the Mercedes, in a field above Fusagasuga.

Chapter 20

Presidential elections

I N COLOMBIA, THE PRESIDENT is changed every fourth year and cannot do a second consecutive term. When I went into captivity, the presidential elections for the changeover fixed for 7 August 2002 were at full speed. The liberals had a candidate, Horacio Serpa, from Bucaramanga, with his huge moustache and a rumoured past connection with the guerrilla. A people's man? The conservatives had become weakened and split. Juan Camilo Restrepo was a competent, humorous and well-mannered man, but he did not have the votes. The other conservative was Noemi Sanin, one of the most attractive ladies in Latin American politics for years, the darling of all the ambassadors and bankers, and once the ambassador in London, and there was a left winger, Lucho Garzon, a trade union man and seen as a communist by the middle classes.

An outsider in 2001 had been Alvaro Uribe Velez, not accepted by his Liberal party, a former governor of the province of Antioquia, whose father had been killed by the guerrilla and who had been doing a sabbatical year at Oxford University. Seen as a creator of self-defence groups, he was a fighter but controversial.

There was to be a first round of elections at the end of May and a second round between the two top candidates in June. Uribe was miles behind in 2001, but started to catch up as 2002 advanced. He was a Liberal, facing the official Liberal, Serpa. Put the two of them face to face, and Serpa was a traditional politician, a bumbler, perhaps tinted with corruption from the time of President Samper, while Uribe was a hard man, who was going to face down the guerrilla and restore security for ordinary Colombians, and who rejected the wasted time of the Pastrana peace talks.

'Uribe is a paramilitary,' said the *guerrilleros*. 'There will be war. We want peace and he wants war, with his friends the Gringos.'

In the elections in May, when I was in the Sumapaz mountains, Uribe won by 52 per cent in the first round, an unheard-of success. Colombians wanted the hard man. They were sick of the guerrilla.

'Oh God,' said Grandpa. 'I hope that I am out of here before 7 August (the handover of the presidency).'

'Why?' I replied. 'What difference will it make? The same guerrilla, the same army, the same need to talk to them?'

Indeed, Uribe had been heard to say that he would involve the United Nations in peace talks, probably knowing that the FARC would not talk to him.

'Ach, you are ignorant,' growled Brutus. 'Things will get violent. The Army will get moving. We cannot stay in Sumapaz. It will be difficult for our families to negotiate.'

'I don't think much will change,' I said.

I was wrong, of course.

CHAPTER 21

Grandpa's story

LIFE IN THE MOUNTAINS WAS MISERABLE. It rained all the time. It was cold. We got wet. We had no change of clothes at this stage in our captivity. We spent too long inside the tent, with the rain pounding on the roof. It got dark by 5.15 every day and the food often arrived after that, because the guerrilla were frightened of lighting a fire in the daytime and leaving a column of smoke to be seen by the Army or the Air Force. The *recepcionista* would arrive in the dark, no flashlights allowed, and we would reach out for the pots, try to find our spoons, and eat in darkness, on our knees. Surely pigs got better treatment than that? The eating would come to an end and there we were, the three of us, in one tent, at half past five, with a twelve-hour night in front of us, lying on the ground.

'Right, Grandpa,' I bullied. 'You can't go to sleep yet. It is too early. Let's talk.'

'*Que?* What, uh?' the deaf old man grunted.

'Wake up. Turn over, Grandpa. Tell us about your life.'

'Eh?' he queried.

'*Hijo de puta*, deaf old bastard,' growled Brutus. 'Just shut up and go to sleep.'

'It's too early. Come on, Grandpa. You are eighty. You were born in 1922. Si?'

'I suppose so.'

'1922. What was Colombia like then?'

'I was born in Arbelaez, near Fusagasuga. My father had a farm. Sugar cane and a *trapiche* (sugar press). He also was an *arriero*. He ran mule trains from the río Magdalena at Girardot up to Fusa and down. Most of the people there were from Boyaca, and had moved to farm the better land in our area. I went to school, but my father took me out after two years, as he needed me to pick the coffee and work with him. I can read and write.'

'Do you remember the 1929 Crash and the big world depression? How did it affect Colombia?

'I remember that the price of coffee fell to a few centavos. The USA had no money to buy it. It was a big crisis in Colombia. We had no money. My father worked with the mules and we made *panela* (brown sugar loaves) from the cane. Colombia should export *panela*, you know. It is so healthy . . .'

After a minute, the huge snores, for which Grandpa was famous, started. It was too early. Poor old man! He felt the cold. He needed to sleep. The rain beat on the roof. Was my bullying of him to talk a selfish act, just to amuse myself and learn more about the country which I liked so much? Did I need to talk to someone? Yes. But also I had to get Grandpa's morale up. He was frightened of the Brute and of the guerrilla. We had nothing to read. By talking about himself, he could gain confidence and remember the good things and have something to live for and get home for. He must not give up and die.

The next day it rained all day and we could only go out for a few minutes. I played chess with Brutus three times. Enough. No coffee.

'No, I won't bloody play chess again. It makes my head ache.'

'Go on, Meester. It helps me forget my troubles.'

'Then sing a song or tell a story.'

'Go on.'

'No. No. No.'

The clothes would not dry. After supper in the dark, I helped Grandpa get into his cocoon of blankets. His nose and white moustache stuck out.

'Go on with your story, Grandpa,' I nudged him. 'We cannot sleep yet. It is only twenty past five.'

'Eh?' he had not heard. So I said again with the decibels increased.

'What do you want to know?'

I thought. 'Tell us about *La Violencia* and Rojas Pinilla?'

'Of course, there was always violence. In our area they were *godos*. There were gangs who took people away and threw their bodies into the river. It was bad. I kept out of politics. When General Rojas came, there was more law and order. He imposed a curfew. If you were caught out after curfew, no question – into the *calabozo*. I spent a night in prison once in Bogotá. I used to go up to the market to buy potatoes and other vegetables for our shop. I had an old truck. It broke down and I got caught out late and was taken to the prison. A friend of mine came and bailed me out the next morning. There were military governors in all the towns. We had a retired sergeant of the Army. He was a rough man. A bad man. He took money.'

'When was that?'

'I don't remember. In the 1950s. 1953, perhaps.'

'But there was less violence?'

'Oh yes. Things got better.'

'Rojas Pinilla got a lot done? He built the new Eldorado airport. And the Military Hospital. What else?'

'A lot. I don't remember. Then the *politicos* got together and made a pact and returned to power. My father had the shop and I helped in it. We had the farm with the sugar cane. And we bought cattle too. I like growing things. Now I have planted lots of trees. Mangoes, oranges, *platanos*. You should come and see.' He fell silent and soon the snores started.

The next day, he went on. 'The road only started up at the top of the hill. We used to ride up and leave our mules, where the road started. The road down to the Magdalena river was made in the 1930s and it was made by the prisoners, the chain gangs. Pick and shovel, chained together and with the guards standing over them. All the way down to the Parrot's Beak. Then the trucks and buses could start to run. It was the end of the *arrieros*. We sold our mules.'

'How was the town in those days?'

'We had the first house of two storeys. Of brick. The houses had always been made of *bahareque*, mud and straw, plastered on to wicker and sticks. One storey. There was a church, of course.'

'When did the electricity come?'

'The church bought a generator. The *cura* put up a loudspeaker and would broadcast music from the radio for *fiestas*. There was radio from Bogotá – the *cadena nacional*, the national network, now RCN. And Caracol. We bought radios with batteries. Then the Electricity Company was set up and came to the town. I think that was in the 1950s.

'Arbelaez has a good agricultural fair. And a bull ring. It was a more important town than Fusagasuga. The new road changed that. We are off the road, but before we were on the mule train route. The *feria* is about now. The people will miss me,' he pondered.

'I used to take my children to school in Bogotá and on the way back, I would stop at the slaughter yard (*el matadero*) and buy a cow's head.'

Brutus woke up, 'That's what I like to eat. You know those stands on the street in the south of Bogotá? Where they sell all sorts of stuff. Cow's lips. *Bofe*. Great stuff.'

'Yes. We could eat the head all week. My wife had died. I had six children. A woman from the town cooked for us. My daughter went to the *gimnasio femenino*. She is a teacher now, in a bilingual French school. She takes the children to France on holiday. My other daughter, she joined the diplomatic service, and was sent to the consulate in Chicago. When they wanted to bring her back, she decided to stay on in Chicago. She is married to a Colombian. They have a newspaper round. He is a total bum. He drinks. She does the work. I went there to stay. We went on a driving holiday with friends of hers. Where? I can't remember. The children, they don't speak Spanish. They are American now. I have my son, Ramon, who works in the shop. I have another who works in a bank in Bogotá. And my other daughter who lives with me. Her husband died.'

'Gosh, Grandpa, you spent a lot on education in Bogotá. And getting up in the morning to drive to their schools. You were not properly educated yourself.'

'But I made sure my children were. When I get out, I think I shall go to stay with my daughter in Chicago,' he concluded, and turned over and snored. I did not think he would. He loves his farmhouse and his trees and animals. The worry is that the bad boys would come and see him again. We all think of getting away from them.

The next day he said, 'When you are out you must come and see me. Your wife would like to see the orchids I have planted in the trees. You can see the *trapiche*. It does not work, because thieves came and stole the pinion. You know the government should help the *paneleros*. The country could export millions. It is the healthiest food in the world, *panela*. Pure sugar. The coffee price is no good. Most people have dug up the coffee, and planted grass, for cattle. There used to be a lot of birds, especially *troupiales*, the black and yellow ones, who sing so sweet. But people hunt and kill them. I tell them not to.'

The Colombian mountain countryside is so beautiful and fertile. No winter, always green, always flowering.

'I don't have money,' he complained. 'I don't know why they kidnapped me. I have fourteen cows. The shop is small. My children are not rich. I am old. It is a mistake. I was driving down from the fields where the cows are, and I was stopped by these people. They got in and made me drive up into the hills. You know, I was driving. There was a young girl next to me, with a rifle. I came to a bridge. I should have turned the wheel and driven into the river and killed us all.'

'Did your sons do military service, Grandpa?' I asked, not a diplomatic question.

'No, I paid the brigade major, so that they got their *libreta militar*.'

In Latin America, every young man has been traditionally issued with a notebook, in which his military service is written up and stamped. If you are asked to produce it and there is compulsory military service, and you can't show it, then you get dragged off to the barracks.

'OK, so you love your sons. You did not want them to go and fight. How many of the middle class do that? I have heard people say that until the upper classes send their sons to the war, they will never really feel strongly about winning the war. The people who live in the big cities, what do they know about this?' I waved my hand around.

'*Si*, right, they don't know the reality of this, I agree.'

'Shut up, Meester,' growled Brutus, 'You're not even a Colombian. *Que te importa*? What does it matter to you that we *negros indios* kill each other. So that you *yanquis* get richer.'

'I am not an *hijo de puta yanqui*. And you are talking balls. I bet you did not do military service.'

'No, I bloody did not. I bought my *libreta militar*.'

'Oh, very brave. You are the one who talks about killing all the *hijos de puta*. And sits at home drinking and . . .' I stopped.

'And what?'

'And nothing. Reading a good book.'

So who are the soldiers? Those who can't buy their way out perhaps.

'I bet you did not do military service, Meester.'

'Well, no I did not, because it had been abolished. But at school, I did army training . . .' I thought I had better shut up. Anyway what has a school cadet force got to do with this? But when I went to Oxford, there were senior men to me, who had served in Cyprus, Malaya, Kenya.

'The guerrilla took over Arbelaez,' went on Grandpa. 'My town. They drove in trucks one morning and blew up the municipal building with explosives. Now it is a ruin. No municipal offices. No Agricultural Bank branch any more. The Coffee Bank pulled out afterwards. They did not stay long and they found a young traffic policeman, a *bachiller*, a school leaver doing national service, and killed him. What do they think they achieve by that? They don't win votes or popularity.'

CHAPTER 22

The family plugs on

O N 3 JULY, JOHN WAS IN BOGOTÁ and went to the Padré's office. They spoke together to the FARC negotiator, for fifteen minutes. They were all more at ease. John reiterated the amount of money that was available. The FARC man agreed that a parcel could be made up to be sent to me. The Padré had stuck for some time at that figure. The negotiator suggested that they spoke the next day at 6 p.m. He expected a higher offer. So our side decided not to make the call at all. The Gaula seemed to have lost interèst and thought that a rescue was out of the question. They could be seen a mile away, up in the bare mountains.

The French government was making a big fuss about their citizen, Ingrid Betancourt. Her case was notorious in France and her book was a bestseller. We had chosen silence and discretion. Could we whip up some political pressure? What use would it be? Several Tory luminaries had already spoken to their contacts and others were sympathetic. But what could the government do? Who in the world had the contacts with the rebels? Who could call in their markers? The UN? The International Red Cross? NGOs? The government had broken off their peace talks, and Alvaro Uribe Velez was going to be the hard man. Uribe had won the election on a mandate of tough action against the guerrilla. He had not taken over yet, but he had been traveling abroad. In Paris, he may have had an earful about Ingrid B. In London, he was invited to 10 Downing Street. One item on the agenda prepared for Tony Blair was . . . this fellow Hutchinson.

Was Europe the way to get through to the FARC? They had been allowed to have offices in Europe and had found sympathetic ears. What did they care about 'image?' Was it about money and to hell with the image?

On 13 July, the *El Tiempo* newspaper reported that the police had arrested six FARC kidnap negotiators in the area of Fusagasuga, under Sumapaz. The committee rang the Padré, who said, 'No wonder I have not had contact.'

'Did you talk to your friend Pedro?'

'No contact there either.'

'Have a go.'

The members of the committee sat back. 'Perhaps the police are doing a crash rescue on David now?'

'Perhaps the FARC are rushing all the prisoners as far as possible in a panic?'

'At least some of these bastards are behind bars.'

Victoria sent an email. 'I saw a BBC programme about kidnaps. One was in Colombia, an American from Cali, who was made to do a double payment and stayed in eleven months and had a hard time. Is the Padré totally committed? Can Blair achieve anything with Uribe?'

CHAPTER 23

The pressure increases

I F WE HAD WASTED TIME IN THE Pines and The Pit, at least from the Patio both
Brutus and Grandpa were taken up to the top of the mountains to speak to their
families. This was part of the process of negotiating the ransoms. It was necessary
to climb as high as possible to get into the line of sight of the masts for mobile
telephones. I suppose these masts were above Bogotá. Brutus charged off and was
back by four o'clock. It was raining hard and he was wet through and tired. He
had spoken to his main wife and told her how much money to get hold of. The
problem was where it was. It was owed to him by business partners.

'Those *hijos de puta* won't pay. They'll hope I die and then they can keep the
money,' he groused. I think he also felt that when he was first interviewed, he
had offered too much money. An easy mistake to make.

Grandpa went on another foul day, but did not come back the same night. I
was preoccupied. He had already been two and a half months longer than us. Why
was he not let go? Was there a problem with the amount? It was easy to imagine
that he had been taken out and shot dead on a hillside. The relief when he
appeared the next day was great. He was exhausted, totally, and lay in a comatose
state for two days but at least he had done it, which would have been unthinkable
in his bad days in May.

'They gave me a mare, and we slept in the plank hut, and went to the top early
in the morning. I spoke to my daughter-in-law in the shop. My son had gone to
Ibague to sell the truck.'

What about me? At least I had made the initial call to my lawyer in the second
week. But would I get the chance of talking to my family? Where was my family?
What was the FARC doing with them?

There was a radio transmitter in the *caleta* of Pedro which was below us on the
upper edge of the Patio. Ferney was camped on the north side. We could hear
the radio at the fixed times of transmission, but it was not very audible. A girl
manned the radio base somewhere in the main military camp and she went around
all the *comisiones* and *esquadras* on a rota. All names were in code. Brutus could
hear the words better than I, being a foreigner, and he stood close to the bottom
and strained his ear to hear.

One evening, the radio was crackling. The voice at the other end was an
authoritative one and it gave an order to Pedro. Something like 'And the
foreigner, get on with it!'

94

It was indeed something like that. I was called down and taken to Pedro's *caleta*. Ferney was there. I had never spoken to Ferney.

'When are we going to agree the money?' asked Pedro.

This was the bombshell, the whole point of this traipsing around the mountains. But I was not the one to negotiate, was I? Surely that was done with the family. Apart from the first interview with the moustached peasant *comandante* on 12 May, money had never been discussed.

'My family will do that,' I answered.

'Things have changed. We have a new policy. I have been given the job of negotiating for you now.'

What the hell? Had the negotiators been captured or killed? Were they keen to get rid of us? It was strange.

'Right. I told the *comandante* in the hut what I could pay.'

Pedro laughed. 'You are not going to pull my leg, are you? I know what you offered. But we know what you are worth. Let's talk real money.'

'I am not rich. I am a pensioner. I am not a businessman. What you think I have is completely false. I told you what I really have.'

'Look, stop pissing us about. Let me tell you, we have all the time in the world. We can hold you for two or three years, we don't care. Or we can sell you to other people who have other ways of getting the money. You would not like that. So let's talk.'

This was not a nice Pedro. Ferney sat silently listening. I should not negotiate. I should be careful. Could I stick out two years or more with these criminals?

'You agree a figure and we take you to talk to your family.'

This was the chance of a mobile telephone call to my home. They could hear my voice. Was that a good idea? Surely it was.

'I shall have to think about it. Give me time and we can talk tomorrow.'

'You have ten minutes!'

Christ, ten minutes! What should I say? I wanted to be allowed to speak with my home. Was an agreement on money the key? Why was it Pedro doing it?

'All right, let's talk now. You know what I said before. How about 300 million pesos? God knows how the family can get hold of so much money. I don't have it ready. It could take ages.'

'Let's be serious, Meester. You want to pull my leg? It will go badly for you. We can keep you for three years. Can you put up with that? We know what you have got. Let me tell you that we have decided a limit (*un tope*) for what we need. It is a million dollars. OK?'

This was going too fast. What was this? An auction at Sotheby's? A reserve price of a million dollars for this fine antique human? What was a *tope*? Should I withdraw now?

'I don't have anything like that. You know it.'

'Make an offer.'

'Then I get to speak to my home?'

'If we agree a figure, I take you to speak to your family.'

'If we don't agree, what?'

'You stay here as long as it takes. We have patience.'

'How can I know how much money can be raised, sitting here in the forest? You have to speak to my family.'

'Hurry up. The time is running out. I can just send you back to your *caleta*.'

What was the situation? I could say some figure that made him happy, and he could give me the telephone call. Then the family would pick it up and play the game. The figure was not important. There would be first-class advisers and friends, tough and experienced. They would know how to play this game. Or I could shut up and stick it out for ever.

Pedro wanted a million dollars. He had been told that all foreigners have that amount of money. He was not a usual negotiator himself. He was a fighting soldier. Why had he been told to get involved? The seconds ticked by like hours. I was in a tough spot.

I offered a bigger amount. He looked at Ferney, who waggled his head negatively.

'No.'

I offered a bit more.

'No.'

This was not a negotiation as the figure was too big. Should I have pulled out and lost the call home? Whatever I said could not be binding on the negotiations. Could it? No.

We split the difference and Pedro got the nod from Ferney.

'All right.'

The figure was too high, unreal, more than I had got to give them. It was lower than the two million dollars of 2 May and the million that was the *tope*. It was a new target for Pedro to use on the family, and was not a bargain. It was not even possible. But what would the family think if they heard this figure? I had to trust them. It was clear to me that I was in captivity for a long time. OK, I could stick it out. The only setback had been the broken wrist. But it did not hurt. It just flopped about and had no strength. I was sleeping and walking well. I felt confident.

'Now you take me to make the call?'

'I shall set it up. Just be patient.'

'Goodbye.'

I walked up the path to our *caleta* and explained a bit of what had happened to the others. Not much. I said that I was going to make my call. I felt that the process had been jerked forward at speed and that was good. But the money was out of any realistic framework still. I hoped that I would never be asked to talk figures again. The information that the FARC had was so wrong. And what could I do to raise money? Nothing. What was important was to make the call.

'What about the call?' I asked Pedro the next day, when I awoke and nobody came to take me for a walk up the mountain.

'Patience. We are waiting for new mobile telephones. The old ones have no battery power.'

I felt happier and more confident of an outcome, after this nasty interview with Pedro and Ferney. Things had come to the boil. The threat was menacing. I was a prisoner of cruel people in an unhuman criminal business. How were we going to get out of it? It was easier for me to stick it out, than for the family to bring it to an end. But I felt that the process was on the move. I was not going to be killed, was I?

CHAPTER 24

I make my call

INSTEAD OF MOVING DOWN TO THE llanos below, our next destination was up into the mountains. We had been for over two months in the original valley. It had been the peak of the rainy season which may have kept the Army away from attacking and the Air Force from seeing us. It had kept us, the prisoners, confined to our tents a lot, and cold and dirty and unwashed. Shortly after my session with Pedro and Ferney, we left the valley and walked south up the river into high country.

'This is the way I came in,' I whispered, 'and the way Epimaco walked out in the third week of May.'

'Are you sure?' asked Brutus.

'Yes. We walked into the hut from up there. There is a farm with cheese and pigs the other side. I was with Laureano.'

But it still did not help me understand the road I took from the day of kidnap to this bit to the first hut. Where the hell were we? Sumapaz, yes. But it was a huge area. Nobody one knows can go there, so it has gone 'off the map'.

I wound my memory backwards to 12 May, when I took this way, with my newly bust wrist and my original clothes and Ramirez, the *arriero*. It had been a hard walk, I remembered. We had been allowed to leave our things packed for mules to carry them. Up and up we went to the crest (the *corona* or crown), which I remembered from the other side. It was bare hillside. On the left a long thin waterfall splashed down, with a lot of noise. Lovely. Little bushes, grass, rocks, boggy bits. We saw some frogs and some lizards.

'Don't touch them,' Hanibal warned. 'They can be poisonous.'

Above, a pair of Solitary Eagles circled, high up. We only saw them twice. They are uncommon. They may have been something else, but their black colour and size and scarceness made this a possible identification. What did they eat? We saw no animal life apart from lizards.

Hanibal gave us some *panela* to suck for energy. Luckily it did not rain up at this height. Our thighs ached with the pumping climb. There was a place where we had to jump over rocks. Behind us, in the distance was a figure, with Ismael. The Woman! It took six hours to get to the top. A cold wind whistled over the pass.

'These valleys run east/west, no?' I asked Hanibal.

'The ridges have numbers in the FARC. This is, I think, 52 and we are going to 54,' he answered.

Then it was all down, which was even more tiring on the thighs, on high stony or clay paths, kept clear or muddy by mule trains. Grandpa had been lent a mare to ride and came past us. He never could have walked it all in one day. We climbed down to the tree line, below which we could see the valley bottom and the cheese farm and the fields with cows in them. And the mountains rising high beyond again. Shangri La. The Lost Valley! For the second time for me but the first for the others.

The guerrilla camped down the valley from the farm. Hanibal made a *caleta* for us three, only one. What about a *caleta* each? No chance. We were on the move. It was lower than the camp of the troops and on the edge of a field which dropped to the river which ran down the middle of this valley.

'You can walk about in the field,' allowed Pedro. It was a large area. There were boggy parts, where we flushed Common Snipe out of the rushes. The whole of it was covered in big thistle plants, not like European thistles, more like pineapple plants. If you kicked them, they came out of the ground. In fact they ruined the field as pasture for cattle, but there were not enough farmers nor herbicides to clear the field up here.

The cheese farm was a working farm. In the morning the farmer's wife and her farmhand rode on mares, loaded with churns, past our *caleta*. The first morning, she saw me and I waved my hand.

'Still here?' she asked. I felt that she was sympathetic

'You remember that you massaged my broken wrist?'

'Yes. How is it?'

'It is not right. I need surgery.'

'Patience. You will get it.'

She did not stop riding. She was not allowed to speak to us, nor was I allowed to speak to her or be seen by her.

The cattle roamed the hillsides. The cows that were in calf were kept in the first field with barbed wire fencing over night, while the calves were separated and kept this side. The calves mooed and came up to the fence in the morning, eager to have their milk. The good wife and her farmhand went and milked the cows, then let in the calves for their share. The pregnant cows were in our field.

The weather was less wet here. We were higher and the rainclouds broke lower, or more in the other valley. We could be outside more in the day and had a bigger space to move about in. The Air Force did not fly over. Even so the *caleta*s were all hidden under the trees. The same routine of *chonto* (in the field), wash in a stream, dry clothes on the bushes, wait for the rice meals. Just at nightfall, there would be a wooshing noise around the *caleta*, which I thought would be the nightjars flying to catch insects, but it was impossible to see them.

I was waiting for the chance to make my mobile telephone call home. I asked Pedro once a week and he said that he was still waiting for the phones to be sent to him. This was a limbo for me, though perhaps not for my family, but I knew nothing of that. The Sony radio had been broken, and I was angry with Brutus for that. There was nothing to read. He was learning chess steadily, when we could get the set lent to us. We occasionally spied the Woman on the path, but she was kept separate. She was now visible as a good-looking woman with long black hair, a strong body, perhaps a *mestiza*, with indian blood.

The guerrilla became dedicated to trout fishing. The two terrible teenagers took it up. Ferney the *comandante* walked into the camp and stayed. He brought a cast-net, round and weighted with lead weights around the edges. He hurled it into the river, and caught tiny little fish. Hanibal was the champion with a rod. He took me down with him a few times. The river had a population of duck, which nested under the banks. They looked white from a distance and quite large. Maybe they were Comb Duck, but it was not easy to get close. The river was close to its source in the mountains above us. It was small, with a deep channel, clear as glass, fast, cold, and had a gravel bottom but with too little food in it to fatten the trout.

'Look, Hanibal,' I said one evening, 'you are sitting on a gold mine. Do you know how much people in rich countries pay to come and have ecological holidays in wild country like this? Riding, walking, fishing. The farmhouse could get a loan from the Interamerican Development Bank to build centrally heated cabins with satellite television and a landing-strip for small planes. You run the fishing. You breed good hill ponies. Bird watchers come. Bingo, you make legitimate money and stop this life of crime.'

'Maybe, maybe,' he mumbled without enthusiasm.

These rebels are so unable to take advantages of opportunities in the legitimate world. It is not that the state does not have mechanisms for starting up small businesses. It is that these people are not educated nor able to take them up. They are a 'socially excluded minority'. The few rich do not oppress the majority. But the few social misfits can make life hell for the law-abiding majority.

On the night of 14 July, the national day of France, a new moon rose over the mountains in the west and set over the mountains to the east, where I had come from. As it set, it shone into the *caleta*, clear as a pig of an orange, in a clear black sky. Spectacular, with the evening star at its side. I thought that at the Palace of Versailles in France the firework show would be over and the people dancing in the squares.

On 27 July, Pedro came and announced, 'Tomorrow, Meester and Abuelo, we go up into the hills and make our telephone calls.'

The mobiles had arrived. The moment had come. In the morning we mounted on mules and crossed the river. On the other side was a stony path, which the mules clattered up and down to another stream which issued from a lake and joined the trout river. We forded that. It's always fun to ford a river on mule or horseback. Pedro and Juan Carlos were with us, walking, with their rifles.

'Your negotiator is some Padré. I have spoken to him.'

This was news to me. Who was this priest who represented me?

'I have no idea at all,' I replied.

We started up the hillside and found another invisible lake. The hillside wound up to what looked like a considerable mountain, wreathed in cloud at the top. Grandpa was a good horseman. Past the second lake we turned left and up. It turned boggy and we had to dismount. At the top, we found *frailejones* again, and sparse grass and rocks and more bogs. It started to rain and was cold, which was worse for Pedro and Juan Carlos who had not dressed for the cold. We dismounted again and left the mules with Juan Carlos, and climbed to the peak. Pedro got the mobile out and took Grandpa to call. Believe it or not, the first call was answered by a Chinese restaurant. The second one was more successful and was answered by Grandpa's daughter-in-law, but his son was out. She gave another number and one of his sons was there and Grandpa spoke to him. Then Pedro took the phone and some angry shouting went on.

Then it was my turn. 'You tell them to pay what we agreed. What's the number?' asked Pedro. Christ, he did not have it? What an incompetent! I did not know the priest.

But he did fish out a paper with some numbers. And dialled. A female voice answered. 'No, the Padré is away.'

'I shall ring on Monday then,' said Pedro, and was on the point of hanging up. But the voice was no fool and kept him talking. He said that I was there, and that he would ring on Monday anyway.

So this meant another trip. 'Look, Pedro, let's ring my home.'

'You have the number?'

'I can remember one.'

'So you are a liar.'

'No, I am not. I gave you a number when I arrived. This is another.'

He dialled and I heard our maid, Ana, answer and say that she was alone. He was about to hang up again, when I said, 'Give me the phone. I shall speak to her.'

Surprisingly, he gave me the phone.

'Ola, Ana, it's me.'

'Oh, señor David. How are you?'

'I am all right. And everything all right at home?'

'Yes. We miss you (*nos hace mucha falta*). How are they treating you?' she gasped.

'Fine. They are Colombians. They treat me normally. I have to tell you that they want you to pay so much and they will release me. Did you hear?'

'Ay, señor David. This is terrible . . .' and she burst into sobs.

'Don't cry. I am all right. Pass on the message. And I shall be back home.'

'Boo hoo waaaa,' she cried.

'You will make me cry,' I said, and it was too much and I started to cry too. The contact with my home and with Ana was too emotional.

'Well, that's it,' I said. I handed the mobile to Pedro. 'The message has been delivered. We don't need to try again on Monday, really?'

'We'll see. Who was that señora?'

'She lives with us.'

'A family relation?'

'No, she works for us. She comes from the coast.'

'She will pass on the message?'

'Of course.'

'Let's go back.'

We walked down to the horses. It was wet and very cold and these two *guerrilleros* were miserable. We had had to get that high to find the signal and it had worked. Suddenly an immense exhilaration filled me. A wild happiness. I had spoken to my home. An electric contact ran through me.

'Can I dismount and walk back?'

'Why?'

'I want to. I feel like it?'

'All right. We shall take the mules and wait for you at the ford.'

'OK, Grandpa, will you walk with me? We have all the afternoon and it is sunny down below.'

Grandpa agreed. I could not go slowly, but bounded over the hillside and had to wait for him. It was sunny as we descended and there were herbs and flowers by the path. I was ecstatic and felt life was marvellous. Before I had felt only the repressed lack of affection, and the fear and isolation. The tears of Ana had showed me that affection existed. The money they wanted was unreal, but my family could handle that and get it down. And there was a priest involved.

The *guerrilleros* had not waited and so Grandpa and I walked peacefully and on our own back across the river and past the cheese hut and to our *caleta*, where Brutus was.

I calmed down and slept peacefully. However, that call made Pedro nervous. It could have been tracked, and our position given away. The very next morning, we were on the move again.

CHAPTER 25

The fourth month: on the move again

W E MARCHED DOWN THE VALLEY, for the first time. Were we going down into the llanos? Would this be like the awful month in the Pines and Pits?
We left the cheese farm, through the gate into the meadow where the cows that were in milk were kept during the day, and along the right-hand bank of the trout river. After a while we crossed the river, wading through, where there was a shallow gravel bank. The water only just came into our rubber boots, for those that did not take them off. Then we were over open ground, squelchy in places, through some smaller streams, up the banks and we saw another stream coming in from up on the right, out of the hills. To get there we crossed a flooded swamp, and there we were on this new stream, with only a patch of bamboo, to hide in. It was a very small space to hide in. The Woman stayed at the entrance and Brutus and I were sent into the middle. *Caleta*s were made and we slept on the ground. Supper was only rice.

The morning was sunny. We had nowhere to walk and it was not clear how long we could stay here. We asked to be allowed to bathe in the stream, which we could hear near us. Pedro said we could and we slipped between the bamboo on to a pebbly beach by the little clear cold stream. Grandpa sat on the beach. Brutus and I stripped off and washed in the stream. Pedro came to see and told Grandpa to get into the water too.

'Come on, Grandpa,' I encouraged him. 'It is cold, yes. But you will get clean and will like it when it's over.'

So he did. Brutus was exhilarated and stretched out to sunbathe. I wandered along the beach and looked at the stones. There were masses of fossils – little clams, embedded in the sandy stones.

'Grandpa, look,' I called him over, to get him involved. 'Just think that we are three thousand metres up in the Andes and we can see that this was the bottom of a sea or lake a few million years ago.'

We collected some. 'Take them back to Bogotá with you,' suggested Grandpa.

'It would be nice to have them. But how long will I have to carry them around before I get home?'

Vladimir came along on his turn of sentry duty. 'What are you doing?'

'Look, *muchacho*. Do you know what these are?'

'No. *Animalitos?*'

'These are shells that lived at the bottom of the sea millions of years ago. Before the Andes existed.'

'*No jode*! You are joking? Really.'

'You should keep some.'

'What for?'

Well, he had a point. A lad without a home or possessions or family or education – how could he own souvenirs or anything?

'You could collect them and sell them to foreign tourists in Bogotá. I bet a tourist would pay twenty dollars for a good fossil from the Andes.'

'Why?'

'People like strange and interesting things.'

It did not mean anything to him. Not even the idea of making money. He was a lost child without a fixed abode or future.

The sky was blue, the sun was sun-coloured, the hillside was green and leaked water, and Brutus was red, like a great hairy prawn. 'Ow,' he yelped, 'it hurts.'

We were clean and warm and relaxed. It was a good day. But it ended in the afternoon and we were marched all the way back to the cheese farm. We remade our *caleta* of the day before. The weather continued sunny. The *guerrilleros* were nervous that the Air Force might fly over and see us. They never did. We dried our clothes. I asked the Witch for needle and thread and she ignored my request in her usual unpleasant style. The cheese lady passed each morning on the way to milk the cows and saw us. It was the end of July and moonless.

A big mule train arrived from the south, and the mules wandered around us grazing. We did not see the muleteers. But an unknown *guerrillero* did appear, and when we were about he turned his back or covered his face. Why did he not want to be seen? He must have been an urban militia from the city, someone we might recognise years later.

Another bossy *comandante* walked along the path. At half past four, he shouted, 'You should be in your *caleta*s already.'

With an hour to lie on the grass in the light, before the interminable night, that was nasty.

But the mules went away. It seemed that they were going in the direction that Grandpa and I had taken to make our mobile calls, where the lakes were. Maybe they were taking stores to a deposit behind the lake? The other men went their way. The farm was a crossroads in the mountains, with heavy traffic on the mule highway.

'I think we are going to be released up that way, where you came from,' was Grandpa's opinion one night.

'But it is not the direction of Bogotá,' I countered.

'Maybe the way to Bogotá has been blocked.'

Quite soon, we moved. Where to? Back up the pass and back to the first valley. So much for Grandpa's idea. It was depressing.

'Why?' I asked the Pancake.

'*Toca*. We have to,' she answered, without explanation.

The climb to the pass is hard and high and short of oxygen. At least we could put our stuff on the mules. We were fitter now.

The Witch was near us as we started off early. She was packing up and talking to Pancake.

'The woman here is anti-kidnapping,' I heard her say. Not for our hearing.

And in four and a half hours we were in the Patio again, that horrid place, remaking the same *caleta*. However, that was not our destination, because Pedro had scouted another much safer hideaway, over the river. We went there after two days for the guerrilla to set it up. We crossed over a tree-trunk bridge, because the river was full and roaring, and then over some boggy ground and up a bank and into a thicket of high rushes. It ended at a wood and that was our home for two weeks. Fredy came to visit us and approved. It rained every day except one, when it rained only half the day.

Pedro wanted us to use a black plastic sheet as a roof and took away the camouflage canvas. He got the boys to cut banana plant fronds as bedding and we slept on the ground. They would not make raised beds. The fronds got wet and then they rotted. I felt under my sleeping bag and it was warm. I looked. The fronds were fermenting and giving off heat. We were being brewed like whisky mash.

CHAPTER 26

The family is getting nowhere

IN JULY, THE FAMILY WERE WONDERING about political pressures and getting nowhere in particular. On 23 July, the Padré rang the *comandante* and asked him if two million dollars was really the figure.

'Si, padré, that's the figure. He has got it.'

'Look, I can't go on unless I speak to him. We don't have anything like that.'

'No way, until you have made the arrangements for the money.'

'Look, are you speaking to anyone else, or just to me?'

A pause. 'Er, well, maybe.'

'You know that I am the only authorised person for this?'

'Yes, but *el ingles* has more faith in another person, maybe.'

The committee met to discuss where they had got to. The family was in England. The FARC had spoken to Ana the maid on 28 July. So had David. She had become so emotional that she could not be sure of the amount of money mentioned.

'So many zeros, señora,' she said.

Was it really him? How much money had he mentioned? What if he rang again? She must be given four questions and the answers, some true and some false. She should write down the answers, if he was allowed to do the test. Nobody trusted anybody by now.

In fact the lack of trust led some of the committee to say that my mobile phone call was a complete fraud. It had never happened. Or if it had, it was a con man imitating my voice. He did not know where I was and was just trying it on to get money. If we paid, I would continue in the unknown for ever. I would never have mentioned so large a figure. It was against all the training manuals. Ana was flustered and confused because she was hiding a plot and lies. She knew it was someone around the corner. Her lover? Why had the first call been to the lawyer? Now to Ana. Did I not trust her either? If the call was genuine, had I gone mad?

This gives an idea of the wild suspicious thinking that is generated by a kidnap.

Friends from Bogotá, Charlie and Lolo, had been in London and brought books and a sweater and a letter from Nanette and Victoria for the 'Red Cross parcel'. Could the Padré deliver it to the FARC, or if we were in a fight, could the International Red Cross do it? None of the family was in Colombia.

News came along the grapevine that the Army was going to do a big push into Sumapaz. They wanted a photograph of me. The peace process had been ended

106

in February and James Lemoyne of the United Nations was doing his shopping on Fifth Avenue again and working in his New York office, with a view of the Hudson River. It was getting near the inauguration of the Uribe presidency, when the war should hot up in Colombia. Of course he would want to recapture the hills near Bogotá. Why had it not been done before?

Three months were up and any chance of an agreement and release seemed far away. The committee got their heads together and felt that they had to stick at the money offered and sweat it out. Be careful. No talking to banks or moving money or visiting or calling the FARC or anything. It is all leaky as a sieve and dangerous for the family. DO NOTHING.

The parcel had not been delivered by the middle of August and the FARC's calls to the Padré had become infrequent. An email arrived. 'Victoria, I am a friend of Gabby's and spoke to Tim P. about a volunteer radio station in Hackney in London. It is a community radio which covers the east of London. It broadcasts in the languages of the communities, and broadcasts by Internet and international- ly. The reason for the message is that is has a huge Colombian listenership and dedicated Colombian programmes. Through an arrangement brokered by Am- nesty International its Latino Hour is transmitted in Colombia. The radio station there has made arrangements for this material to be broadcast to the 4,500 kidnap victims, for them to listen on transistor radios which have been provided en masse to the kidnappers. London residents can broadcast messages to their loved ones. You might be interested?'

CHAPTER 27

The presidential inauguration

WHAT WITH THE CLOUD AND RAIN, and being in the trees, the Air Force was not going to see us. In these wintry conditions, the guerrilla felt safer and was more relaxed. They also felt that the smoke from the cooking fire was not going to give them away, so they could cook earlier and we could eat while there was still light to see with.

One day, in the rain, there was a noise outside our front door, and we peeked out. Three wet figures were being escorted up to the camp. Then a new *caleta* was made on the way to our *chonto*, between us and the Woman. We went to meet the newcomers, three men. One was a lecturer at several Bogotá universities, on environmental engineering. He and I had colleagues in common and he could speak some English, in fact was about to have an article published in an English academic review. He had missed the deadline to correct the last draft! One was a retired army sergeant, who was a trader now, and one a very fat man. They had been picked up in an ambush (a *reten*) on the road from Bogotá to Villavo, at the top of the hill. The lecturer had been in his car, the others in a taxi. It sounded like a 'fishing trip' (*una pesca milagrosa*) and the guerrilla did not know who they were. Then, they said, the Army was told and a patrol was sent to catch the guerrilla and a helicopter arrived. The poor captives had to run off into the hills with the helicopter shooting at them and Army in hot pursuit. At some stage, they had to climb a wooden ladder, up a cliff. They got away and had been walking for several days. They were in a bad way, with huge blisters on their feet and thighs, and tired and filthy. The sergeant, who had a very oriental face, being a *mestizo* with a lot of indian blood, thought they had got to La Cabrera, across the hills, where we were, but we did not think we were so far west. The rivers still flowed east. These were not people with money. They stayed two nights and then the Witch took them away into the rain again. They told us that their backgrounds had been checked and, because they did not have money, Pedro was sending them back home free.

'Lies,' said Brutus. 'Their families will have been told to bring money. These *hijos de puta* do not release anyone without stealing their money.'

So it was back to us three. It rained and rained, the peak of the rainy season. The worst was when we spent five days in the *caleta* without being able to go out. I would sneak out to pee, and my jacket, a rotten camouflage jacket that Epimaco had left me, would stay wet for days. The guerrilla had dammed a stream that ran through the camp, to create a pool for collecting washing water. They stripped and soaped in the rain and rubbed a towel over their body and changed clothes – all in the cold rain. I had not washed for a month. All that one had to do was get into the stream, drop one's trousers and wash one's middle. If it stopped raining for a while, we got out of the tent and hung up our clothes on the branches to dry and walked up and down the tiny area of clearing before the *chonto*. Ten paces up, ten paces down. Brutus worked out a way of placing the chess set on four thin sticks, stuck in the ground, at chest level. We played too much chess – inside the dark tent, outside on the sticks. Grandpa had a penknife that had not been taken off him. Brutus used it to carve chess pieces out of wood. He was good at that. We could have our own set but we had no board. He thought about that. Could we get a piece of cardboard or a cut-off plank of wood? Where from?

We were all three sleeping in one *caleta*, with a black plastic roof. The floor was leaves of wild banana (*platanillo*) which got wet in the rainy weather. Brutus and Grandpa suffered from the cold at night. I was lucky and generated enough body heat to sleep well, and actually take off my socks in bed. Brutus was obsessed with stretching strips of plastic sheet around the sides of the *caleta* to keep warm. I did not see how that would raise the temperature. It was always going to be as cold inside as outside. He got angry if there was a chink. He got angry if Grandpa and I snored. I had to sleep in the middle to keep the peace. But if I snored or breathed heavily, Brutus would bang my head. Grandpa confessed that he was afraid of Brutus who had borrowed, permanently, his penknife, and had threatened to stab him. Was it the snoring?

The guerrilla passed in front of our door as they went out on patrol. Pedro acquired a dog, a shy sheepdog. It had the ridiculous name of Transmilenio, which was the new bus lane in Bogotá, like calling it Central Line. But it showed how the Colombians were impressed by the new public works projects in their capital city. Antanas Mockus is an excellent Mayor and Bogotá impresses visitors nowadays, much more than ten years ago.

When Pedro went for journeys of more than a day, he twice lent me his radio.

'I am lending it to you, and nobody else,' he warned. 'Don't give it to anyone. It is for you.'

Did he think that the other *guerrilleros* would ask to borrow it? Or he favoured me over the Colombians? The first time I switched on Caracol Radio FM to listen to the news programme and daily chat shows, intelligent voices filled the silence of the forest.

'Put on music, Meester,' pleaded Brutus. He wanted to hear *vallenatos* all the time.

'No, I won't. It was lent to me and I want to hear normal people talking about normal life.'

'Don't be an *hijo de puta*. I need music.'

'Bad luck.'

The second time, it was the day of the inauguration of Alvaro Uribe as President of Colombia. 7 August 2002. Did Pedro lend me the radio on purpose, for two days? The guest list for the inauguration included Prince Felipe of Spain, politicians from USA and Europe, and fellow presidents from Latin America. Not Fidel Castro! The FARC had not been pleased with the decision of the Colombian voters to elect Alvaro Uribe. They had declared him a 'military objective' some time before. So they set about doing something about it.

They rented a house not far from the centre of the city, with a drive-in garage. Inside, the explosives expert rigged up a line of launch tubes for home-made rockets. These were cabled together for a series launch, and a mobile-phone detonation system was wired in. As the swearing-in ceremony started, the expert opened up the garage doors and walked down the street a prudent distance and dialled his mobile. Four of the tubes fired, and twelve failed. The rockets zoomed off towards the presidential palace. One fell behind it and was audible to the guests. Others fell further away in the poor slum of El Cartucho and killed some miserable beggars. One killed some children in a street. All in all, there were nineteen dead innocent civilians.

The police were alerted by a neighbour and a policeman ran and caught the expert, within three minutes. Excellent work. In the house, the police found forty unused rockets. Before this attack, a shower of mortar bombs had been fired at the military academy, a bit further away.

A general made a statement, 'There is no doubt that behind this attack is the training of the IRA. It reminds us of the IRA attack on Downing Street in London in 1991. The first rounds were designed to distract the police, far from the principal target. We did not know that the FARC had this know-how, so it was difficult to prevent.'

I could listen to all of this on the radio all day. Did Pedro know that it would happen? I remembered the words of Hanibal. 'We have rockets too.'

After fifteen days here, when the bedding had fermented, Ferney appeared to look around and the word was that our clothes should be dry. Grandpa's and mine, not Brutus's. Grandpa was excited. I was not unhappy that Pedro himself came and took my clothes and my towel up to dry on the fire. The next day we were off. These fifteen days had been calm, and we were nervous again. Where were we off to?

'There are no mules,' Pedro warned. 'You will have to carry everything. And you two, take Grandpa's stuff.'

This was bad news. We had accumulated as much as we could to survive sleeping out on a cold mountain. Brutus had scrounged seven blankets. I had three

Map of Colombia

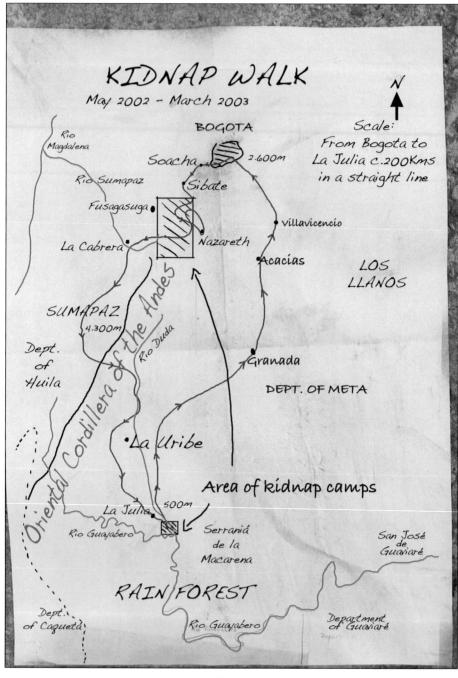

Map of kidnap walk

Aerial view of the Andes mountain range

Bogotá's bull ring

Colombians harvesting coca leaves in the jungle

Coca leaves drying in a hut after being harvested

DC3, fully loaded with marijuana, failed to take off in time

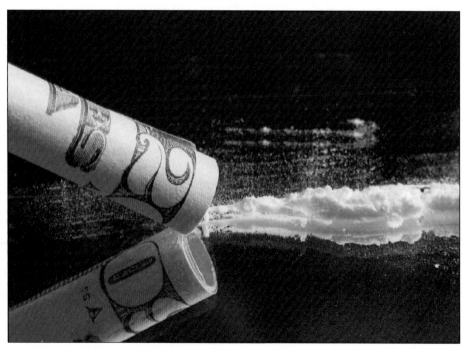

Snorting cocaine through a dollar bill

Colombian guerrillero

Colombian guerrilleros *walking through a village as locals look on*

The AK-47, the favourite weapon of the guerrilla

Andean mountains near Bogotá

Frailejones, *found only in Colombia and the Northern Venezuelan Highlands*

Mountain hills near the Savannah of Bogotá

A hummingbird rests momentarily on a branch

Mountain cloud forest

A Colombian orchid – Stanhopea

Juan Pablo Montoya, Colombian F1 racing driver

Colombia's President Uribe meets Tony Blair in London

Tree frog in a heliconia plant

Lizard basking in sunshine

Waterfall

Fossil in rock

Western Cordillera rising through morning mist

Mountain jungle hillside

Sunrise over the Savannah of Bogotá

Walking cattle to market in the llanos

Mule being loaded with provisions

Local shop, trading in basic food supplies

Toucan in the rainforest

Howler monkey

Poster asking to free Ingrid Betancourt

Green tree snake on palm tree

Meandering lowland river

Orchid – Cattleya

Anaconda

Piranha

Wild pig or peccary

Baby cayman, common in many lowland streams and rivers

Chiguiro *with babies, found in the Ilanos plains*

Red and blue macaw

Freshwater stingray

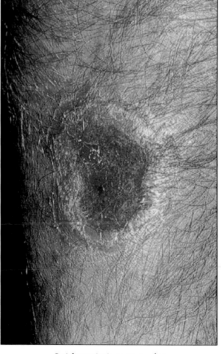

Leishmaniasis sores on leg

Local bus, known as a chiva

Army roadblock to check passengers and bus

One of hundreds of village churches in Colombia

Young girls playing outside

Che Guevara at the start in Cuba

Para Miguel Urra:
Recuerdo de este 9 de Octubre 1967 en "La Higuera", Bolivia, donde quizás se cambió un poco la historia a nuestro favor. Con especial afecto a mi compañero Brigadista. *[signature]*   Miami   Enero 07, 1999

Che Guevara after being captured in Bolivia

David after his release

sleeping bags and all the black plastic strips that Fredy, the prisoner, had left and Brutus valued to keep the wind out of the *caleta* at night. They had to be left.

'I'll take something,' offered Grandpa.

'No, old man. You can't. We'll take a little pack. Your washing things and some clothes.'

Brutus and I had huge packs. We set off across the boggy ground. I tried to stay with Grandpa, but the Witch made me go on faster. We were going back to the cheese farm but we were starting from further away and had the packs. It was going to be tough. Luckily it was a fine day. It always was when we had this particular march to do. Brutus went fastest, being stronger. The bridge was unpassable, as the high flood-water was washing over the logs. So we went along the bank until Juan Carlos found a fallen tree that we could scramble over. It was near the waterfall, which was huge and noisy. Then it was just a three-hour slog up the slope. In the middle is a stream to be crossed. Either you can jump or wade. Our guards had gone. I felt that I could not jump, with the big pack, so I started to wade over a rock ledge with slippery green weed on it.

'Brutus, *hijo de puta*, help me,' I called.

Miraculously he came back. I held out my stick and he grasped it.

'Whatever you do, don't pull. Let me walk slowly.'

I shuffled across the slippery rock.

'Nearly there,' he called. And pulled. I slipped and fell on my knees on the rock, got up and he pulled me out. I looked at my knees. Blood ran down my right knee. It was cut from side to side and the skin and flesh flopped loose. Damn. The knee hurt too. Could I walk? I had to. I bound my handerkerchief around it and walked on. All right.

'Why did you cross there? I saved you. Look down below.'

There was a waterfall, with a strong volume of water and noise, and large rocks.

'I was doing all right.'

'*Hijo de puta*, you might have been killed. Idiot. Lucky I saved you. If you had been swept down that you would have died. And I would have been in deep shit. If you had died, I would have been blamed. And they would have shot me. You f---ing idiot.' He was shouting.

'Calm down. I am all right.' I felt that his pulling had been the cause of the fall. He had not saved me at all. He was such a clumsy man.

'Calm down! *Hijo de puta*, you nearly had me killed.'

'Shut up. It is me that is injured, not you.'

'You nearly had me killed, *hijo de puta*,' he bellowed wildly.

I walked off, faced with this mad reaction. My knee worked. It was hard to lug the pack up the last bit before the crest of the pass. But there Hanibal caught up and gave us *panela* to suck. It was cold and windy as always. We could see the lake over the other side, far below. Grandpa passed us on a mare that Pedro had borrowed. He could not have done it otherwise. The downward path was endless.

I lost my way and wandered to the right alone. Juan Carlos came to find me and waved me back on track. My thighs ached with the weight of the pack and the downwards stepping. We reached the bottom and went to the cheese farm, not to the old camp on the left. Brutus was there. I took off the backpack and pitched forward on my nose, as the weight went. We were given a room and potato sacks were spread on the wooden floor.

'Rest. We have a long walk tomorrow,' announced Pedro. I did not want to talk of my knee. Would it swell up and get infected?

Where was Grandpa? Had he gone to the camp? He must have arrived earlier, being mounted. The darkness came and then a figure staggered into the farm. It was Grandpa, exhausted.

'I asked to get off the mare as I was afraid of falling on the downslope. I was walking but Juan Carlos left me. I got so tired that I sat down and could not get up. I thought I would die. I crawled down the last bit on my knees.'

'Christ, I am sorry, Grandpa,' I said guiltily. 'I thought you were ahead. Otherwise I should have looked for you. Sorry.'

We were responsible for the old man. He had to survive.

I went to see Pedro in the kitchen of the farm where I had slept in May.

'Grandpa cannot go on tomorrow. He is whacked. He is eighty and this was too much for him. Have a look.'

Pedro looked stern and did not comment. But the next day we stayed. It was a lovely sunny day. The Woman was sleeping in the room next to ours and she came out and lay on the grass near us. We were left alone. Brutus went and bathed in the freezing river. I washed some clothes, to get the blood and dirt out. They dried well spread on bushes and on the barbed wire. We played chess. It was a splendid day of relaxation to rest our aching legs. Grandpa had to pick up strength. I concentrated on the chess.

'Eh, look at that,' Brutus called.

I had spread out my English woollen sports jacket on the ground to dry but I had kept in the inside pocket some pieces of *panela* and *cancharina* for the walks. The huge white sow, with a piglet, was eating my jacket! I sprang into the air and shouted at her. She dragged the jacket away with her at a trot. I ran after her. Grandpa and Brutus roared with laughter. When I got the jacket, the inner lining had been eaten and the cloth was torn from top to bottom. My marvellous English jacket, which had kept me warm for four months, was chewed up.

'I shall come back and eat you, you fat pig!' I cursed the swine. She had got me again! First the soap, now the jacket. I asked the Witch for a needle and thread and she obliged. The afternoon was spent sewing. I could not afford to lose any warm clothes.

The cheese lady came by. I saluted her. 'Here I am still.'

'Good luck.'

I showed Pedro my knee and he brought the first-aid kit.

'I won't put stitches in,' he declared. 'Better that it is open and heals without dressing.' He sloshed antiseptic on it.

'I think you had better put a dressing on if we are walking. It will get dirty and stick to my trousers.'

'All right then.' He was good at first aid.

'Can you walk?'

'Oh yes.' But I did not know. It would be bad news if I could not. I would see on the morrow. It was 15 August. A new moon.

PART 3

Towards the Rainforest

CHAPTER 28

The long march to the forest

WE LEFT THE MOUNTAIN VALLEYS OF Sumapaz, where I had been hidden since May, going round and round in the same area for four months. The road was still backtracking the way I had been brought in. We marched up the stony path which I had come down, with my newly broken wrist, a hard uphill slog. Grandpa had his mare and we had mules, so we did not have to go on with the big backpacks. At the top, we turned right and passed between rock outcrops, higher and higher, to bare hillside. There was a high flat plateau with a lake. Time to rest and have rice and water. It was sunny and clear. The way was down and along and up the other side. The other side was steep. There was a traverse across a rock face which was difficult for me with one hand. I called out. La Negra came back and pulled me over. At the top of the rocks, I could look down. The bones of two mules that had fallen to their death could be seen underneath. There was a long flat traverse, before the descent to a different valley. We were very high, on top of the Andes. A new lake came into view in front, but it was far enough for a day. Pedro stopped us. We had to sleep on the bare top of the mountains, where there were no trees. He found a trickle of water, a chain of pools and a few bushes. Thick yellow grass (*pampas* grass?) abounded. This was cut to make beds and made a soft mattress. The *caletas* were guyed up to the bushes, very low. The mules stomped around. A *rancho* was set up and we had rice and beans, what else? The sun set and the big full moon rose. It became cold. It was a new experience, lying in the moonlight, on the bare mountain.

The next day we marched down to the lake. From the lake ran a fierce river, which we had to cross.

'Look,' I whispered to Brutus. 'It runs west, not east. We have crossed the Cordillera.'

'Bollocks,' he answered elegantly. 'You are wrong.'

'No, I am not. I know where the sun rises.'

That is the truth. One has to see where the sun rises and sets and relate all the scenery to that. So you can tell west from east. But it is not so easy to tell north from south. Of course you knew where north was, but how far north compared to Bogotá?

The way across the river was on horseback or mule. The horses could swim but the current was too strong for us and even the horses got scared and one turned back. The dog, Transmilenio, was with us. He got scared and turned back

117

in mid-stream and had to be thrown back in higher up. The mules crashed their hooves on the rocks at the bottom of the river and lurched and swam over. Exciting stuff.

We walked up the other bank. There was a brace of duck in the lake. Teal, I thought. The march was long, but pleasant, and took us to a new valley which also sloped west. We came to the tree level and a hut and fields and a herd of splendid cattle, with ear-tags. It was possibly an abandoned farm, or stolen cattle. The clouds were moving up the valley. We went down and crossed a stream and came to a farmhouse with a muddy corral. This was our objective. We were told to lay our bedding on the plank floor of a room, where food was stored, on shelves and on the floor. The Woman was put in the next room. There was a kitchen and a balcony on the inside, where the tack for farm horses was stored. In our room, the packs for mules, called *enjalmas*, were hung up on the beams. The *guerrilleros* bedded down on the balcony.

Above the corral, there was a stream along the fence and a hosepipe had been stuck in it. We used that water for our washing. We could walk around the corral, if the Woman was not out herself. The rule of separation applied. It rained often, as the clouds moved up and down, fine rain that was not tropical, more like Bogotá rain. We had left the Orinoco/Amazon climate. The trees had orchids in them, *odontoglossum*. The guerrilla went in and out of the forest behind the farm. There must have been a cave and storage there. I found a pink comb under a cowpat. Luxury. I could comb my hair and beard.

A group of very young *guerrilleros* marched in from lower down the hill, with a leader. They saluted. '*Hola, companero!*'

Christ, I looked like a *guerrillero*. 'Che' Hutchinson!

Their leader came into the storeroom and greeted us. '*Retenidos*? Eh? Well, it is your own fault. You should have paid up what you were supposed to.'

What an idiot! Did he really think that Colombians had to pay a revolutionary tax or knew what they should pay or how or where? Or accepted that they either pay the FARC or deserve to be kidnapped? The attempt to issue guerrilla tax laws – the Law 002 and 003 – were pathetic imitations of the real laws of Colombia, an attempt to argue that if we paid to the State, we should pay to the alternative state *La Nueva Colombia*.

Ismael and Hernan went away on a mission. Brutus had worked out how to whisper to the Woman through a chink in the plank wall. She said that the mission was to take explosives to Bogotá. This farm she called The Lugubrious House, because over fifty corpses of *guerrilleros* were buried here.

We three men slept in the storeroom. The temptation was too great. I started to eat bars of drinking chocolate, until I got a stomach ache. Brutus liked eating the milk powder and so did Grandpa, and we all ate sugar. One of us stood at the door to watch for the guerrilla, who were only a few paces away. The other two stole the food. We got overconfident. Grandpa was gulping milk powder, when the Witch came along. We put everything back and assumed poses of innocence. She came in to get a bag of sugar and said, 'What's going on?' in a schoolmistressy way.

'Nothing.'

Brutus and I saw that Grandpa's beard was covered in milk powder. We burst out laughing as soon as the Witch left. The air was full of milk powder and laughter. A good moment.

At night the storeroom had visitors. I woke up. 'Aaah! Ughhhhh!' Little cold wet feet ran across my face. Mice.

If the sun came out, we played chess and dried our clothes and walked around. If it rained, which it did every day, we came in and played chess on the balcony. After a bit, I found that we could sit in the kitchen, on a bench and get the warmth of the fire, and watch the cooking, if there were not too many *guerrilleros* around. The radio was next door with the Woman, although later Pedro built a *caleta* on the other side of the corral and took the radio there for privacy.

Pedro called Grandpa and me to have hot baths. That was good news. He cut Grandpa's hair. Better news. He did not cut mine. Bad news. The next day, Pedro called Grandpa to the radio and they talked to his family. Pedro was angry. I talked to Pedro.

'How is my thing going?'

'Fine. They are having trouble getting the money together, they say.'

'Why don't you let Grandpa go? He is not rich. And he is old and tired. It is cruel.'

'These old buggers say they have no money. But they always have a pot of savings hidden away, even if they can't remember where. He has to pay more.'

What a bastard!

Grandpa was called to the radio a second time. He came back and said that he had been asked questions and they had been transferred to a telephone by the radio operator.

'Proof of survival,' said Brutus. 'You are going home.'

That night Pedro came to the storeroom and said 'Grandpa, get ready, you go home tomorrow!'

'Hurrah!' I cheered and slapped the old man on his back. Even Brutus loked almost pleased.

'*Hijo de puta*, you will be with your family in – let's think – three days.'

We helped pack his bag. I asked him to get in contact with my embassy. He had made it. We slept and in the morning, a rainy morning, he mounted a mare and went off with the Witch. So we were three! But we only had one more night in the Lugubrious House. A day later, we walked down the hill, into a wood and over to another valley. It rained hard. We had to find a cable and basket bridge over that river and climb the bank to a ridge. The sun came out and we had our lunch of rice on the top. There were swallows and humming birds and lizards. We took off our boots and socks to dry them out. The next valley had another river. It was a more broken and precipitous landscape. I got left behind and went into a farmhouse, where a woman with small children told me that she had not seen the others. I was actually having a conversation with a normal human. We were entering a populated region. This river was bridged by a real concrete and brick bridge that could take truck traffic and it led to a farm and another farm and fields and fences, the high grassy cool farms of the Bogotá savannah, but over the hill on the Magdalena river valley side. We stopped at a wooden building with sacks of potatoes on a balcony. A fenced kitchen garden had broad beans and blackberries planted in it. There was a big clay oven in a separate hut. The Woman was put there. We stayed on the balcony. Pedro appeared with the horses and mules, from a different direction. He decided to stay here. The grass was thick. Real farmers passed taking their cows to pasture or milking.

I found a letter nailed to the door. It showed that we were in the municipality of La Cabrera. That is above Fusagasuga, on the highway from Bogotá to the Magdalena valley and Cali, the gateway to Sumapaz from the west, a frontier where the State and the FARC battle for control. Real civilian farmers lived here in an uneasy coexistence. This hut belonged to the heirs of a man who had died and his children did not come, but left it locked up. La Negra smashed the locks and we had one room shared with the teenage truants, while the rest went into a potato store. The supper was potato soup. After supper, I walked with Brutus to the gate of the field, and looked at the tall pines and eucalyptus. We argued about where we were and where we were going. We had crossed the Cordillera, no doubt, and were near Fusa and heading south. He thought we would go to the province of Huila, south of Tolima, the valley of the Magdalena river.

The march continued next day along the hillsides. We stopped at a farm with a new galvanised roof. Then we passed to another valley over a crest and along a path through green fields. There were more new roofs. It was a sign of the FARC area, was it? Money being spent. Ahead of us we saw a school and a flagpole. We turned in to the schoolyard. It was full of *guerrilleros*. Lots of them!

CHAPTER 29

Castro, El Che Guevara and Venezuela

'YOU KNOW WHAT I HEARD?' said the Woman, much later, when we knew her. 'Pancake was talking to La Negra and said, "The one that I am most sorry for is el Mister. He has done nothing, just come to live in Colombia."'

It was Pancake who had talked to me before that remark in the Lugubrious House, and sighed and said, '*Sabe*, Meester, my idol is el Che Guevara.' She fished out a little book on *The Life of Che Guevara*, with the famous bearded face on the cover, as it had been on the T-shirts of a thousand students in the 1960s.

'Who the hell is he?' had retorted my thirty-year-old golf companion, some months earlier, in Bogotá, when we were talking about this and that.

'There you are! You thirty-year-olds did not go through the stormy revolutions of the 1960s, the Bay of Pigs, the death of Kennedy forty years ago . . .'

'Steady on, mate. I know about Kennedy's death,' he laughed.

'You were not a gleam in the milkman's eye, young man. We lived through Danny le Rouge in Paris in 1968, the Red Brigades in Germany, the Montoneros in Argentina, the Shining Path in Peru, the murder of Aldo Moro in Italy, Salvador Allende, the marxist who got hold of Chile. We had to thank General Pinochet, the generals in Argentina, Fujimori in Peru, for getting us out of that mess. And now they are all being done for human rights violations. War is a dirty business and you don't keep democracy alive by wearing white kid gloves.'

'The thing is that politics in Latin America has been a big pendulum,' added Bertie, who was born in Argentina. 'We have lived through it. The pendulum swings too far from one side to the other. The liberals and conservatives swapped power in 1929. The populists like Perón arose in the 1940s and gave too much power to the unions. The generals took over. The marxist guerrilla had a go in the 1960s and in Chile won power. They were squashed by the military, who waged a dirty war. Democracy came back and market economics. That is fine. But the past was dragged up again by the human rights crowd. What next? The pendulum is swinging and we can never settle down.'

So what was this sixteen-year-old Colombian girl doing, worshipping this wild Argentine doctor, tracked down and killed in Bolivia, a perpetual revolutionary, a failure in the end, but two generations later, an icon for later revolutionaries?

Ernesto Guevara Lynch de la Serna, son of an architect/engineer from Cordoba, up north of Buenos Aires in some hills west of the great river Parana, and a communist-ish wild mother, Celia de la Serna. 'El Che' – a famous Argentine, or 'infamous'?

'I have a theory,' my Argentine brother-in-law said to me over an *asado* (barbecue) of sausage, sweetbreads, and beef ribs, washed down with a Valmont red wine, some time afterwards in Argentina. The sun was shining in the *Pampa*, the *carancho* birds screaming, the horses stamping, and my great-nephews kicking a football around the lawn. We looked at the clouds. Would it rain? The road was a mud track and we would not be able to get out if it rained.

'The conversion of Che happened when he read Jack London's book *War of the Classes*. Nobody reads it now. I grew up with the Guevaras, in Alta Gracia in Cordoba. His mother was a bohemian. Their house was a mess. I was more friendly with his brother Roberto. We were in and out of each other's houses. His mother had a collection of left-wing books. She was a communist. I know that he read that book when he was young.'

'I read a biography of him, which said that he was upset when he visited the Chuquicamata copper mine in Chile, on his famous motorcycle trip,' I interjected. 'He could not see the importance of the huge American investment, the new exports for the country, the employment created, the tax and schools and hospitals. He only saw the Indians and compared their wages to the style of life of the *Yanquis*.'

This is how some people get obsessed with seeing 'exploitation' in everything, I thought. Every white man who goes abroad to build a dam or set up a mine or drill for oil or plant a banana plantation is an 'exploiter'. And the Yankees are 'imperialists'.

This is how Fidel Castro thought, as he grew up in a part of Cuba, where the United Fruit Company had their estates. *Yanqui imperialistas*. By the time that he had been in power, with his anti-*Yanqui* rhetoric, half the Cubans wanted to flee to the USA to find the jobs and wages that capitalist investment creates. And in Colombia, Gabriel García Marquez saw the United Fruit Corporation and the banana plantations the same way, which he wrote about in his *Hundred Years of Solitude*.

Che Guevara was an asthmatic, so he could not smoke and drink hard, and could not indeed be far from his medicines. But he conformed to the rest of the pattern of the adventurer. And the anti-*Yanqui*.

'Oh yes, his mother was the communist,' said my friend Amalia, as we had supper in Buenos Aires, later on. We had got back before the rain, this time. The city of Buenos Aires was at its loveliest. It was November and the jacaranda trees were in purple bloom in the city avenues. It was sunny and would have been hot, if it were not for the breeze from the River Plate. Supper was a cut of beef – a *vacio* – with roast potatoes and salad. The wine was a Norton, from Malbec grapes, the *vino tinto* of the house.

'*Eran locos los padrés*. His parents were nutty. I used to work for his father. I heard him say "Celia, this is the last time that I bail you out of jail. The next time you stay there and rot." She used to go on the streets pasting up posters against the government of Uriburu. You know they separated. But they were not rich enough to have separate houses, so they went on sharing the same bedroom. Each one had a revolver under the pillow. One night they each heard a noise in the house and crept out of bed, grasping their revolver. They bumped into each other at the door and found themselves pointing a revolver in the face of the other. The house was always a mess. Of course, when Che became an important man in Cuba, they were pleased. They went out there to see him and were honoured guests. You know, I was the *novia* (fiancée) of Ernestito (el Che) when we were both seven years old. We were the same age. He was good looking. It was his big eyes and his curly hair. They say they were from the Irish blood of the Lynchs.'

'There is a famous story about Che and the Central Bank,' I remembered.

'It's true,' nodded Amalia, as we ate cheese and the last of the wine. 'Roberto, his brother, told us all. Castro had called a meeting of the revolutionaries and had said that he needed a head for the Central Bank. "*Quien es economista aqui?*" he asked, "Who is the economist here?" And el Che misheard it as "Who is the communist here?" "I am," he raised his hand. So he became head of the central bank, as a doctor, knowing nothing of banking.'

This is a 'Freudian' slip. He really did think that he was the only communist among the Cuban *barbudos*. He had imbibed it with his mother's milk.

On 10 October 1967, el Che was dead. He had walked into an ambush set by the Bolivian Army, as he led a few rebels around in the mountains of Bolivia. Was this his destiny? His father had written in a preface to Che's *Notes on a Journey* (1951):

> Now he left . . . to follow the routes of so many legendary expeditions. They would leave behind comfort, love, family, and search for new horizons . . . Ernesto bound to the mystic certainty of the inevitability of his destiny. Now Ernesto and his companion had to follow the road of the Conquistadores, only that instead of the desire for conquest that was their banner, these boys marched with another destiny.

Written with hindsight, this was a dramatic way to describe a Gap Year journey!

If 'Che' Guevara had survived as an idol, the country of Cuba was a much more solid example of a Marxist paradise. A totalitarian dictatorship of course, with no freedom of the press, no private property nor private businesses, lots of political prisoners, no free elections but a high degree of equality and universal education and good public health – a tiny rebel hangout which had cocked a snook at the mighty USA and got away with it? In his old age, Fidel Castro was being invited to presidential inaugurations in Brazil, Argentina, Ecuador. A mythical figure and a heap of trouble.

The balance of political factors had been further tilted by the election in Venzeuela of Hugo Chavez as President. He dreamed of a 'Bolivarian' movement.

In 1820, Venezuela and Colombia had been one country, Grancolombia, and the
Liberator, Simon Bolivar, was alive still. The FARC loved Chavez and he seemed
to support it. Their joint guerrilla leadership with the ELN had been called the
Coordinadora Simon Bolivar. I heard the *guerrilleros* chanting '*Vivan las FARC. Viva
Venezuela*'. After all he was the enemy of his oligarchy and the friend of Castro.
And anti-*Yanqui*. He could sell oil to the USA and, at the same time, be rude
about their presence in Iraq.

Did the FARC leadership find a safe haven inside Venezuela? Were kidnap
victims hidden in Venezuelan territory? Was Raul Reyes, the brains of the FARC
secretariat, really seen in a café in Venezuela and having a medical operation there?
Hum?

CHAPTER 30

The family and the committee struggle

THE FAMILY WERE OUT OF Colombia at the end of July and the channel of communication was Padré Rodrigo. The FARC were calling up and making demands. He was a very busy man, who travelled a lot between his churches and charitable foundations. His mobile telephone was not always on. The family and the committee wondered whether the FARC would lose their temper. On the other hand, they had not lowered their demands at all.

The lady on the committee felt that his recall of what was said when he talked to the FARC was not clear. His style was accepted to be exceptional – the way he talked to them. But they had not dropped their demands and even he felt that that was not normal. What the hell was going on? His offers were not being taken seriously. How much did the negotiators think they knew about the funds available? Was the Padré going to be able to make a deal?

And then Pedro had called the number of the flat in Bogotá and put me on the line. Only Ana was there. Were the FARC cutting out the Padré? Did they want to involve the family? That was not on. Ana was briefed as to what to say if they called again. They must ring the Padré's number. Should any of the family travel to Bogotá? NO!

The Padré wrote a letter on 12 August. 'But seeing that we have not advanced much in our dealings, I feel that I should say some things.

'I confess that I am somewhat obstinate and pragmatic, and, analyzing the situation, I become suspicious about third persons. I feel that I should warn you, so that you can take measures, if necessary. I anticipate further difficulties, and, perhaps only for a while, you should get rid of Ana and the people in the farm. You may think I am overbearing and an ogre, but this is what I think.

'The "friends from the mountains" are not disposed to drop a single cent. They seem to have information – perhaps erroneous – about your lives and are not going to drop.

'I ask myself, "Who makes them so sure about their extortionate demands?"

'I see that in the negotiations they show that they know things that are not guesses, but the result of close observation. Is Ana involved? There is a saying that "if you think the worst, you will be right".

'The only objective is to end this kidnap. I must say, however, that in other cases, I have found out that close acqaintances or family members have been involved in kidnappings.

125

'I have asked, insistently and unsuccessfully so far, to speak to David, but they dodge the question, saying that that is only possible when the ransom is ready. These people are heartless and soulless and don't want to show any kindness to anyone, above all when they are being pressed so hard. But I shall continue.'

Three months after the kidnap, the lack of progress was maddening the family and committee. They knew that it was going to take a long time. But even so this intransigence on the part of the FARC was difficult to cope with. And it made everyone's heads spin and suspect everyone else.

The Padré had said that the FARC were being pressed hard (by the Army?). Had he heard this from them? Were they angry and determined to take it out on the innocent civilians? Would I be left to rot and die? He had felt a total lack of compassion and soul in them.

The committee was aware of the change of political atmosphere, with the coming of Alvaro Uribe, who had the people's mandate to solve the problem of armed subversion. Would the Army be sent out to fight the war? Lots of friends thought so. One of them advised Bertie to get in contact with the General of the Fifth Division. He spoke to him, and wrote a letter at the request of the General.

'From a kidnap victim who was released in June, we know that David was taken by mule up into the Sumapaz. Since than we have no news of where he is, but we suppose that he is in the same area. I enclose two photos of David and confirm that he is tall and rather corpulent (thanks Bertie!) but may have lost weight. If the Army has plans to retake the Sumapaz, I hope that you will take into account the chance of coming across David. As we all say, it is a pity that an Englishman who has retired in Colombia and loves the country has to have this happen to him.'

CHAPTER 31

The long march

THE SCHOOL WITH SO MANY *guerrilleros* around it had a big camp behind it. We were marched up through the camp and pointed at a *caleta* already prepared in the bushes at the top. The Woman was given a *caleta* even higher up. We had climbed up the hill and it was cold and high. It was the edge of the *paramo*. Bare hillside stretched above us. It would have been easy for the Air Force to see us. This was a serious concentration of rebels. It started to rain. The sentry at our *caleta*, doing the correct thing by standing facing us and looking at us, was Hernan, with a very short haircut. We tried to talk to him, but he made a negative gesture with his head and kept silent. We found out later that he was doing his punishment for having overstayed his leave a year before. He indicated that we could not look at the Woman and could not leave the *caleta*. Very strict. The guerrilla is afraid of its *comandantes*. We had to ask permission to pee.

A girl came up with a good supper of meat and potatoes and rice. An army marches on its stomach, said Napoleon Bonaparte. This was an army and we were going to march?

It was a cold night, lying on the earth, with no sides to the *caleta*. The morning dawned clear and the sun rose. We saw lots of horses and mules. A jolly man was in charge. I heard him say, 'I am not a *guerrillero*. I am a muleteer, but there is no work, so I am helping out here.' Later, the Woman would find out that he was the husband of the lady of the cheese farm.

We were taken to bathe in a stream. There were lots of new faces in the guerrilla. No other prisoners were visible. Lunch was good. A pig had been slaughtered and we ate lots of pork.

'Steady on,' I warned Brutus. 'Your stomach will not be able to handle so much.'

He ate some more. 'Delicious.' In an hour he was asking for permission to go urgently to the *chontos* and was sick. We spent a second night, a clear and freezing night. Were we going to stay with the fighting troops? We were usually kept separate.

Voices carried to our *caleta*. A *comandante* of importance was addressing the junior officers, including Pedro. He congratulated Pedro on his mission. Why? Was it ending? What had he done but guard us? Or had he done other things?

'We have to change our attitudes towards the civil population. They have to like us. We have grown in numbers, but we don't know where to go. We are an armed movement but it is not by arms that we can win the hearts of the people.'

127

That is all that I could hear but it was electrifying – a glimpse of the political problems that face an armed political movement which must know that it cannot win in open warfare. Could it win the hearts and minds of the Colombians? He was saying clearly that the FARC was cocking that chance up.

Hernan had been replaced by a very young boy, maybe sixteen years old. He stood looking at us. I asked him where Bogotá was and he indicated over the *paramo*. We may have been as close to home as at any stage. He said that there was an advance guard up there in the high *paramo*, freezing their socks off, protecting us.

The second night was very cold. We were high in the mountains, where the *paramo* starts. The dawn was pink, then blue sky. After breakfast and toothbrushing, we sat in front of our tent. Another sentry, a boy of some fourteen years old, stood watching us and would not talk. This was a military camp, with military discipline, and everyone was packing and the *comandante*s were moving around. Our stuff was taken away to the mules. No aircraft overflew. The *guerrilleros* had their uniforms on, backpacks, rifles. We were told to walk down to the school. The *guerrilleros* were lined up four deep and across the schoolyard. They looked so young, boys and girls. The commandants watched them. 'Guerrilleros . . . attenshun! Form groups. Ready. March.'

Off they went in groups, down the hill. 'You too. Off you go' and we marched with our commission, in front and behind us, three *frentes* (fronts) with three senior *comandante*s, perhaps 350 *guerrilleros*, on a march across the *cordillera oriental* of Colombia. Was this a planned retreat from Sumapaz, so long 'Our Country' for the FARC, faced with the new president and the propect of an army advance? I could not know what was going on in the real world. My family had no idea where I was, but they could have known that the historic reconquest of the Sumapaz was on. So I was unwittingly swept up in a strategic retreat and a historic moment.

On the first day we marched only until midday and camped in a bamboo grove, with a little stream. On the other side of this stream there was a rise, on which the *comandante*s sat and watched us. We bathed in the stream and thought of washing clothes. Pedro said that the washing of clothes was the duty of the *recepcionista*, so I gave my washing to Pancake. It was the last time that anyone washed my clothes for me and was only because the top *comandante*s were there. There were lots of new faces, from *frentes* we didn't know, including two really pretty small brown girls, with perfect pert faces. I asked for a nurse to patch my knee, for the walk. 'We have a doctor,' I was told, and Ruben, a *paisa*, probably a medical student, came. He was friendly and asked how we were.

'You are a gringo?'

'Fine, thanks. I am English, not gringo. Can you put a plaster on this knee, because we are going to walk a lot?'

'Better that it is open and heals naturally. But for the walk, all right.'

On day two, we were awoken before dawn and packed in the dark. I had to be helped with the tent, which is difficult to pack up small, if you don't know, and everything was taken to the mules. Breakfast of soup and *cancharina*.

'The *cuchos* must go ahead; we have a long walk.' Someone called out.

It was mountain weather – cold at first, big clear sky and huge views, sun that burns your skin later. We climbed a hill, but we were still on a cattle track, through gates, and across fields. The boys and girls struggled with their heavy packs. A fat girl – Carolina – lagged behind. Pedro's wife, the Witch, dogged our heels and urged us on. We got to the top and rested. The Witch kept sure that the Woman was behind and could not talk to us. Below us a column marched down to the stream at the bottom. There was one stumbling figure who lagged behind. Ahead, a long column climbed the bare hillside, on the other side. To the right, huge rock formations piled up, at the top of a mountain range, slanted and sloped, tossed by ancient volcanic forces. Not a house, not a road, not a field in sight. We were going south-west, away from Bogotá. Surely we had lost any chance of being released now? The weather was different. It was not the rain shadow of the Orinoco rainforest any more but drier, sunnier, a big sky, free of hanging clouds. There was no sign of watercourses, the birth of great rivers. At the top, *guerrilleros* were resting on the ground, by a fence. One was *Comandante* 'Milton'. A cold wind chilled our sweat. The mysterious Woman was made to sit well away from us, again.

'Eat your lunch,' Carolina said. It was rice and beans, in a plastic bag.

When Milton's *escuadra* got up, shouldered their packs and started down, we followed quickly. The ground bent to the left, and a little stream came into view. A wisp of snipe called in the boggy ground by the stream and got up and flew away. Below there was some cloud underneath us and we could see where we were going to. It was downhill. We had crossed the back of the cordillera, from east to west and would be following the water down from its birth to the big rivers – but was it the rivers that run to the west, to the Magdalena, or those that run to the llanos and into the Orinoco? After some eight hours of walking, we could see a river that rushed from right to left (north-east to south-west?). Perhaps if one were to walk up-river and over the hill, there would be the town of Fusagasuga, and the Panamerican highway from Bogotá west to the Magdalena river valley and to Cali? But how wrong could one be, disoriented in the mountains? We stood aside as the mule train passed, with the baggage. Pedro was the chief muleteer, with Juan Carlos. As always, the muleteers walked fast, at the pace of the mules, cheerfully cursing at the mules. But as they thundered down the steepening slope, one of the mules went head over heels, and lay there with four legs waving in the air. It was overloaded and it was 'our' mule, with our sacks, full of our blankets and clothes. The two *compañeros* leaped down and heaved at its lead rope, and the noble beast rolled and rose, none the worse. Soon we were down by the river, racing green and cold over the huge rocks. To our right there was a high concrete bridge, suspended by steel wires, anchored into concrete blocks a government bridge, built by the Ministry of Public Works and on the high ground above it, on the west side, a substantial green-painted wooden ranch house, with a patio in front. '*La Casa Verde*'. It was heaving with people. As we came into the patio, leg-tired and dirty, we could see a series of tables and *ranchos*, at which sat or leaned senior, tough *guerrillero comandantes*. We had not seen them before. Clearly there were several *frentes* and lots of troops. This was a major crossroads on the guerrilla trail. No government aircraft overflew us, despite being on the bare mountain. Where were we all going, in such numbers? As usual, we the captives were to be put right at the back, away from the *comandantes* and kitchens. We scrambled up a steep clay bank, and into an open field, overgrown and uncultivated for ages. The *guerrilleros* started to put up *caletas* and cut the scrub with their machetes. We lay back luxuriously, staring at the sky and resting our tired legs. The baggage was brought from the mules. 'How many ants are there where we are to sleep?' The Brute and I were in one *caleta* and, very near, the Woman. Water for washing was a difficult scramble down a bank, and the water was muddy already. Hernan brought supper of rice and lentils.

'I don't eat these *hijos de puta garrapatas* (ticks = lentils),' roared the Brute, hurling them into the bushes.

We climbed up the back of the field. If you pulled up the *escobilla* weeds, the grass underneath was excellent. This was good country for cattle or sheep.

'*Mierda*, this countryside is exactly the same as where I was brought up. I recognise these plants. My father used to pull them up too. I feel at home.'

We slept on the ground, like logs.

It was dark when the guerrilla got up. The duty sentries clapped their hands, at half past four, the dangerous hour before dawn. The *comandantes* came and stirred everyone into activity. The backpacks were packed, the tents were untied. By pulling the special guerrilla knots, they undid themselves easily. This was the trick of an army on the move, ready to wake to the arrival of another army, a bombing raid, warfare, and run. The camouflage canvas was shaken and rolled up. They could do it into small squares. For me, it ended up as a huge loose roll, so Hernan had to do it again. Lucky we had the mules to carry it. Hot coffee arrived. I headed off into the bushes to pee and let out wind and got back without falling over in the dark. We stood in the darkness and waited. The Woman was nearby. This army did not march at night, in the moonless days in the middle of the month. You can't. The *recepcionista* arrived with our pans full of rice and beans.

'Are the *cuchos* ready? We have to go,' said Pedro. 'Come on.'

The sheepdog Transmilenio was at his heels. So Pedro was walking with us? What about the mules that he liked to handle? Was he being punished for the mule that fell yesterday?

We went down to the stream and forded it and then out of the perimeter of the Green House farm, south, back to the river, but on the north bank. Up and up a path, with Pedro striding out, first the Brute, then me and then the Woman. We were together still. Pedro kept up a brisk pace.

'Hurry up. We shall never get there before dark.'

Groups of *guerrilleros* passed us, with heavy backpacks, going faster. Luckily our own stuff could be loaded on to the mules. We were exposed, high on the bare mountain. On the left was the river, below us. We were marching south-west, away from Bogotá. How far were we to go? It was unnerving to think that we were heading away from home and far into the wild country. They were not going to let us go. Grandpa was the last of us to be freed. We should be captives for a long time more.

This was a long march and called for a marching song, to cheer us up. Not that you can get a marching rhythm, if you are on a narrow mountain path, where it's more of a scramble, but I started.

Hitler has only got one ball
Goering has two but very small
Himmler
Is very sim'lar
But as for Goebbels
he's noballs at all.
Da da, da da da, daa daa da . . .

'The March of the River Kwai' – sing at the top of my voice, and whistle the second verse – Sir Alec Guinness in captivity in the Burmese forest.

Pedro approved of the song. When I stopped, he told me to go on. So I did. With a change.

Up to mighty London came an Irishman one day
As if the streets were paved with gold so everyone was gay
Singing songs of Piccadilly, Strand and Leicester Square
'til Paddy got excited and he shouted to them there.
It's a long way to Tipperary, it's a long way to go
It's a long way to Tipperary, to the sweetest girl I know
Goodbye Piccadilly, farewell Leicester Square
It's a long long way to Tipperary, but my heart's right there.

The passing groups of *guerrilleros* laughed. 'El Meester is singing his gringo songs,' called out Pedro. The FARC does not have marching songs. Could I get one of my songs adopted as their official march? I started to compose words in Spanish.

'Tirofijo has only . . .' I stopped and decided that the new words could be undiplomatic. Back to the British version. Tra la, tra la la, la la la.

The ground rose and the river fell further below. We were getting hot and my legs were aching. Then we came across a large group of *guerrilleros*, sitting on the ground, at the top of a rise. It was a rest. We sat down. Next to us was the medic who had patched my knee in the bamboo grove. He was drinking from a bag of saline drip.

'Hey, Meester. How are you?'

'Well, thanks. Look at my knee when we get to the end of the day?'

'Right. What do you think of us? We are not bad people?' He was a normal enough young student, well spoken, polite.

'Well, all right, but why are you doing this to us?'

'I believe that people should be equal. Not rich and poor. Equal. Like in Cuba.' He was a juvenile utopian communist.

'But people don't want to be equal. Or they would vote for you. And Cuba is poor and oppressed.'

'Here in Colombia, we need equality. That's what we are fighting for.'

I thought that I had better stop. It could be dangerous to get involved in arguments or to be seen to be corrupting the younger troops. Marxism is not about discussion or voting. It is a religion, the sole purveyor of the truth – the False God.

'Let's go,' called Pedro. We were the slowest and had had to go first. I stood up.

'Where do we go?'

'There,' he pointed ahead. There was nothing to see but sky. I walked forward and looked down. The river was miles below. There was no path, just a rock face.

'Jesus.' My scrotum tightened and sweat broke out on my hands.

'See that ledge on the rock? Put your right foot on it and swing your left foot out and over on to the ledge and jump to the other side.'

I could see the ground on the other side of the rock face and the beginnings of a path. It was a long way down to a certain death. The ledge was less than the width of a boot. Hernan stood on the other side and extended a hand. Christ, grit my teeth and go. My right foot caught the ledge and I was suspended over the river. A swing and push and Hernan grabbed my hand and on we went. This must have been the top of this range, but it rose to the right, vertically, with no other way to get over it. Now we went downhill.

After a couple more hours, we were being passed by more groups at a good pace.

'Hurry up, *cuchos*,' called Pedro. 'Do you want to get there before dark?'

Then we saw a dark patch below, a small wood, a hut, people. It was only the middle of the day.

'Are we there already?' I asked Pedro. He laughed. He had played the hillwalking trick, telling us that we had to go a long way and hurry, when it was not so far. The guerrilla likes to arrive early, to have time to set up *caletas* and start cooking the last meal of the day. We had to be in bed by five and up at four.

'Get behind the hut and wait,' ordered the Witch. The Woman was taken the other side of the hut. We could not be with her. We had to be apart from the *guerrilleros*. We were the responsibility of the *comision*, and nothing to do with the fighting units.

Later we were taken up into the wood. The *comision* had an area and we had a *caleta* for the two of us men and one nearby for the Woman. Food was brought, and there was meat. The fighting army likes to eat well. Where was our baggage? The mules could not go over the rock face that we had traversed and had taken a longer route. Just before dark the baggage came up. We opened it to get the blankets, sleeping bags and washing things out. The blankets were heavy. As I shook mine out, a couple of mortar bombs fell out.

'Here, Juan Carlos, what do I do with this? Can I throw it at you?' I made to toss one over.

'Don't worry. It won't go off, unless you twist the screw on the nose.' I looked. There was a threaded nose cap, a safety device and maybe a timer.

In the *caleta* of the two madcap teenagers were the tube of the mortar and a belt of heavy machine-gun ammunition.

The next day we were got up in the pitch dark. It was the middle of the month, the new moon time, the dark time.

'Pack up, we must go,' called Pedro. No breakfast. I could not see anything. I stuffed what I could feel around me into the sack. Pedro came over and shone his flashlight to help a little. Juan Carlos folded the tent. We had to carry the sacks down to the hut.

'Go, go,' urged Pedro. We stumbled to the path. The first light was showing over the mountain to the east. Was the Army coming up behind us? We were walking south and a little west. A spout of water splashed from a hosepipe.

'You can wash here,' he said. I searched in my pocket. Damn, my pink comb had disappeared, but there was no use going back. This was the price of getting up in the pitch black. Damn. I ran my fingers through my hair. My beard was long and matted. Brutus looked like a bush. We washed perfunctorily and a minute later were on our way. The guerrilla was urgent and rushed. Maybe it was to be a long walk. The path wound downhill on the edge of the hill above the river. Every now and again, huge landslides had crashed into the river and scarred the high bank. The path found a way over the fallen rocks. The river became brown and muddy beneath these landslips.

'I want to walk with Meester,' announced Pedro. 'He sings. Come on, Meester.'

'Hitler has only got . . .' The song got me swinging along. We stopped for some food and water. Groups started to pass us. Brutus was the strongest walker, and the Woman was kept behind. Our group became stretched out. It became clear that there was a rearguard. We were not supposed to fall behind them. We were in the vanguard and somewhere in front there would be a forward unit and side units in the hills to each side. Later we were told that at this stage, the Army had come to within a quarter of an hour of us. I don't believe it. But we certainly got going early and pushed on fast. I was amazed that there were no aircraft overhead. We were so exposed.

The path went uphill and arrived at a hut, set up as a store, full of sacks of rice, potatoes, sugar. There was a kitchen and benches, hoses of running water and a little garden, with a barbed wire fence around it. We stopped and drank water. In the mid-morning we walked through a hillside of red ground-orchids – *sobralias*, tall as lilies, thousands of them. A spectacular sight! If we had been at peace, tourists from Europe and the USA would have paid a fortune to see such a sight. The mules could take the same path, and when they came up from behind, there was a shout and we had to get off the path quick. A mule train of loaded beasts at full speed will knock you for six.

We were slow walkers, but not the only ones. The shambling figure that I had seen the first day was at times behind, at times ahead, and increasingly sitting resting with us. He had a name – Morales. He was a figure of fun to the young fit men but he was not old. He was overweight, with longish curly hair and a brown beard. To the peasants, he was a *mono*. He was on his way into the heartland of the fighting guerrilla. From where? What duty? He was cheerful and carried a full pack, and rifle. But he was not in training as a walker. He said that he had been on a battle course the year before, running with all his equipment on and had fallen off a tree and damaged his knee badly.

'Hey, Meester, how are you? Enjoying the walk?' he asked.

'If it was voluntary and I was on holiday, I probably would love it.'

'Yes, I know. But don't worry. You pay and go home. Unlike me, ha!'

'When?' I asked Morales.

'It won't be long, I'm sure.'

'Why do you kidnap people?'

'The revolution needs money,' he replied. 'Goodbye. I must go.'

When you rest, you take your backpack off and cool down. When you are ordered to get going, you stand and feel the cold wet shirt on your back, freezing and wet. You put your pack on and set off and are soon in the swing of it. A merry song rises to your lips. A jolly walk, ho ho. The weather here was not as cold as we were descending from the high mountain. It did not rain. We were west of the rainshadow of the Orinoco/Amazon therefore, but this was a really long walk. We crossed the river, while it was small and shallow, then we climbed the other bank, by a hard upward path that left us tired at the top. We stopped and sat down several times, often with Morales. When we were at last on a downward path, there was a hut on the left, and it was working as a country shop. The guerrilla were queuing up to buy junk food, fizzy drinks (*gaseosas*), and biscuits and sweets, the kind of food that could be transported on mules and stored, yet was a luxury. The Witch gave us some. She had paid for it with a roll of banknotes. I had a Tetrabrik of fruitjuice and a packet of biscuits. What a pleasure.

One of the guerrilla had a Japanese face. Really? I looked at him again. It was. He must have had a Japanese father, an immigrant, and a Colombian mother. His mates called him. 'Oy, *japones*. Come here.'

The path went downhill and was dry. We kept the empty bottles for carrying water on the march. The river was below on the right. There were no trees, just open hillsides. The mules came past. We rounded a corner and saw two men walking fast up the hill towards the shop, one white, with a toothy face like the English comedian Lance Percival, and one black. Both had drawn pistols in their hands. Why? They greeted us cheerfully and kept striding on. They are mysterious these young men, who live in the hills, in guerrilla areas, and run farms.

'What's mysterious?' frowned the Woman, at a later stage, when I commented. 'They are guerrilla.'

'But what do they do there? They are given land, without title, stolen land, to farm?'

'They feed the guerrilla and store arms and clothes?'

It was late when we came down to the edge of the river. We had walked for about thirty kilometres. The river was getting deeper and faster. On this side were a meadow and a hut, with pigs in it. The grass was full of *guerrilleros*, putting up *caletas*, collecting wood for cooking, cleaning their rifles. We waited by the pigs and then were led up into a wood. We always got the furthest back and worst campsite, sleeping on rough ground. There was a stream, beside which the *rancho* had been built and cooking was in progress. We could go there and wash. Brutus and I stripped naked and splashed the cold water over us. It gave us a naughty pleasure to prance around naked in front of the guerrilla. They bathed in their underwear, but did not stop us being naked.

CHAPTER 32

The march continues to the hot country

In this meadow with the pigs, the FARC decided to stop for a day. They must have felt safe from the Army. They were given permission to wash the blankets and sleeping bags, and dry them in the sun. Luckily we did not have to do the washing, and the Witch took everything away to the river. Brutus asked for the chess, but Pedro said that it had got broken in the sacks on the mules' backs and the pieces could not be found.

'He's lying,' said Brutus. 'He threw it away.' And in fact, when our stuff was brought up to us, a lot was missing. Pedro must have wanted to lighten the load, so we had nothing to do all day. Below us were more tents. We watched some people, including One-Eye, erect a canvas screen around one tent.

'Keep away,' he warned. Then a number of the girl guerrilleras walked up and went in. Something was going on. Ferney appeared looking fussed.

'I don't want to see that Negra ever again,' I heard him cursing. I realised that it was an abortion session.

'Well, it may not just be abortions,' said the Woman, who was with us. 'You know what they call Ferney? *El Conde* – the Count.'

'I don't understand'

'*Conde. Condilomas.*'

'What is a *condiloma*?'

'It is a sexually transmitted infection. A kind of wart. He has the instruments and medicines to cure them, so he is the Count – *el Conde*.'

'There is an English word which has the same double meaning, in every sense, but modesty forbids me and I hope your school teacher never got that far. Come to think of it, it is the same in French.'

Cries and groans came out of the tent. And in fact, that day, la Negra and also Ismael left and we never saw them again.

This was warfare and so we had proper sentries, who had to stand over us all the time. Most of them we did not know, but in the late afternoon it was the turn of Morales. Brutus and the Woman and I were sitting on the ground and here was an educated *guerrillero* to talk to. The Woman let him have it. She was 'Pati', but since we had never been allowed to be with her and talk a single word to her, her mystery persisted. Now she became a *compañera*, a fellow sufferer, someone we were being allowed to know.

'Am I a political prisoner or not?'

'You are a politician, yes.'

'So am I here for a swap of political prisoners or not?'

'Perhaps.'

'What the hell do you think that will do for the reputation of the FARC, when the people who voted for me know that I was taken by you? I tell you, they will hate you.'

'It is all a stage in a political process. You have to understand the historical inevitability of the popular struggle.'

'What do you gain by subjecting me, a Colombian woman, to this cruelty?'

'Patience. I know it is not nice. But you must understand that life goes in cycles. Nothing is for ever. This is a bad experience. But you will get past it. And it may even teach you things. Life is a continous process. You are part of it.'

'Balls. I am a democratically elected Colombian, and an honest politician. You can ask anyone in my constituency. And a mother who should be with her children. I was tricked into a meeting with you people and you cheated. Who can I speak to?'

'Patience! You will get past this experience. It is part of the process.'

He was a political thinker, a Hegelian and believer in the proletarian revolution, a commissar in the ranks of the FARC.

Brutus interrupted. 'She is a politician. But what about me? I have no money. Why do you kidnap ordinary Colombians, who are working and creating jobs and trying to improve themselves. I was born poor and anything I have, I won by my own efforts. You *hijos de puta* are just stealing from the poor people. Why don't you kidnap the rich bastards?'

'I don't know your case. But you will get out. Patience!'

'What about me?' I asked. 'Why kidnap foreigners? Do you want the whole world to see you as criminals?'

'I don't know, but don't worry. You are in a popular revolution and we have nothing against you. Personally. But you are here because you are British. You are a military objective. I know about you.'

This made me think. Was I also a political bargaining chip in an international terrorist war? I went on, 'You use criminals and corrupt policemen to kidnap ordinary people. And that seems all right to you?'

'Who do you think got you?'

'The police?'

'Perhaps it was our people disguised as police,' he suggested.

'Or policemen who belong to the FARC?'

'Maybe. But not necessarily. Plenty of them like the money and are friends of ours.'

'What are you trying to achieve?' asked the Woman. 'You don't have the votes to elect even one senator. You can't win by force either.'

'The only path is the revolution. When we do politics in the open, our people get killed. That is why the Communist Party of Colombia has become the Clandestine Communist Party of Colombia and lives here in the guerrilla.'

'Clandestine *hijos de puta*,' roared Brutus. 'Why do you treat ordinary Colombians like me in this way? I am not a politician. I just work. If I have my money stolen, I shall have to fire my workers, and they will end up jobless.'

'We only ask for some of your money, not all of it. You can go on working.'

'What kind of country do you want?' I asked.

'An egalitarian society. Not one oppressed by seven rich families and a press monopoly and Gringo aid.'

'That is crap. Don't you know that communism is a total failure. The Russians have given it up, and the Chinese communist party has allowed private business and property rights? Only Cuba remains and they are as poor as church mice, those that have not swum to Miami.'

'Look, Mister. It is a historical process. Maybe we don't want communism. We want a socialist country like you have in England. But how do we get there. The oligarchs block the advance of the rights of the people and hold on to the wealth. We can only advance to modern socialism by taking up arms against the oligarchy. There must be war to overturn the government and its *yanqui* backers, and then we can construct the right society for all Colombians.'

'But we got Tony Blair by a peaceful democratic process, not killing people.'

'When Colombians go on the street to reclaim their rights, the Army kills them (*les echa bala*).'

'Balls,' protested Pati. 'This is a democracy. I should bloody well know. I was elected. You weren't. I work for peanuts to get funds to spend on my people, schools, roads, drains, water.'

'It is not popular justice. Society is controlled by the rich.'

'Rubbish,' I said. 'There are at least 460,000 members of the upper middle class. There are over five million active members of the Social Security System. There are more holders of bank accounts than that. The middle class is over ten million is local terms. Anyone can find land to work and in fact most people who have it cannot sell it to anyone. There are twelve million registered voters. We want more of those, not less. And nobody will invest and create jobs if you carry on the way you are.'

'Wages are peanuts and the *campesinos* cannot get land or borrow money. The country is in the hands of the World Bank and the *yanquis*, while the Colombians stay poor.'

'Then why don't they vote for you?'

'The bourgeoisie has to decide, as in all pre-revolutionary moments. Do they support the oligarchy or do they throw their weight behind the revolution for social justice and equality? It is their decision and they must pay the price.'

Was it dangerous to go too far in this argument with this tin-pot Lenin. He knew that we were not going to agree, but better not to be too rude. He had the rifle in his hands, and we had a spoon each and a toothbrush. Prisoners don't argue.

We drifted away. At least he brought us a big portion of supper, with meat. He sat and watched us eat. He brought out a pipe. The stem was broken, so only the bowl was left.

'Do you smoke a pipe?' I asked. It was somehow typical of his academic style.

'Yes. I have this Italian friend in the guerrilla who brings me pipe tobacco.'

'I have a pipe too. I like to smoke it in the farm, in the evening with a rum and coke, looking at the stars, after a day's work picking coffee or whatever.'

'Look Meester, do you want this pipe?' He stretched over and handed it to me.

'No thanks. Keep it and get it mended when you are back in a city. I bet you have books too. Poetry?'

'Ha. Half my pack is books. I can't live without them.'

He finished his sentry duty and was replaced by a sixteen-year-old boy, who stared at us silently. The Witch came up and said, 'You can only keep one blanket or a sleeping bag from now on. Choose.'

We were out of the cold country and heading down to the hot jungle. Brutus complained, 'I have a bad back. I need the blankets to sleep on.'

'Tough luck. You won't need to keep warm, where you are going.'

I decided to carry one sleeping bag. The prospect of being warm was attractive, after the cold mountains.

And next morning, we marched along the left bank of the river for a while and came to an extraordinary cable car, over the river again. A wooden box was slung on a pulley under a wire cable, stretched over the water. We climbed up a ladder and sat in the box. Whoosh, off along the cable to the other side. The path climbed up the right bank, up and up, a hard slog. I looked back at Pati and she motioned with her hand to go slower. Brutus was ahead, being a strong 39-year-old. These paths are bumpy and worn down in the middle by water flows and made of red clay. Luckily this was dry. It took two hours to get to the top.

I was closer to Pati, but still not allowed to stop and talk to her. Carolina, the fat girl, was with us. I sang a new song, a marching song.

Allons enfants de la Patrie – ie-ie
Le jour de gloire est arrivé
Contre nous de la tyrannie
Da da dada dadda
What the hell are the words?
Marchons
Marchons
Dum dum da dumde dum

It reminded me of a rugby match in the Stade de France, with Serge Blanco charging down the wing.

'Oh, *La Marsellesa*!' said Pati. 'We learned that at school.' And she took over in Spanish. We had almost conversed normally.

The music took us to the top. There we found tall trees and a crossroads in the path, which was wide and getting wet. We took the right turn and moved along the crest. Soon we had views on either side downwards. We veered left and then on the right there was a large dark lake. The path began to go down and turned into a morass. A traffic of mules must have mushed up the clay ground and the water had nowhere to run off. It was very dirty, slow going, with mud pools up to one's knees. Horrible. It went on for hours. The mules came past, crashing into the mud. This was what the army called the Guerrilla Motorway, from the Sumapaz, the Andes, to Caqueta, the rainforest.

That night we slept in a wood and set off in the dark next morning. The countryside opened up and we walked on a bare hillside, then back into the forest, and through many small streams, flowing left to the river. It was warmer. I bent down and scooped up handfuls of water.

'Don't drink water,' called Pedro. 'It weakens you (it takes away your *aliento*).' This is the wisdom of the guerrilla.

'We shall stop and prepare water and sugar,' he said. 'Wait.'

Like a British soldier's 'brew up' of tea and sugar, the guerrilla on the march needs sugar in the water for instant energy.

Suddenly a tremendous rainstorm started, real tropical rain. We had our waterproofs (*carpas*) and had got to a wooden house. Our group stood under a tree. The visibility was a few metres, such was the rain.

'Come here,' ordered Pedro. I was not allowed to stand with other *guerrilleros* under the eaves of the house. We, the captives, had to be quarantined and could not mix. When the rain stopped, we all moved off and the speed picked up. I was walking down a hillside, when a squad charged straight down the hill at speed.

'Elite troops,' commented the fat girl, who was behind me. We rounded a bend and I saw a vast view to my right, of the llanos plains far below. To my right? How could that be? Had we veered round to the east? We were now on the east side of the Andes. Well, I never! I had not noticed our direction change. We came to a newly-built wooden house, surrounded by *guava* trees. So we had come down to about 1,400 metres above sea level. It was the best climate in Colombia. Warm, not hot.

There was a pile of planks that the owner of this farm had cut. Hernan cheered and said that they were his favourite bed. We laid planks out and stretched our tents over them and relaxed. I can't say that sleeping on planks was my favourite bed. In fact, one's hips hurt like hell after such a night. The *comandantes* chose rooms inside the house. The owner fussed around, with his uninvited guests. He had a wife and small son. He had planted maize and yucca and bananas. It was a lovely place. The mules and horses were let loose on the hillside to forage.

'Don't damage my planks,' called the farmer. He had cut them himself, with his motorsaw, to build his house.

It rained like fury in the night. The Witch and Pedro had the *caleta* above mine. She had rigged the roof in such a way that it filled with rainwater and then tipped it all over me. I got up and tightened her guys, to get it to tip over her. No luck.

We were up and away in the dark and continued to walk downhill through *guava* trees and *escobilla* weeds. The trees cleared, just before a field, and everyone was sitting, resting, including the three *comandantes* of the FARC columns, the big chiefs. One was Milton, whom we knew; one was an older man with a deeply lined face and light hair, not very Colombian looking, who had a German shepherd dog, and a special mule, because he had a bad back; and the other was a quiet man, with a pipe and a retriever dog. They smiled at us and said hello. It was not the time or place to talk to these senior men, in charge of moving three columns of troops in safety to God knows where.

We kept going and at the bottom of the long slope there was a stream and, on the other side, the guerrilla was setting up the camp. It had not been a long day. On the left was a wood, bordered by a barbed wire fence, and on the right was a big grass field. It was a hot country cattle farm. The field had tall termite towers of red mud all over and the ground was alive with ants and their underground nests. It was hot. We took off our packs and shirts and laid down our *carpas* and lazed on them in the sun. The guerrilla was on active service, and we could sneer at them as we sunbathed and flicked off the ants. There was one *comandante*, the number two to Milton, who was a pain in the arse. Oscar was his name. He always had full uniform and his beret on. He was endlessly calling for a parade of his company and inspecting them. One of his men was the luckless Morales, and he took every chance of humiliating the shambling intellectual.

'Did you walk to the kitchen without your rifle?' he bellowed.

'Yes, my *comandante*.'

'You useless fool! How many times have I told you? To be more then a pace away from your rifle is unsoldierly conduct. It is a court martial offence. You may think yourself cleverer than the rest of us. You may be going to work with *Comandante* Jorge. But here you are a soldier and a bloody useless one.'

'Si, my *comandante*.'

'Right, I will tell you your sanction later. The rest of you, aten . . . shun. *Guerrilla colombiana*, slope . . . arms! Clean your weapon, get your tents tidy, check your schedule for sentry duty. Fall . . . out!'

Better not laugh. Just look away. Oscar passed us and said, 'Meester, how are you? Long time since we met.'

'Do I know you?' I asked without thinking.

'Don't you remember? I was there when you came in.'

So he was where? When I met Laureano? When I got to the hut? I did not remember him. But he knew me.

We could wash in the stream, which we had crossed. The beds were made up inside the wood. There was a poor supper of rice and beans, as we were on the march. It was warm. There were no mosquitos yet.

The next morning, we were heading downhill and leftish, until we found the river on our left again, and the path was quite dry and reasonable. It got warmer all the time. We came to a wide bridge with wooden planks on a steel frame, old and rusty. The planks were rotten but it looked as if it was made for vehicle traffic. The other side was a large clearing, with hundreds of *guerrilleros* setting up. It had been a short walk. This was a major campsite. The bridge was over a small feeder stream, which fell into the main river. A big *rancho* was being set up. We found our allotted area and dropped our packs.

'Hurry up and have a bath first,' said Pedro. So we followed him to the river and jumped in. It was good. Pedro was relaxed and watched us. He came up and gave me a new comb. The *guerrilleros* came and went, fetching water and washing the food. It was a long afternoon, doing nothing. I saw Milton, at the highest point of the clearing, which was his favourite position. He could look down on everyone. He had a laptop computer, thin and black, perhaps a Hewlett Packard. He was using it. His technical gopher, Alexander, was with him, the one who had to carry the spare batteries and know how the PC worked. Did he have a satellite link-up? I don't know. I had read that Carlos Castaño, the head of the *Autodefensas*, did have a satellite phone and used it every morning to read the news in the forest.

Sleeping in the midst of the guerrilla means that you can't talk freely. The chess set had been lost. There was nothing to do or say. A number of butterflies flitted around the clearing, including the 'Eighty Eight', the *Diaethria Neglecta nymphalid*, so typical of South America. The guerrilla all bathed. The beady eye of Milton was on us. The odious Ferney was sewing a leather *pechera*, for which he carried around a roll of leather and needles. Pati was near us. Could we speak to her? Better not risk it. There were hundreds of *guerrilleros* there – all of them except for the advance guard and rearguard, who were out of sight, protecting us.

The following day, we continued along the river. It was flatter. The road was dry. It led by a large banana plantation, in terrible condition. The presence of the FARC must have driven off the original owners. Someone said that on the right was a kind of tree that made you come out in a rash, if you went near. We entered a grassy field and stopped at the end. There were lemon trees, uncared for. We ate lemons. Acid they were, but we needed the fresh fruit and its vitamins. There was also a *guava*. The fruit was unripe and hard as stones. The climate was definitely warmer. Juan Carlos and Ismael disappeared into the banana plantation and found some miserable small bananas. What a pity that it was abandoned! The day wound on and we came to a steel bridge over the main river, to the left. We crossed it and found a house, then a school, with a large playing field, and behind it a farm shed, with a *trapiche* and pigsties. Behind it was a considerable banana plantation. That is where we were to camp, among the banana plants. The guerrilla found a pig and we ate roast pig that night. Luxury.

For some reason, the FARC was unable to decide to travel the next day. We packed. We unpacked. We packed. We stayed the second night. What was going on? We gained a whole warm day, doing nothing. Ramirez, the *arriero*, appeared with his mules and his fat 'wife'. He set up a generator set and plugged an electric hairclipper into it and set up as a barber. Pedro appeared, walked over to us and said, 'Brutus, Meester, haircuts!'

This was an electric moment. Our hearts thumped. A haircut was the preliminary to being released. Brutus was ecstatic.

'Meester, we are going home.'

'Ah ha! Don't get illusions. The disillusion is much greater.'

'Don't be a wet blanket. I am sure. Tomorrow we go.'

'I don't think so. This is not the right place to release us. We are on the march.'

'Perhaps we are near the llanos. We could get to Villavo. Our families are probably waiting.'

'Don't get disillusioned. Better to think that we are not being let free, then if we are, so much the better.'

'*Hijo de puta*, miserable bugger. You may not, but I am going home.'

It is a fact that if you get excited and then disappointed, your mental state is not tough enough to cope with it. We may think that we are managing well in captivity, but underneath we are frightened and unstable. No illusions!

Brutus asked for the clipper and Ramirez gave it to him. He shaved his beard and then all his head, until he was bare, like a Turkish wrestler. Unusual in Latin America, but I saw bald pates often enough when I got to England a year later.

I had my beard removed and a hair trim.

'Why?' I asked Pedro.

'Orders,' he answered. So Milton had taken a dislike to the sight of these shambling tramps in the middle of his army? Or did we have to look like *guerrilleros*, if the Army saw us?

In the dark of the next pre-dawning, Brutus was still elated. We were off, after the inexplicable delay. Had the advance guard seen trouble ahead? The Army?

'I have news,' announced Pedro. 'No more mules from here on. You have to carry your own stuff.'

'Oh shit.'

So this was bad news. The big sack, hitched with rope, was full of bedding and clothes and usually they wanted us to take some of the food – bags of rice, beans, a bottle of oil – weighing some forty pounds. Maybe the SAS carry twice as much on campaign, but this was enough for a sixty-year-old pensioner in the jungle. Goodbye Ramirez and the helpful mules.

'Follow the paths marked with sticks,' someone told us. Ha ha! Had they mined the banana plantation behind them? Was the Army after us? The Army suffers a lot of injuries from mines in this horrid war.

We went back through the school and the shop. I saw that there was a Telecom satellite telephone office, with its generator. What was written on the school? *La Estrella.* Was that the name of this place and, if so, in what province? Instead of crossing the bridge, we turned right, along a wide path, and walked back uphill and up river. It started to rain and the *carpas* were put on. We were under tall trees. The long crocodile of *guerrilleros* stopped. There was a bridge ahead. We were made to go under the trees and wait. We heard the sound of helicopters, then a small plane – a Fokker maybe – flew low over. Was it about to land at a nearby airport? Would that be Granada in Meta province? The column was frozen and exposed. I ate my breakfast, a piece of cold pork crackling and some rice.

'Start walking, but leave fifteen metres between each person,' was the order. 'Space out.'

What was it that we had learned in the school cadet force when I was fifteen? 'Shape, shine, shadow, silhouette, spacing and movement.' How to avoid the enemy seeing you in warfare.

We passed over the bridge and ducked off the path into the thick forest. This became a hard steep walk. The ground was clay and slippery and long shoots of creeping bamboo and lianas tripped me up. I learned how many ways there were to fall down.

1. Your back foot gets caught in a creeper. You fall on your bum.
2. Your front foot gets caught in a creeper. You fall on your nose.
3. A creeper makes your back foot cross your front leg. You fall on your nose.
4. Both feet get caught in creepers. You fall sideways into a prickly bush.

The guerrilla were going past at speed. At the top, the ground sloped vertically down to a stream. There were steps as tall as a man, requiring one to slide on one's posterior, while hanging on to a tree root – not easy with one broken wrist and a backpack. At last we reached the bottom and walked down the stream bed. Around a corner was a group of guerrilla.

'Right, we shall have water,' said Pedro. Big pots were filled with water and sugar and Royal fruit jelly powder. It was now hot and humid. We were getting down to the rainforest level. The glade was full of spectacular butterflies, really spectacular. Big blue *Morphos*, floating *Heliconidae*, completely unknown *Nymphalids* with orange/black/yellow/blue markings. What a sight – the dirty, thirsty troops and the huge trees and the remarkable butterflies!

We had left an exposed track and inhabited area and were safely hidden in the thick forest; not the forest of the high mountain, but a new thick rainforest, hot and dense. I got up to ask for some more water.

'Sit down there. I shall bring it to you,' ordered Pedro. 'You are not allowed to mix with the guerrilla.' He sounded fierce.

They were unknown to us. Other *frentes*. We were a secret to be kept away from them.

CHAPTER 33

The walk continues

WE SCRAMBLED OUT OF THE BUTTERFLY GLADE, up a clay bank and arrived at the edge of the forest. There were fields of grass, made for cattle, with barbed wire fences. In this guerrilla territory, presumably the old *zona de distension*, the barbed wire was often new and shiny and tight and difficult to crawl through or under. We slept in a wood on the edge of a field. We had walked a long way, to get out of danger, and were tired and filthy. The backpacks were now large and heavy. We fell heavily asleep.

The next day was flatter and bordering fields. It was the edge of the cattle country of the llanos. We advanced a bit and stopped in a wood. We could see a few farm buildings and earth roads leading to them. The three *comandantes* were with us. We waited. Then some men came with sacks and unloaded them, revealing bottles. Beer and soft drinks. What a luxury! There had to be a road and a town not far off. I was given a bottle of Aguila beer, and Brutus as well. Biscuits were passed round. We waited for a long time. It was clear that we were in the vanguard and could not advance until the advance guard radioed their go-ahead.

When we moved on, we came to a clearing in a wood, where tables had been set up with big pots of water. The 'head waiter' was a familiar face, from this long march. He must have been the organisation and supplies man. We had to wait again.

'Look at that,' said Brutus. A *guerrillero* had belts of fat shells with copper noses. In what weapon did they fit? An anti-tank gun? A RPG? Two strong older men were carrying heavy machine guns, with tripods, and belts of bullets. These are used to fire at aircraft and helicopters.

The go-ahead must have been received, for we moved on, across a lot of fields. On the edge of one field were a few flame trees, sure sign of hot country and in one of them a number of noisy birds, with hanging nests.

'*Oropendolas*,' I remarked.

'*Guapuchonas*, we call them,' retorted Pedro.

And on the fences, I saw fork-tailed flycatchers – the scissor birds (*tijeretas*) – of the open cattle lands from Argentina to the Caribbean llanos. We walked around, through and over the fences, and along the edges of the fields. We arrived at a farmhouse.

Beyond the farmhouse was a stream and a bridge of bamboo trunks, not bamboo, as we call it, but the famous *guadua*, a much taller, stronger type of

146

bamboo that is used for building houses and furniture and as scaffolding, especially in Antioquia. It grows in the warm country, in large groves by the watercourses, and is a lovely sight, with its tall waving plumes of leaves. And across this bridge was a plantation of *cacao* trees (cocoa as we call it) and, on the trunks, the flowers and the pods from which chocolate is made. *Cacao* is from Mexico, and grows easily but this plantation was not well maintained. Rotting pods lay on the ground and the trees were covered in fungus. Under the trees it was so shady that it was dark and damp and no grass grew on the ground. We were assigned an area and set up the *caletas*. Maybe it was for one night, maybe more. Brutus picked up a bean and split it and chewed some of the white beans. He spat them out. They do not taste of chocolate, not until they are dried and roasted. If he knew, he was so desperate to eat something different that he took a risk.

There was still some meat with our rice for supper. The plantation was full of *guerrilleros* and we were all under cover. We went to bed before dark, as always, and the grove was quiet by eight o'clock.

Suddenly a terrible roar burst upon us. Vrrrrrrrrrrrrrrrrm. Deafening. We were being attacked by the Air Force. One or two attack jets had dived on us at low level. This came as a complete surprise. Everyone jumped up.

'*Cuchos*, come, NOW. NOW.'

I put on my boots and trousers and grabbed my shirt. Where were my glasses? Ah, here.

'NOW! NOW!' Pedro appeared. It was pitch black, the middle of the month, no moon. He took my hand, and I was dragged under the trees.

We crossed the *guadua* bridge and climbed up the other side. A press of *guerrilleros* crossed the bridge behind us.

'Let the *retenidos* go first,' Pedro called.

'No lights, no lights.'

The bridge cracked and half a dozen *guerrilleros* fell into the stream.

'*Hijo de puta.*'

The jets had roared over and were turning up in the sky. They would surely turn and dive and drop their bombs, now that they had us marked.

What could we do? We climbed to the hut and were pushed under a tree. It was very dark. We awaited our death.

We waited. But the jets did not come back. Why? They had practically parted our hair. It was not an accident.

'They know that there are hostages here,' whispered Pati.

'Surely not,' I thought. 'Anyway, they should kill us too. This is too good a target.'

I supposed that the pilots had to report to their general to get permission to engage the enemy. Was bureaucracy our friend? I did not know.

So we went back to bed.

'We shall set off at 3 a.m.,' Pedro warned.

But at 1 a.m. we were awakened and we packed in the dark.

'Hurry, hurry, we are off.'

'I can't see bugger all.'

'No lights, no lights.'

'How the hell can I pack?'

'Shut up. Hurry. We are off.'

We started off in line,

'Ow, shit, bugger.' I had bashed my head on a branch of a *cacao* tree. They grow horizontally at about five and a half feet high, which is OK if you are a Colombian peasant, not if you are a lanky Brit. I felt my face. Thank God the glasses were still there but they had dug into my nose and eyes and blood ran down my face.

'Hurry, Meester.'

The line snaked into the open country outside the plantation. We held on to the shirt tails of the man ahead, like a crocodile of children on a Sunday walk. I had Juan Carlos ahead. I held on to a strap.

'Shit, meester, stop pulling me over.'

'I can't see anything at all.'

'Hurry!'

The ground was slippery and uneven, and also invisible. But the jets had gone. We walked for two hours and came to a *guadua* suspension bridge, over a deep clay-banked stream. On the other side, we stopped in the dark.

'Sleep for a while here.'

It started to rain heavily. We had to put up the *carpas* any old how and pile in. I lay down and the water flowed into the *carpa* and soaked me. In the next *carpa*, Pati was squashed in with four *guerrillera* girls and a certain amount of giggling erupted. By four o'clock, we were up after an hour's rest and someone had made some coffee. We had to make more distance from where the Air Force had pinpointed us. The *comandantes* were anxious to escape death from the air. Surely they would come at dawn and kill us? We started off again in a crocodile, holding on to the man in front. By five, there was enough pre-dawn light to see. Would the jets come with the dawn light? No, they did not. We went on. The order came that there be fifteen paces between each man. Each one of us had a guard in front and another behind, named by Pedro. A bridge appeared, a splendid construction of wood and wire suspension cables. A noticeboard stated that it was built by the parents of the local school to get their children to school. An hour later, we had to cross a river, not the main one. How deep was it? It had a very narrow, feeble wooden suspension bridge over it. There was a big queue to cross. I joined a line of troops wading across. The water tugged at my legs, but the bottom was gravelly and firm. The water flowed into my boots. At the other side we took off our boots and poured out the water and wrung out our socks.

Soon we arrived at a large wood, where everyone was waiting. We could not go on. At the far side of the wood, Milton, the *comandante*, and Alexander had a radio receiver with a very long aerial. Milton was listening. A voice spoke from time to time. Suddenly the noise of machine-gun fire was audible. The voice rose over the chatter of the guns. The advance guard was being attacked by helicopters.

One of our machine gunners put his gun down and took a belt of munitions off his shoulders.

'If the *hijos de puta* come, we shall let them have it,' growled Oscar, the keen-as-mustard type, with his beret on his head.

Was our adventure to end here and now? The Woman told us later that the guard who was placed behind each of us had orders to kill us if we were attacked. In my case that meant that Hernan would have shot me.

We waited for hours, then we moved on. We came into a field with a large herd of white cebu cattle.

'Look at that!'called the older *comandante*, who had ridden on a mule on the way down, and was accompanied by a German shepherd dog. He walked with a stick. He pointed at some water buffaloes, mixed with the cattle. He explained about them, but I could not hear. This was a fine herd of several hundred cows and bulls and calves. We were marching on flat land across big fields. In the afternoon we came to a farm, with big wooden barns and a corral. Milton consulted with a man who appeared to live there, and we turned across the field. It was flooded after rain and the water lay on the hard laterite earth, which did not absorb it. The dog got excited and ran off barking. I saw that it was chasing an armadillo (a *gurre*), which scuttled into a hollow log. We went into the wood on the other side. It was full of fern trees with long fronds, which were cut down to make the floors of our *caletas*, to sleep on. Milton and Fredy and Pedro were right next to us.

'Meester sings his gringo songs,' Pedro warned Milton. So I let rip. I could not disappoint the boss.

Oh Mary, this London's a wonderful sight
There be people here working both by day and by night
They don't plant no baccy nor taters nor wheat
But there's gangs of them digging for gold in the street
For all that they find there they might as well be
Where the mountains of Mou-ourne sweep down to the sea.

I was not John McCormack, nor was there any applause. I wandered around in the small radius allowed, when we were with the troops on fighting duty. Behind a fallen log, I found a tin of Chilean clams. So that smiling *comandante* was tucking in to special delicacies! There was some arguing with the man who lived on the farm, about killing a steer, but supper was just rice and beans. We were called to clean our teeth in a stream and to bed on the fronds, Brutus and I, in the same *caleta*, back to back.

The departure next morning was delayed for ages. It turned out that the steer was being cooked and had taken much too long, so breakfast was at about ten o'clock, with masses of good meat. The rest had to be carried on top of the backpacks, wrapped in plastic.

Where had the fighting gone off to? Had the advance guard driven off the Army? Had we taken a detour and escaped?

CHAPTER 34

The family loses contact

SINCE MY MOBILE PHONE CALL on 19 July something had started but petered out. As September advanced, the guerrilla had not telephoned the Padré for a long time. Nanette had lost patience with waiting in London. She felt that she could be of more use in Colombia. This worried the Foreign Office, not to mention her friends and the family, but she went back at the end of August and was reunited with Ana and the dogs and the farm. Her orchids were to bloom again.

John had been back. A parcel had been left with the Padré for delivery to the FARC. This contained two books in English chosen by Victoria, the literary member of the family, brought from London. Banks had been talked to. The car had been recovered and was in the Mercedes workshop, but nothing could be done as the insurance company needed all sorts of papers signed by the owner, who was bird watching in his rustic prison. It had been taken apart and even the seat belts had been cut out (I can understand that because straps are precious to the guerrilla).

The Padré tried all his numbers for the FARC again and only one answered, and that was some young girls in a town, who were nothing to do with this affair, just the new owners of a cloned third-hand mobile.

Nanette received a telephone call from a former neighbour at the flat we had lived in ten years before.

'Nanette, listen, I have a friend whose husband was released recently from kidnap. Would you like to meet her?'

'Of course. Tell her to ring me and she can come to the flat. I am very keen to hear her story. We are getting worried.'

This lady came round. She sat down, accepted a whisky, the dogs were pushed away, and she talked.

'We spent eight months negotiating and had got nowhere, then we were put in touch with a retired police general. In three and a half months more, we had my husband back. We paid much more than we wanted. The general saw us and asked how much money we had. He rang back in forty-eight hours and said that he had contacted the guerrilla and had been told which group held my husband. They were ready to do a quick deal. Then he asked for proof of my husband's wealth: bank statements, tax declarations, valuations of properties, statements of debts. The thing is that he plays both sides and gets a percentage of the ransom paid.'

This conversation was reported to the committee, who exploded. We would have to show documents to a dodgy man in Bogotá, who could check up. The price could rise if he fixed a false idea of the amount payable in his mind. Two of the committee had heard of his way of operating before and said, 'Don't touch him with a barge pole. He leaks information and is a crook. However frustrating it is for us and the Padré, stick with him. He is honest and on our side.'

Victoria's husband, Tim, had a terrible accident in England at this stage. He was driving with Victoria on a road and saw a crashed car. He stopped to help and was himself hit from behind by another car, driving too fast. He was hurled into a field, unconscious, with one leg almost severed. He was months in hospital while surgeons repaired his leg. The pain for Victoria and the family was doubled.

John and Nanette had to go to see the *Fiscalia* (Attorney General's department), and asked a friend to drive the car, and wait. They walked into the 'Bunker' near the airport, and along the cold grey concrete corridors. In offices, staff were writing statements into word processors, and interviewing people. They found the office of the officer in charge of the case, a young lawyer.

'Oh, by the way,' he said, 'there is a man who works here, who says that his father has just come out of kidnap. He thinks that his father was with your husband, because he talks of a foreigner, whom he calls 'El Meester.'

'Can we meet him?'

'I shall call him now.'

And this other *Fiscalia* employee appeared quickly and said, '*Mucho gusto*,' looking with great curiosity at these two foreigners.

'Nice to meet you.'

He shook hands and sat down. 'My father has just come back home after being kidnapped. He says that he was with a Meester, and I think it could be your husband.'

This was very exciting and a great surprise.

'Can we meet him?' asked Nanette.

'He is in his farm. I shall have to talk to him.'

In fact it took some time, as Grandpa was adjusting to life again. John had gone back to work.

'We can meet in the Salitre shopping centre,' said the son, one day. 'I can't be there, but my other brother will take our father there. He will be wearing a green shirt.'

All that was missing was that he should say that Grandpa would have a huge white false moustache on, but Grandpa had that anyway. Or had he shaved it off?

The next day, they were all sitting in a café together, having coffee, the best coffee in the world – *Café de Colombia*. Grandpa and his son were very nervous. Nanette and the other committee member were excited.

The deaf old man reassured them. 'Meester is all right. He has lost weight. And his wrist is broken. I am grateful for the help he gave me all the time, carrying my things and walking with me. I am eighty years old. They made me walk and I was too weak. I thought I would die. When the aircraft flew over, I hoped that they would bomb us and I would die. *El Meester es una persona fuerte.* He will survive. The guerrilla lets him go to the *rancho* and talk to them, when they don't let us. They are better with him than with us.'

'Where is he?'

'In Sumapaz. They took me across the sierra again and let me go in the llanos. They gave me money for a bus home. I'll tell you something. El Meester keeps food in his pockets. One day he was sitting on a rock and had put his English jacket on a bush to dry. But a pig appeared and smelt the food and ate his jacket. He ran all over the field chasing that pig, but his jacket was ruined.' Grandpa laughed like a drain at the memory. 'That Meester, *que comico!* Shouting at that pig. I shall never forget.'

'Thanks for the news. It means a lot to us.'

'Tell him to come and see me when he is out. El Meester gave us courage to believe that we would come out alive. *Un buen hombre.*'

They went home and Nanette was happy at the news and felt better. But she also felt lonely at the thought of me up in the cold mountain for how much longer. She knew already about the broken wrist. It had not been mended.

CHAPTER 35

Arrival in the rainforest

WHEN WE LEFT THE FARM, where the steer had been killed and we had the late breakfast, we went into the fields again and along the edge of the woods, until we hit a wide path, more like an unpaved road. It was wet and muddy, with an annoying feature. There were ridges across the road and in between pools of water that could not run off. So we had to step on each ridge, and when the water had made pools, on to the side of the road by the barbed wire fence, a tiring and annoying style of marching. It was hotter. The road joined another wider one, past some newly-built wooden huts, with women and children moving around inside. There was a school and a shop, then we were back to wilder country. The trees became thicker.

We were spread out. Then, over on the left, I saw a helicopter, a small one with a clear bubble body, flying low in the opposite direction. I crouched down. The *guerrilleros* near me stopped. I hid behind a bramble bush in the fence. How could it not see us?

I heard Pedro say, 'It is a sprayer,' meaning the *coca* eradication programme fumigators.

It went away and we stood up and walked on. We left the fields and went into the trees.

'Look, a *marimba*!' called a *guerrillero*. I saw a large monkey walking along a branch. A toucan flew into the same tree. We were on the edge of the rainforest. These different birds and beasts were exciting. It started to rain fiercely. I came across Brutus and our people and we waited for Pati. Pedro told us to turn right and into a field. We came into a grove of coffee bushes and then suddenly into a large wood. The earth was bare and trodden and flooded, with the signs of many *caleta*s. There was even a wooden hut, a sort of canteen or restaurant. It was obviously a major camp from the time of the *zona de distension*. Thousands of troops must have been based here. The rain belted down. Should we put up a roof? Pedro came over with a *guerrillero*.

'This is Tiger,' he said. And fell silent.

'Come on,' said Tiger. We followed him and crossed the camp. I realised that this must be a handover. Pedro had finished his job with us. Pati ran back and said goodbye to him but I did not feel like doing the same, nor did Brutus. What was this? Was he a friend? No. To hell with him. I looked back and saw the adolescents who had been with us since May. It was September now. They waved. I stared. We went on.

154

Tiger was a cheerful, educated chap. He brought another *guerrillero* with him. It stopped raining. We crossed several fields, recently slashed and burned. It was certainly a *coca* plantation. Then we saw the *coca* cuttings in the ground, what they call 'the true Peruvian'. A civilian in jeans and a T-shirt joined us, to guide us. He took us into a farmyard, with buildings. We saw a shed with plastic barrels of chemicals, cement bags, and cans of diesel. This was where people made *coca* paste. We kept on walking fast and crossed a plank bridge over some ponds and into the forest, along a good path. Tiger was talkative. He said that we were on the border of two provinces. Pati thought that they were Huila and Meta. I thought that they might be Meta and Guaviare (a big *coca* province). I asked the other *guerrillero* what was the closest town. Miraculously, he replied.

'San José de Guaviare,' he said. That was a town right down the Guaybero river to the east.

'Not Granada?'

'Oooh, no. That is a long journey.'

So it was possible that we had walked right to the Amazonia area, the great rainforest. Three weeks on foot. As far as Caqueta? Surely not.

We seemed to be walking westwards. Strange. The sun set. We stopped in a field.

'We have to wait,' said Tiger.

There was no moon and the stars were bright. The others lay down on their *carpas* and tried to sleep. I was alive and nervous. I did not like being with new *guerrilleros* in the night in a field God knows where. I could see the outline of mountains in the west.

Much later, there was a sound of a motor but no lights. Tiger made us get up and walk to a hut, which we had not seen before. A truck drove up with its lights switched off. Several people jumped out. They were uniformed *guerrilleros*, on a night-time mission, to pick us up. But first, food. They had brought urban food – polystyrene boxes of chicken and coleslaw and rice, and big plastic bottles of Pepsi Cola or *Colombiana*, the fizzy drink of Colombia. My goodness, there must be a town nearby. The food was delicious and exotic. Fancy eating chicken, US-style junk food in the dark field under the stars.

'We are going to have to blindfold you,' Tiger apologised. He put us into the back of the truck, and the *guerrilleros* climbed in and we drove off. It was a proper road, unpaved, but made for traffic. We could not use lights. The night belongs to the guerrilla, but the sky to the Air Force. A man shone a flashlight through the windscreen, and we drove fast, bouncing along the stony surface. Then the blindfolds were put on and we must have driven through a town. We stopped in front of a hut on the road and got out. There was a conversation with a man who lived in the hut and the *comandante* of our new captors. He was a tall and educated man with a neat beard and a polite manner. We set off along a path, probably a cattle path, which became a pool of mud. In the pitch dark and with short bursts of a flashlight, it was a nasty dirty walk. We arrived at a river. Nothing. We walked back to the road. What was that about? More conversation. The man in the hut was angry.

'Come along,' said the tall *comandante*. 'We shall have to find a place to spend the night.'

I supposed that he had expected a boat on the river and it had gone wrong. We walked along the road in the dark and found a large farm with good quality buildings. We lay on the plank floor of a barn.

'If you want to get up and pee, tell us first,' said the tall man. 'We don't want one of these men to shoot you by mistake.'

It had been a long day. We slept well. It was warm and the need for blankets was over. Goodbye Pedro, you rat! Welcome to a new chapter of our kidnap.

The next day we awoke to sun and a dry day. We had been walking for three weeks and done perhaps 300 kilometres. Had we arrived? Where?

The new *guerrilleros* were young boys, plus the tall *comandante*. They had sent away for food and made a breakfast of eggs and sardines and coffee. What an improvement! We had apparently missed an appointment with a boat and would have to wait until night. This boat only travelled at night so we had a whole day free. There was a stream where we washed ourselves and all our clothes. I washed the camouflage jacket which Epimaco had left me, for the first time in its life. Twice. Everything dried in the heat. We were getting to know Pati better. There was a big tree with *sapote* fruit hanging all over. It is an orange-sized fruit with a hard green skin and yellow fibrous pulp and was sweet and juicy. The boys climbed the tree and brought back a sack of it and we each ate more than twenty, until we could eat no more. Lunch was chicken and vegetables and rice, with bottles of fruit juice. Luxury. We sunbathed and walked around the farm. There was a Ford tractor, banana plantations with no fruit, and new concrete pig pens, with no pigs. It was an abandoned farm in the war zone. What a pity.

Before dark, we packed and marched to the river, where we had been in the dark last night. We found a long dugout canoe, with an outboard motor and a boatman. The tall man, who was a bit of a John Cleese character, walked towards it and sank in the mud up to his waist. When he had been pulled out and had lost a rubber boot, the canoe came in closer and we got in, the three of us, and several *guerrilleros*, and pushed off into the current. The river was in fact a creek that came into a much bigger river and we headed downstream. It was shallow, gravel bottomed, with large driftwood trees stuck on the banks that came and went in the middle of the waters. The river went by tall trees and banana plantations. There were big iguanas and small alligators (caymans), the Amazon kingfisher with its tufted head, ibises, black and white, and sandpipers. The sky was wide and blue. We had set off in the light, but we needed the dark. The river descended in shelves of gravel and then fell over the edge to the next shelf. There might be a deep channel. If not the canoe grounded and the boys jumped out and pushed it clear.

'I thought the caymans had been hunted out of existence,' I asked the tall man, with the muddy legs.

'Ah, it's the Japanese. They set up a croc farm, and the beasts escaped.'

This is the general belief of the guerrilla, and I read that there is a Japanese research facility in the forest of Colombia, with an ancient professor who speaks no Spanish. They are doing a species count and inventory.

The bottom of the canoe was crowded with fuel cans, sacks of plantains, boxes, and overflow river water. The seats were planks laid athwarts. One lean back and the seat tipped up and deposited you in the bottom and its dirty water. Where were we going, down this tropical river into the rainforest?

The darkness fell with a red sunset that lasted all of fifteen minutes. We stopped and backed into a creek on the left. A pair of *guerrilleros* were waiting on the bank. The boatman unloaded some boxes and barrels and we pushed out into the river again. After two hours we pulled into the river bank and some lights flared up and figures came down. It was a strange scene: black night, the figures moving about, the forest.

'Maybe you stay here tonight. For the night and go on tomorrow,' said the tall man. He was not the world's best organiser. We were a day late and unexpected and late in the day for the hotel check-in.

On 11 August 2001 a very curious item of news began to circulate. Three Irishmen had been detained by the police at Bogotá's Eldorado airport. They maintained that they were tourists and had been holidaying in the rainforest. After a while, it surfaced that their passports and their real identities did not coincide. I suppose that their photographs had been circulated to the secret services where you circulate such photos and a fit was made. They were Niall Connolly, the representative of the IRA's political arm, Sinn Fein, in Cuba, and Jim Monaghan and Martin McCauley, allegedly IRA explosives experts. They had been known to travel under the aliases of David Bracken, Edward Joseph Campbell, and John Joseph Kelly. David Bracken was the name of a baby who died in 1966. Connolly had been involved in arranging a trip to Cuba for Gerry Adams, the Sinn Fein leader. Perhaps Adams wanted to enjoy the beaches and music of that lovely island. It was soon reported that traces of explosives were found on their clothing. They maintained that they had been holidaying.

The telephone rang in my flat. 'David, it's Mick. How are you?'

'Fine. And you?'

'Have you seen this news? Oi mean about the Irish lads?'

'Yes. What do you think?'

'Chroist, the phones are ringing. I got a call from a mate who said that his visa says that he came to work in a bookshop, but he is teaching English now. Do you think he should go to the DAS and change his visa?'

'What? Do you think that they will be checking up on all Irishmen at the airport now?'

'Too roight, they will. What a cock-up. And my visa says that I came to teach English and you know that I spend all the time in my electronics company now. Shit, what if they catch me? Do you think that I should go and change my visa?'

'You want me to tell you? You can't win. You don't tell them, problem. You go and tell them, you get caught up in the bureaucracy, problem again. Imagine the DAS full to bursting with Paddies waving their visas? Ha, ha.'

'All right for you. They will think we are all IRA boys.'

'Relax. Don't do anything while the fuss is on. You've got a Colombian wife and you have been here for ages. You have a *cedula* (identity document). Relax.'

'Ah Chroist, but everyone is jumping up and down.' He rang off.

What a joke, all the Paddies in a panic, ringing around from their language schools, shops, the Irish pub, their church groups. They love Colombia.

In April 2002, the US House of Representatives called a hearing on this matter, for 24 April, and invited Gerry Adams, president of Sinn Fein, often called the political arm of the IRA, (or the IRA is called the private army of the Sinn Fein.) Imagine the embarrassment of the US politicians, trying to manage the Irish situation in Ireland and Ulster, to find Irishmen, who might have been helping their arch-terrorist enemies in the narco-guerrilla of Colombia. Adams replied that he had better things to do for that day. He did not show up. On 2 April, a member of the Irish parliament suggested that if Adams were not to explain himself in the USA, he might like to do so to the Irish parliament. Since the guerrilla in Colombia is a clear and present threat to the USA and its nationals, it is easy to see how this matter got the knickers of the USA in a twist. Richard Haass was the US special representative for the peace process in Northern Ireland. By May, he was reported to have expressed himself forcefully to the Irish and in the USA and to the press.

11 September 2001 is not a day that anyone will forget. I was up and moving around my apartment in Bogotá. The television was on and, by Direct TV, the BBC World Service was being transmitted, as I moved around and Ana, the maid, cleared up the breakfast – papaya, coffee from our own farm, brown German bread from Europan, the German bakery down on 5th Street. I had wandered into the bedroom and something caught my eye on the screen – the World Trade Centre towers in New York. There was a column of smoke. What was it? 'What is that?' echoed the television. 'We just have a report in from New York . . .' People in the street were looking up, then there was film of the first aircraft flying into the tower. This was the birth of 'global terrorism', of 'the evil axis', the

stiffening of the sinews of President George W. Bush. Someone had hit the USA below the belt, inside its frontiers. There were dead from many countries. Even Colombians.

Earlier that day, in Dublin, Richard Haass had a meeting with Gerry Adams. Could he make progress on the decommissioning of arms? After a few minutes of careful talk, Haass is reported to have snapped, 'If any American, service personnel or civilian, is killed in Colombia by the technology that the IRA supplied, then you can f--- off. Don't tell me that you know nothing about what's going on there. We know everything about it.' The pressure was on the IRA. Its supporters in the USA would not take American deaths in Colombia. Are the Irish in the USA involved in drugs? No, that is not in their culture at all. And a few hours later the world changed, as the towers collapsed and people died. Before, the IRA had said that the British army should be 'decommissioning' and leaving Ulster. Now Bill Flynn, the Chairman of the Mutual Bank of America, began to say that after 11 September, the IRA had to disarm. Sinn Fein has an office in Washington and funds are raised in the USA. Indeed the guerrilla of Colombia has offices abroad, in Europe, and a website, and friends in the union movements and NGOs of many countries. The FARC publishes a magazine, *Resistencia*, and its website is translated into other languages, including Russian and Japanese. How do they do it?

Mr Flynn is reported to have said that the IRA contacts with the FARC are devastating. 'Colombia is a place that peddles drugs into this country.' This underlies the belief that the guerrilla in Colombia lives off drug money, that it is a narco-guerrilla, a very damaging accusation.

In Colombia a deserter from the FARC was found who testified that he had helped Monaghan unload missiles some time before from a private plane in the distension zone. It had already been rumoured that Nicaraguan Marxists had sent SAM missiles to Colombia. Obviously, a guerrilla armed with surface-to-air missiles is a different kettle of fish to a footslogging infantry army, hiding under forest cover. And if the FARC had access to cocaine, how better to pay for weapons, instead of paying money across bank accounts, exposed to freezing by foreign governments.

As the trial in Colombia dragged on, this affair was to be mentioned in the difficult negotiations of October 2003, as Tony Blair attempted to put the Irish peace talks on the tracks again. The Colombian involvement played into the hands of those protestants who have never believed the IRA. The decommissioning, supervised by the Canadian General De Chastelain, was derailing itself.

This fatal linking of terrorism with drugs points to the enigmatic drama of drugs themselves. They are illegal substances, under the laws of most countries of the world, and obviously the USA, but the richer countries are where the consumers are. Drugs are stronger than humans. Not always, but enough to destroy people and families. But so are cigarettes and alcohol and driving too fast and eating too much. How much of the budgets of our countries are spent on the illnesses and crimes that arise from alcohol, smoking, overeating, taking drugs, driving cars too fast? No wonder that periods of ascetic religion – Puritanism, Methodism, Quakerism, Islam – have been good for the members of certain societies.

Making drugs illegal necessitates a huge police and customs effort and expense to stop people doing what they want, but should not do, and the trade falls into the hands of criminals. Often the consumer is allowed a 'personal dose', as long as he does not sell to others. Marijuana is close to being tolerated. The list of illustrious men and women who favour 'decriminalising' drugs is long. The battle to eradicate the production of natural drug plants – *coca*, opium poppies – has clearly not been successful. Afghanistan, Thailand, Burma, Colombia, Peru have all suffered casualties in their armed forces, corruption of the police and judiciary, expense. I think that it was in the Superbowl football finals in the USA in 2001 that a wonderful advertisement (costing the earth?) was shown linking the deaths in battle in the Colombian forest with the use of drugs in USA. 'By using drugs, you are killing soldiers.'

So are drugs a matter of personal responsibility or a cause for international warfare? The USA spends money and time on Colombia. Why? Because *coca* comes into the USA, and heroin, and marijuana – or did until people could get away with growing it in their own flowerpots – and the politicians are convinced that the voters want the drugs to be eliminated, rather than the users to be educated. Or both. So *coca* and poppies are illegal crops and thus are handled by the drug mafia and latterly by the guerrilla, not by Philip Morris and BAT, or United Distillers and no tax can be collected.

In a not-untypical cock-up of Colombian justice, the Irishmen were released by a lower court judge and then the government appealed and a higher judge convicted them of coming to train the FARC. By then they had disappeared. You may bump into them in a bar in La Habana, drinking rum and coke instead of Guinness. I think the governments of several countries are glad that they are not in a Colombian jail. I am.

PART 4

Six Months in the Rainforest

CHAPTER 36

The *frente* 40 takes over

THE FIRST MORNING IN THE rainforest found the three of us huddled together on the ground under one roof in an undergrowth of *heliconias* and wild bananas. Above were the tall canopy trees and by the river bank the *yarumo* trees, which let in a good deal of sunlight. Where were we? The camp of the guerrilla was very close along the path that we had come along from the river. One of them – they were new to us – brought coffee. The *comandante* – he said his name was Edwin – came with a girl and a notebook (*cuaderno*). He asked us one by one our names and addresses and telephone numbers. She wrote them down in the notebook. Perhaps he was illiterate. This was depressing. They did not know who we were? My God! It was 11 September, so had the negotiating stopped. Did the FARC have to start again? Did they not have our telephone numbers? Oh, hell. When would we ever go home again?

This was a moment when we could catch a hint of the limbo that is the FARC. We could be passed around different groups and marched around the country ad infinitum. It was the huge world 'through the looking glass', half of Colombia. No one knew where we were. There are kidnap victims who enter this limbo for years. Where are Jose Eladio Perez, Mahmud Salem and so many others whose names one hears on the radio programmes and sees in the files of *Pais Libre*? Since we are not told how the negotiations with our families are going, we have no clue. But we had a clue now. They did not know who we were! Not a moment to despair. Chin up.

Then a tall, thin *guerrillero*, an older man, sauntered up the path. Oh no! I could not believe it. It was Hanibal. We had said goodbye to him at the cheese farm. We had understood that he was on his way – to retirement or to *orden publico*. The bad penny turned up again. He said that he had been here for three weeks or so. He knew that we were coming.

'I thought that you were going to retire and go home?' queried Pati. '*Que pasó, viejo?*'

'No, it did not work out?' replied Hanibal, uncomfortably, I thought. 'I am working on it.'

'Who is in charge here? What *frente* is this?' she went on.

'I can't tell you, *doctora*. Don't ask,' he said. He seemed to be relegated to a junior level and not to have the confidence of Edwin. He had to watch his mouth.

'*Que tal*, Hanibal?' I hailed him.

'Hey, Mister, how are you? Long march, no?'

'Just a stroll. But I suppose we can stop now?'

'I don't know if you are here to stay or just for a night.'

'Christ, can't we stop. Three weeks moving. When can we go home? You said up in the mountains that we would be out in a few weeks.'

'Don't worry. You pay and you go home.'

'But when?'

'Won't be long. Mister.'

'Anyway, nice to see your ugly face.'

'Eh, *paisa, buenos dias*. Good day,' he saluted Brutus.

'*Que hay de bueno?* What's good, *hijo de puta*?' growled Brutus.

The guards, doing this 'commission' of looking after us, were:

Edwin, the *comandante*, a tall, thin, quiet 28-year-old. Later we were told that his nickname was 'Cat's Meat' (*Carne de gato*);

Sandra, his 'wife', a beautiful, tall girl, with a fine face, tipped-up nose, and long dark hair;

Olmedo, a polite, quiet young man, with a pet parrot on his shoulder.

Hanibal, our 51-year-old friend;

Adriano, probably late 40s, a rough fellow from near Cali, sometimes friendly, sometimes silent;

Polo, an old man, said to have been the village drunk;

Patas Chitas, a 15-year-old Indian boy;

Jonhatan (*sic*), an 18-year-old mulatto, retarded boy, from Valledupar, in the north;

Colacho, a lanky amiable 17-year-old, of mixed blood, born on a farm in the llanos;

Ramiro, a 17-year old, bigger Indian boy;

Carolina, our 16-year old fat friend;

Yasmin, the black girl, with no front teeth;

Yesica, a brown, pretty, busty girl of some sixteen years;

Jaime, a thoughtful, more educated city man in his thirties;

Andres, from the march, a tall, better-class 19-year-old.

The routine of a commission for kidnap victims is sentry duty, usually one hour on each twelve hours. One person is the cook (doing *el rancho*) for one day, then the cook does the job of *recepcionista*, being the waiter, serving the food and drink to us, and washing up. They sleep when they can. They have plenty of free time, for games or fishing. One person is the medical orderly (*enfermera*). This was Sandra, when we came, but Yasmin took over. She had a gentle touch and was a good nurse. Some came from other parts of Colombia. Some had come from the hills, in advance of us, like Hanibal. Some had marched with us – Yasmin, Carolina, Andres. A lot of them were recuperating from battle wounds. Colacho had been caught by a burst of machine-gun fire across his stomach, and had lost metres of intestine and could not eat normal food. He was very thin.

'I was at the storming of Las Delicias,' he told us. I seemed to remember that that was an isolated army base in the southern province of Putumayo, which was attacked by a superior guerrilla force, and overrun. There are Army prisoners in the jungle from that defeat, who have been over five years in captivity, and are part of the never-happening 'exchange of prisoners' idea.

'We were five or six *frentes*. We charged up the slope towards the soldiers, shooting and telling them to surrender or die. My friend next to me got killed. After the fourth charge, we had to decide whether to go up again. The Army had machine guns. We went again and they ran away or gave themselves up. But I caught a burst in the stomach. Look. My guts were hanging out.'

His scars were impressive. I imagine that medical attention is rough – cut open, throw away the damaged guts, bung a bucket of antibiotics in, sew up.

He said that he had been born in the llanos, but that his family had moved up to the *Sabana*, near Bogotá. The *Sabana* (or 'savannah') is a high flat valley floor, 2,400 metres high in fact) in the Eastern Cordillera, running north-south, where the Spanish had finally set their capital, in the land of the Muisca Indians. The names are Indian often: Zipaquira, Ubate, Teusaquillo, Neusa. The cool landscape reminds one of Switzerland. A temperature range of 20 centigrade at midday to 8 at night. Not what we would call tropical hot, but tropical temperate. It is always the same. Every day dawns at six and night falls at six, with a bit of variation between December and June. We are in the northern hemisphere, just, by seven degrees or so. This is the Andes, green and cool, the home of maize, of the potato, of the tomato, which the Europeans only knew when the Spanish brought them back to Europe in the 1500s, and of a heap of fruit, such as cactus fig, tree tomato, *pitahaya*. Colacho left school young and reads with difficulty. That is to say that he does not read books or papers, and listens a lot to popular music. He got a job manning a stall on the road, selling the vegetables and fruit that a woman with a farm produced, near Zipaquira. He was good at it, he says. The woman said that she would finance him to be the owner of the stall. He was making 800 pesos a day, more than the minimum wage. He could buy clothes and give money to his parents.

So why was he here in the forest and not a prosperous greengrocer, near Bogotá? Good question. The most likely answer is that he got into trouble with the law? No? He was philosophical about life. One day, he was on sentry duty, and talkative, which was forbidden.

'If I live until I am twenty. That will be long enough. I have lived a full life. I don't want to be old.'

'Don't you want to have children? Have a home and a wife and family?'

'No. I hate living in a house. I get bored.'

'But you are an ordinary Colombian. You were born in a house, in a family? What do you do if you live in the forest? If you get sick? The Indians know about natural medicines and how to hunt, not you. They are the people of the forest.'

'No, Meester, we are people of the forest too.'

That left me speechless. He did think that he was a forest dweller. He had regressed as a human to a primitive life as a hunter-gatherer. His life expectancy had reverted to that of a European of five centuries ago. And voluntarily?

The prisoner of the FARC experiences poverty. What does that mean? I had to survive a life with nothing and worth nothing. Maybe that allowed one to tune oneself to the mental state of our captors. Of course, we had a possibility of getting out into the middle-class world, whence we had come. Or were we to die here? We had no money and nowhere to buy anything. We had no house, no bed, no electricity, no means of transport, no pen, no paper. What was the minimum? We were given food and some clothes. A spoon and a pan. A toothbrush, a towel, soap. A comb. A sleeping bag and a blanket. We were no better than the companions of Odysseus in 1000 BC.

This was brought home to me abruptly in another way. Yasmin, the black nurse, was chatting one day.

'I like to sleep in my *caleta*, on bamboo. I can't sleep in a bed. I remember once that we were marching through farms in the Meta. We had to spend the night at a farm. I was given the bed, but I could not sleep a wink. So soft! That is how the *richachones* live, but not me.'

So for Yasmin anyone who sleeps in a bed is a *richachon*, a rich man, a moneybags! Poverty is managing to live with almost nothing. I was doing that. All you have is what is in your head – poetry and songs, and a sense of humour. And the earth – plants, ants, monkeys, parrots, fish in the river. In fact, I got fond of Yasmin, as she did have a sense of humour and was a good nurse with a gentle touch and got ill and felt sad and felt jolly. Of course, she was also illiterate and lazy, with no skills.

'Why did you become a *guerrillera*?' we asked her.

'My father was killed by the Army. I always wanted to join the guerrilla. I asked to join when I was twelve, but they told me to wait until I was fifteen. But I went on asking and they let me be a camp-follower when I was thirteen.'

That seemed to be the end of the conversation. What could we say? How could the State get her to rejoin society and behave? Many *guerrilleros* don't see how they can fit in to civil life. If they deserted, what would they do? They are useless. Who would employ them? Would they be promised retraining by the State and then dumped into a world where they feel alone and unemployable? So they stay on in the forest.

It was a false line of thinking to say that the poor are poor because the rich are rich. We, the prisoners, were people who had started without capital and had got a better standard of living by education and hard work. Brutus had it right. Why take from us? Were we not doing the right thing? Society was not stacked up against the Colombians. The opposite was true. The open economy did give us chances. It was just that the *guerrilleros* were unable to take advantage of opportunites. They were the losers, and they could not blame anyone. Brutus did not sympathise with them. He despised them.

What did I feel all those months as a prisoner of these people? If I could believe that they would agree after a year or two to release me for a sum of money that my family could pay, then I just needed patience. I was being robbed and could not fight back. They were far from brutal. It was easy to get on with them, although they were forbidden to be with us for long. Every now and then, they were told to be tough and stand far away and not talk to us. Did the *comandantes* not trust them? Would we weaken their convictions? Did they hate us? Not that I could see. The rich just had to pay the poor, by force, and put up with it. I was not going to die, any more than I would let Grandpa give up, or Pati. But if they wanted more money than we had, then they would get annoyed and would kill me. It was later that this feeling was confirmed. They do kill. My life was worth nothing. But meanwhile we could crack jokes and play games with them. Colombia had divided into two camps and we were the captured enemy.

The nights were long. The sentries changed every hour. The one on duty woke up the sleeping relief, who got up and walked around the beat with the one going off duty, flashing the flashlight in to each *caleta*, to see that we had not run away or died. Sometimes this woke us up. Sometimes we slept through. The sentry was left alone. Some of them would talk, and it was Pati who was the best listener.

Bad Boy told a tale of a sentence of popular justice passed by the FARC on a local bourgeois in some country area, for collaborating with the Paras or the State probably. The condemned man was taken by Bad Boy and another (they always have to go out in pairs, as the *comandantes* don't trust them alone). He was made to dig his grave. He pleaded for his life. Perhaps he offered money. 'We decided to let him go free,' said Bad Boy. 'We filled in the grave, and he ran off. Then my *comandante* came and asked if we had finished. He became suspicious and asked us to reopen the grave and show the body. What could we do? I started to dig. We would get shot ourselves. Suddenly there was a sound of gunfire. "Back to the camp," ordered the *comandante*. "Leave that."

'Christ, that was a close one,' summed up Bad Boy. Why did he tell us? Was it true? It was possible that he had a better character than others. He was more informative but he was a liar and a thief.

Pati took a chance to ask him to buy a radio for her. It was so important for her to get messages from her daughter and sisters. That could assuage the terrible anxiety about her children, mostly her young son. Bad Boy said that the boatman could get a radio. She gave him forty thousand pesos. The radio never came. The money was never returned.

Someone told Pati one night that there had been a Court Martial (*Consejo de Guerra*) after the arrival in the forest. This is normal procedure, when the troops are in base camp, in the presence of the big chiefs, to tidy up pending disciplinary matters. How would you run a rabble of youngsters and ex-convicts without discipline? This one was dramatic. On our march, we had noticed a smartly dressed but worried young man, called V . . . He had been brought up to face a charge of misbehaviour towards some civilians. He was found guilty. The verdict is in theory arrived at by his peers, the *guerrilleros*. Like the Roman Emperor asking the public at the gladiator arena to put their thumbs up or down. He was found guilty and taken out and a pistol was fired into his head.

There was a girl who was seven months pregnant when we reached the forest. We had seen her and her big belly. A nice girl. The FARC had a policy of no pregancies and maternal leaves and babies. The *comandantes* wanted to build up the fighting strength.

'Get rid of that baggage in your belly,' was the sentence pronounced by the *comandante*. An abortion at seven months!

'And Vladimir had better watch out,' the voice in the night said. 'He has a charge of killing civilians pending.'

The Colombian nation has always voted in referenda against capital punishment. The FARC has no such compunction. Its law is not that of the Colombians. It is a hard and murderous law, but no harder than the law applied by Castro and Guevara when they took power in Cuba, or the communists in Russia and China.

It is widely believed that the *guerrilleros* are paid wages, which is why they join up and stay, and from that it is easy to think that narco-traffic generates the money to pay these wages. Thus the guerrilla is a narco-guerrilla, a big business, running a big payroll. They can pay higher wages than the minimum wage or than the cash that subsistence farming produces. However, we were told that the boys and girls get no wage at all. None. They don't seem to carry any money on them but they do get hold of certain articles that usually cost money. The girls get some feminine things. The boys? Well, I don't know. Having radios is common enough. It is possible that if they are allowed home or into the real world, they get an allowance. If they are pensioned off, do they get a lump sum of money? Do they get money for medical treatment? I bet they do. However, it is probably not necessary to offer wages to recruit these waifs and strays. They only ever talk about the companionship, the food, the clothes, the cigarettes. Ths *comandantes* carry a roll of cash in their pocket. I saw it once or twice. The Witch was the cashier of the *comision* up in the hills. I saw her pay for biscuits and drinks at the shop on the march.

Cigarettes, President brand, are the only luxury. Transporting them around must take space and time in the difficult logistic of the guerrilla. But it is allowed by the bosses, as a morale booster. When the cigarettes arrived, the boys brought them to us too. I did not smoke, but the other two got their packs. After a while, the cigarettes made both of them sick and gave them headaches.

'Don't smoke then,' I said, with the superiority of the non-smoker. Once or twice Brutus threw his cigarettes in to the *chonto* and said that he would never smoke again. But he did. When the canoe did not bring any, he asked the sentries for one.

'Lend me one. I shall pay you back later.'

Getting a light was even more difficult. There were no matches, only lighters, which broke down and lost their flints and were repaired. They were precious and not given to us.

It was strange that in our undernourished state, our bodies could not cope with nicotine poisoning. No, it was a good sign. We were being purged by our basic diet.

CHAPTER 37

Brutus's tale

OVER THE MONTHS, BRUTUS TOLD US his life story, in the periods when he would talk, or when Pati would talk to him, or to me. Our relations were not always easy. We were so different, and so much on top of each other.

'I was born on a *finca* in the countryside near Guarne, outside Medellin. We were poor, poor, poor. We slept in one room. I have six brothers and sisters. My father was very hard on us. I was the difficult one. He used to beat me. Once I ran away, then I got frightened and came back at night, but he made me sleep outside on the terrace. We handed down the clothes between the brothers. I know all about the countryside (*campo*), the plants and animals. We grew peas and potatoes. But I don't like it. Once I was sent to stay with my uncle. He had a nice *finca* and some cattle, but he lived alone. I saw a big snake there. I hate snakes. Then some men came with guns. They said that my uncle had killed a man. I think it was someone else, but they blamed him, because he had had arguments with his neighbour about his cattle eating his grass. So he had to run away, and not come back. I went home. I did not like school. My father would beat me if I did not learn, but I did not see the point. When I was fourteen, I ran away to Medellin. I lived in the street. I made a living by being a street photographer, selling photos of people who were walking about – country bumpkins and other things. When I was twenty I decided to go to Bogotá. There was a man, an older man, who befriended me and helped me. I started in the clothes business. It went well.'

Another time he reminisced, 'I used to go by train to La Guajira to buy clothes.' This was and is the centre for contraband, smuggled in from the Caribbean and Panama, by sea, often by Arabs, the experts at textiles in Latin America, from before the rise of the Chinese. 'I would fill up my suitcases and get back on the train. Sometimes the police would come, *hijos de puta*, and take away all the stuff so I had to start again. Then my friend helped me, and I put up a factory to make clothes – shirts, underwear. I had up to four hundred girls working for me, and eighty sewing machines. I was doing well. I travelled all over Colombia, selling the stuff and taking the orders.

'I have four children by four different women but I have never given my name to any of them. I have never married. Yes, I am a Catholic. I believe in God. Don't you? One of my women runs the office I have. I met her in Pereira, where I was selling. She worked in a clothes shop. You know, the women of Pereira are

170

good-looking. You can find very fine women, who will do it for very little money. Fine women. She had a girl, and when I went back, I did not like how she treated the girl, so I brought them to Bogotá. The girl is sixteen now. She wants to go to university, and she has her *bachillerato* exams soon. I want to be at her graduation, but here I am. Do you know any good universities in the USA? How much do they cost? I have a son too. He is a little dumbo, ha, ha. The rogue! He says, "What have you got for me, Papa?" He can't read yet, although I always buy him pencils and paper. I buy food at the market and take it to my women. I have a new woman, and she is younger than my daughter. I think she is pregnant. I hope it is mine. She is going to school. I wait for her outside the school. What do you mean, I am a dirty old man? She is old enough to know what she wants. She is over fourteen now.

'I make good money, but I spend it all. I like to drink, probably too much. Whisky. I start drinking on Tuesday and go on, especially over the weekend until Monday. I get totally pissed. The only thing I regret is having shouted at my daughter. I came back home once and was noisy, and she said, "Papa, why do you not stop drinking? You make us very unhappy." And I roared at her and tried to hit her. Perhaps, when I get out, I shall stop drinking? I do like to smoke a good spliff. I built a Jacuzzi on the terrace of my house, with a hi-fi, and I love to sit there and smoke grass.

'I have a visa for the USA. Oh, yes. The last holiday I had, I took my woman to Miami. I liked the food and the shops. I got a cold and wanted to buy medicine, so I asked a man on the street where I could buy drugs. You know here we say *drogueria*. I guess I should have said – what do you say, Meester? – pharmacy? He looked astonished, me a big man from Colombia asking for *drogas*. Ha, Ha. When these *hijos de puta* asked me to answer some questions to send to my woman, one of them was "Where did we spend our last holiday?" and I put "In Miami." Oh shit, that was not a good idea, was it?

'I have never worked for anyone. I could never do it. I am lazy. I scarcely do anything. I have a good income and I spend it all. I think you could say that my whole life has been disorganised. I like to go and gamble. I end up losing, but sometimes I win a lot. I know lots of people with money, real money, more than ten thousand million pesos. Oh yes. I have this Iranian friend who gambles big money, but he has just been imprisoned for smuggling people into the USA. I was going into the USA, through Mexico, once, but I changed my mind. I have this friend. He is a big man. In contraband. He and I go out and drink and take cocaine and have a great time. Once he got mad at a man and ran him over with his car, several times. An effing great Mercedes.'

Another time we were talking about 'low profile', how to avoid being known. I mentioned telephone numbers.

'I have ex-directory numbers, sixty of them,' he said.

'Why?'

'My business is telephone calls. Porno calls. That is what my woman manages. It brings in good money and I don't have to work at all. I am building an office block with a penthouse on top. In the Sanandresito South. I have closed down the factory and stored all the sewing machines.'

'I was in Madrid recently. I went to a nightclub, because I wanted to meet girls (*comerme una vieja*). I was having a great time and dancing like mad. I got hot and took off my leather jacket and hung it on the chair. When I left, I had had all my money stolen, six thousand dollars.'

After these soul barings, a sense of puritanical repulsion came over me. My God, I had never met a person so morally degraded. How could he call himself Catholic? How could he treat women so badly? He was a complete *machista*. Not a serial monogamist, as men are said to want to be, but a serious polygamist. But he was so like the *guerrilleros*, that he and they spoke the same language.

It was awful. 'He is probably suffering from withdrawal from hard drugs,' said Pati. 'That is why he is so difficult. And missing sex.'

'What was he doing in Madrid, with so much money? He must be a drug mule or mule organiser. How did he get the capital to set up a textile factory? It must be drugs.'

'Christ, get on the wrong side of him, and when we are out, he will come and kill us, or kidnap us again!'

How to live with him? How to humour him? How to avoid telling him anything? I could, as a foreigner, manage a relationship of a sort. That is why I had always slept between him and Grandpa, to defuse the proximity of two Colombians of different styles. Grandpa was correct and polite and well-spoken and a good family man. Now it was the relationship with Pati. Much more tricky. She was for a start a woman, of the same age as he.

'He already proposed sex,' she told me. "If we have to live together, why not have it away together. It will help," he said. I told him that he had got me wrong and no thanks.'

He became a problem for her. Either he was moody and walked alone, or he came and confided to her about his legal and matrimonial problems and she gave him good advice, or he got playful and schoolboyish. He hid behind a tree and jumped out on her, waving a stick. She screamed and cursed him. This was not a treatment that she was used to. He went on. The second time he did it, she said something that she should not have said.

'Do it your wife. She is used to it.'

'This is what I do to my wife,' he shouted, opening his fly and waggling his willy. 'I bet you would like it.'

Well, after that there was no way of mending the relationship. She complained about him to the *comandante*.

'Take me to another camp. Even if I am on my own.' She did not speak to me for several days. Another man. All men are swine.

Brutus sulked in his *caleta*, like Achilles in his tent. I could not speak to him either or take sides. He had the penknife that he had inherited from Grandpa. Edwin came to ask him to hand it over.

'But I need it to cut my nails.'

'Hand it over.'

'No, I need it. And I am making a chess set.'

Edwin backed off.

Were we frightened? Of dying? We must all have thought of it. Brutus was angry and aggressive with the guerrilla. He was also worried about how to raise money to pay them. He had talked of escaping already.

The Woman was in a terrible position, being a politician and running the risk of long-term captivity. She was tortured by thoughts of her children. Her body did not accept all foods and she was eating the wrong diet.

I had the philosophy of age, I discovered. My children were launched on life and I had retired anyway. I trusted my family and friends to do their best. If I died, so what? I had no difficulty dedicating my efforts to getting on with my captors, observing the forest, exercising. I had a woman companion. She was agreeable and good-looking. My male companion was difficult. Very difficult. We were each very different, but there were things we had in common or could do together. I had to make the best of it.

Would I live long enough?

CHAPTER 38

Life in the rainforest, monkeys and toucans

WHAT IS THE RAINFOREST? Not when you are sleeping in a tourist hotel but when you sleep in the forest and live every waking moment in the forest. Can you live off the forest? Is it full of fruits? No, it is not. You would starve quickly, and the Indians have their villages and plant yams, yuccas, tapiocas, plantains. They hunt for meat, and fish.

By the river, the first line of trees is *yarumos*, like tall weeds, with twelve-fingered leaves and pale bendy trunks. They are hollow inside, and full of nasty red ants. The wood is useless and fibrous; well, it is not really wood. The flowers are long thin fingers. This is what the monkeys like. All day, the monkeys swing through the *yarumos*, when they are in flower, that is to say, the spring, when we arrived. But this is not proper rainforest and these trees are weeds.

'Look, the *micos* are coming,' I would say, at first, to the guard. 'Which ones are these?'

I would get a lesson. There were five species of monkeys. The *ti-tis*, very small, sprang from even weak branches, in large gangs. They whistled or squeaked like little birds and would move quite close to the ground, in the bushes – leap, crash, squeak – moving fast and covering a large area of forest in a day. When the eagles were overhead, they would stop dead and go silent.

The *maiceros* or maize monkeys were not so common. They were acrobatic swingers, rather solitary, or one pair, and they had a nasty temper. Their black face was framed in a paler ruff.

The big ones were *marimbas*. They were in small groups or alone. They stood on the branches and walked along, with their arms and tails holding on branches above them. The females carried babies under their stomachs, clearly visible. They liked to squash into the forks of trees and curl up and rest. They were so like humans in so many ways, and not afraid at all. They would bark loudly, like dogs, if worried about something and the tribe would move on.

The invisible ones were the howler monkeys, the *araguatos*. These make the most dramatic noise of the Amazon rain forest. We joked about taping it and sending it as background to our messages to our families. 'Here we are in the forest, in the middle of the tigers ...' Not every morning, but often, after the first light, the *araguatos* would start up at the top of tall trees, not far away. 'Rrrrrroar, aaaarrrrr, roarrrrrr, grrrrrrrrr'. The forest shook. But they did not come close. And before night fell, again, 'Rrrrrrrrrrrr. Aaaaaaarghh. Grrrrrrrrr.' Magnificent. Invisible.

But our closest companions were the *choyos*. They loved the fingers of the *yarumos*. They hated us but did not fear us much. They came right over us and insulted us and tore off branches and threw them at us. Legend had it that if you stood still under them they would pee on you. There was always a leader, a big male, who came first and stayed last. We saw their babies, either on the backs of the mothers or freely springing around. They hung upside down by their tails, while they ate. They swung by their arms, from branch to branch.

The monkeys knew how to eat in the forest. They were predominantly vegetarian, living in the *cupola*, the tops of the tallest trees, because the flowers and fruits were up there. But I bet they would not turn down a baby bird or a lizard. Nor would I have, if fried and placed on my rice.

Would we have eaten a monkey? Long pause. I don't think so. Nearly all the guerrilla had eaten *mico*, or so they said. 'Yum, yum,' was the opinion. But I did not notice them doing so. On the whole, the feeling was that the forest was there to be shared with the monkeys. It was theirs. Let's get on together. It would be a bore if they got scared of us and disappeared. Maybe this feeling came from the Indians?

I asked Cat's Meat to let me go and see the *araguatos*. We could only hear them howl. What did they look like? But I should have had to walk further than the perimeter of our camp, accompanied, of course, but Cat's Meat was an inflexible man. He smiled and smiled, like Iago, but never did anything for us. A cold stern man, like Mister Winterbottom.

There were more birds than animals. Colombia is the best country in the world for variety of birds. Everyday one could hope to see a new bird, and often one did. There were the quiet *trogons*, the red-beaked nunbirds catching insects, the antbirds following the columns of ants, the toucans at the top of the trees first thing and last thing in the day, the omnipresent hummingbirds looking for flowers, of which there are not many in a rainforest, and the treecreepers, with their long curved bills.

At five-seventeen in the evening precisely, we awaited the call of the *panguana*, fat little dark ground bird, very difficult to see. It must have been a little *tinamou*. I never saw it, except once as a vanishing shape. We learned to imitate the four notes of its song, like the start of 'We're swinging along, singing a song, la da de da . . .'

'You can see it if you stand completely still in the bushes and wait,' advised Hanibal. 'It is good to eat.'

Once, a Capped Heron, stocky and white, flew in and stood under Pati's *caleta*. It must have been ill. Brutus came and threw sticks at it.

'Leave it alone,' I protested. 'Let it stay. It is friendly.' He drove it away. It was his way. A bad boy.

And there were the parrots, especially the *Loro Real*, the royal parrot, which is probably the Mealy Parrot. It makes a great screeching and you can talk to it and it answers. Flocks of little parakeets would come and go, chattering away.

Here were large red-crested woodpeckers, and smaller greenish ones. Everyday we could hear their tap-tap and look for them on the tree trunks.

The noisiest arrivals were the *guapuchonas* or *oropendolas*. They did not have a nest tree in sight, but would come in gangs and rush through the treetops, making a great noise. It was a similar noise to the *choyo* monkeys, and could be confused. They came close and we could see the black and yellow colours.

Brutus was the one who saw the *guatin* first. It is the size of a spaniel dog, and looks like a cross between a mouse and a rabbit, with little round ears and it sits on its fat bum. It lives in a hole and is an herbivore. It came from the forest towards our *caletas*, and at first was nervous. But if we stood quietly, it would graze and not run away. We put out spare rice and beans, which it ate. Actually it did not like the beans much, sensible beast. Then Brutus saw that there were three different ones of different sizes and colours. A family? He also saw that there was a bird which came and ate the rice, a ground bird, which he called a 'chicken', with a long beak. Putting the food near our *caletas* encouraged the mice, let alone anything else. So we started to put it in nearer the *chontos*, then we could silently creep along the path and watch the *guatins* munching.

The huge Amazon rainforest is the home to large land tortoises, as well as terrapins in the water. 'They get so big that you can sit on them and go for a ride,' said Hanibal. 'They live for two hundred years.'

The ones that lumbered into our camp were small and could be picked up. The theory is that you can tell their age by counting the plates that make up their shell. These ones were all thirty-six years old. Maybe the theory was not true? They had the most amazingly huge ticks (*garrapatas*) on their shells. The only place that the ticks could suck blood was right on their necks and the ones on the shell must have been in a queue to get to that soft place. We flicked off the ticks and they scurried around in the sand.

'Quick, kill them, 'cried Brutus. 'What if these *hijos de puta* get on us and bite us?' The normal *garrapatas* are tiny and red or black and climb up one's legs or drop off the trees and bury themselves in one's most private parts. Every morning and in the river baths we had to look and pick them off. We must have looked like monkeys.

When it rained, the path to the *chontos* got damp and the dips where the water puddled became muddy. Since I was an early bird, I could see the animal and bird tracks in the mud. I would call the *guerrilleros* over to have a look. After all they were the country boys.

'What is that?'

'A mouse.'

'A tiger.'

'A rabbit.'

'A *guatin*.'

'Well, make up your minds, at least.'

If it had been hoof prints it would have been a tapir (*danta*). There was a female tapir with a baby that crossed the river at night. The tapirs make distinct paths. Nobody likes to shoot them as their flesh does not taste good.

It is a fact that humans are more scared of snakes than any other beast – the ancient legacy of the Garden of Eden. And we were sleeping out in the open in the forest, where they hunted. The first snake that we saw was when Pati was going to the *chonto* and shot back saying, 'Snake, snake!' It was a coral snake, poisonous, or was it a false coral, harmless? They are black and orange-ringed and don't move fast. Colacho came and killed it. That experience stopped Pati going to the *chonto* in the dark.

The most dangerous is the *bothrops* family of swamp adders. They are long and wide and slow and wait for you to tread on them. They are not scared of anything. Their venom has toxins in it that attack your nerves and you die bleeding at the nose, mouth, eyes, ears and any other unmentionable place. I have seen an indian boy, after one had bitten him, in Amazonia. His leg was swelling and blackening and he had a tourniquet to stop the blood circulating with the poison. The usual one is called Four Noses (*Cuatro Narices*).

Then Brutus saw a long, thin, brown snake sliding into the tree that marked the turning point in our walking track.

'Snake, snake!' he shouted and grabbed a branch and flailed at it. It accelerated into the leaves. 'Lend me a machete. It is a Four Noses. *Hijo de puta*, I am going to kill it.'

He spent two hours slashing at the undergrowth and bashing at the snake when he saw it. It was spread on the path in a bad way and the guerrilla came to see it.

'It is a hunting snake – a *cazadora*,' pronounced Colacho. 'Harmless.'

'Better than harmless,' I said. 'Surely they eat rats and insects and birds. Well, not good that they eat birds, but otherwise they clear up the vermin, no?'

'Yes, they are not dangerous.'

'Poor old thing.'

'I am not going to sleep with *hijo de puta* snakes,' Brutus closed the subject. Before we had quarrelled, we had our moments of schoolboy fun. He would creep up to my *caleta* and roar like a tiger. I would swat him with my towel. I might, if the mood took me, creep to Pati's *caleta* and hiss like a snake, causing her to shoot up with a scream.

One day, when we were not on talking terms, but sitting on our beds, a frog jumped across the cleared space between the *caleta*s at great speed and stopped. Behind him came a snake in a S-shaped wriggling run. The frog stopped in fear and puffed himself out. The snake grabbed him in its mouth. I watched the event. Brutus grabbed a stick and belaboured the snake, which had to drop its prey.

'Let the poor bugger have his lunch. He won't attack us.'

'That's what you say. I bet it is poisonous.' And he killed it. Humans are the most dangerous animals in the jungle.

Hanibal came and looked at it. 'It is a *sapera*. A frog-eater. Harmless.'

But in fact animals did approach our camp without fear and the guerrilla say that that is well-known. The guerrilla is ecological and has rules prohibiting killing of animals and birds. And they chase off commercial fishermen from the rivers.

The exemption for this rule was the day that they decided to kill a monkey to have bait for fishing. Bad Boy waited until a group of *choyos* were in a big tree behind out *caleta*s and aimed with his AK-47 at one. He kept shooting until we saw that one of its arms was shattered. But it hung on to a branch with its tail. The group was upset and screaming. A baby came to the dying monkey and cried. So it was a female with a small baby. More bullets thudded into her. It was nauseating. Her grip relaxed and she fell to the earth far below. The group screamed and ran about and departed, not to be seen for a couple of weeks.

The odd thing was that a week later, a single *marimba* monkey, came to the same tree and put up a tremendous show of anger. He stood and shook branches and looked at us and screamed. He must have smelt the death. He was telling us that we had done something wrong and not what we normally would do and had broken the law of the jungle. We felt guilty. Well, I did.

It was lucky that I liked nature and the jungle. It helped me in captivity. I kept myself amused and could talk to the *guerrilleros* about the animals and birds. I made it a rule to see something new every day – a butterfly, a bird, some ants. It was a Robinson Crusoe existence and I must have looked like a shipwrecked mariner with my straggly beard and torn clothes and broken wellies. Would I ever see my family again? The day passed, but the night tormented me with dreams. The dreams were real and the day was unreal. Or was it the other way around? I was through the looking glass.

CHAPTER 39

A woman in captivity

THE WOMAN HAD BECOME A COMPANION. She was one of us. She was Pati. Had she been reclassified as an economic prisoner? Why could we talk to her? Or could we talk to her? Or was it all dangerous for us? When she arrived in that wet night in The Pines up in Sumapaz, she was a shape in a sleeping bag. I had learned that she was called Pati and was 39. The guerrilla pretended that she did not exist, so she was The Woman. She marched separately, until the long march, when she closed up with us two men. At the Green House, she had whispered that we were going to *abrir*, or be separated, for different destinations. Brutus thought that would be a good idea. It was not good for us to be tied in with a politician. But when Pedro left us, we were obviously a group of three. As we ate the fried chicken dinner in the night, we were together. The day in the plantation house by the river, in the sun, we relaxed and spoke. We got in the same canoe and were put in the same tent in the forest. So what was going on? At least each of us had not been able to complete our negotiations for release. She was a political hot potato. I was a rich foreigner. Brutus was a special case – and how! The others had gone home.

Over the days and weeks, she told her story.

'Meester, you must understand that I am not like you. I was born in a *pueblo*. Look at me. I look like a *campesina*, no? I have two sisters, no brothers. My father left us. He lives in Venezuela. Perhaps he has another wife, we don't know. But he has come to see us once or twice. I married when I was fifteen and I had my daughter when I was sixteen. That's how it is in the *pueblos*. My husband was at school with me. He went on studying and became a lawyer. Now he is a judge. When my daughter went to school, I decided to finish my education and at least get the *bachillerato*. Do you know, my daughter and I went to the same school, wearing the same uniform? I have a great photo of us. I fell out with my husband and we separated. We had married too early. I did not want to be a housewife and he did not help me to study. I went to the *Universidad Libre* in Bogotá and qualified as a lawyer. I liked to work in my town and had a clinic for women with problems. When I was still a student, my friends asked me to stand for elections to the town council, and I was elected. I worked with the *Liberales*. I helped people, and made a little money, not much. Then my husband and I got together again for a while and I had a baby boy. He is eleven years younger than my daughter and he was born with a skin cancer, and needs treatment all the time. He has a special diet, and if I am not there he will not go to school.'

She cried a few tears and sniffed, but stopped and pulled herself together. This was not a crying lady. She was tough.

'I am a lawyer. And I am a woman. I take a lot of cases of women, who are reclaiming their rights: separation, support from their men for the children, labour law rights cases. I help them for free, if they have no money. I also deal with land problems. I know that there is a land reform law on the statute books. The *Incora* exists to give title for land to small farmers but the process is very slow. You have to provide so many photocopies of documents, legalised by a public notary. How is a *campesino* living in a hut in the country going to do that? Where does he get the money for the copies, without even speaking of lawyer's fees? And if he does not get a clean title he cannot borrow from the bank, even if there is a government cheap loan scheme, the *Finagro*.'

'I was working for the coffee bank once, as their lawyer,' she recounted another day. 'They had to execute a mortgage on a farm, as the farmer had never paid the loan. We arranged to meet the secretary of the local law court on the road and draw up the execution document. I went with a driver and someone from the bank. The court secretary did not turn up. So I took my laptop and said that I could write the document and take it to the court later, so as not to waste the trip. The bank official was dictating and I was writing, when a jeep came down the road, full of armed men. "Oh ho," I thought. "What have we here?" One of them got out and asked, "Who is the lawyer here?" Luckily I was writing. "He did not come," the banker said. "So who is she?"

'"Just the secretary."

'"Oh. Stop writing and go away. We do not allow the banks to take away the land of the people. We are the guardians of popular justice. The land is for the people, and the FARC is the protector of the people. Go and tell the lawyer that if he comes back he will answer to us." We left and they went back into the hills. In fact they wander about as they will. I escaped by the hair of my teeth. I cannot go back there though. Or should I? I am their elected representative.

'There are politicians who can go around as they wish. They pay contributions to the guerrilla. I don't. That is why I am here. I fell into a trap. I was invited a dozen times to go and meet the guerrilla. I always said that I was too busy, but would listen to them whenever they wanted. You know that there is a woman who wanders through the government offices and collects money for the guerrilla. I have seen her. She has a Mitsubishi jeep. Nobody denounces her. One day, the phone rings and they say that it is time that we have a talk. I drive with my nephew up to the mountain and meet them. "Come and talk and stay the night and go back tomorrow," they say. But I never went home and here I am. I was tricked.

'The paramilitary have come into the area. No one has seen them. But I saw a copy of a letter warning another politician to stop paying the guerrilla or face the consequences. The civilian population, we are the cheese in the sandwich of a civil war. The president promised to protect us. How many mayors and town councillors have been murdered by the FARC? If you accept invitations from the Army to their fiestas at the barracks, does this mean you are a target? We are Colombians and support our president and our soldiers. Now I shall die here in the forest and never see my children. I know that my son will not go to school if I am not there. The other children laugh at him. He needs me: What will my mother have done with him? How will they pay the school fees for next year? If I live, do I go abroad? Be appointed to a consulate somewhere?'

'But you don't speak English,' I demurred.

'Or do I go on being a politician? Or resign and move to Bogotá and be a lawyer. Start from scratch. It will be difficult. I don't think the Governor will accept my resignation. He is a target himself.'

She was agonizing over the dangers of being a democratically-elected people's representative in one of Latin America's oldest and best-regarded democracies, faced with a Marxist insurgency, aiming to win power by the gun not the vote. It was not fair.

'Let us have a daily routine to use our minds and not go on thinking about these things,' I suggested.

'What?'

'OK. I can give you English classes. And we can have discussions about the country and economics and anything. You can teach me law. And we can do charades. And in the night, when we have gone to our *caletas* but it is too early to sleep, we are going to talk and sing. Well, I can't sing in tune, but you can. What else?'

If we walked in the morning and bathed after lunch, the classes could take place before supper, in the afternoon. I started, with a scheme. The class would have a little play, like a meal or a talk to her daughter, then a grammar and vocabulary session. 'Say after me, "The hat is in the hot hut. The cat is cut and must go to the cot. I go, you go, he goes. I went. I want to go but he went so I won't."' After a few sessions, the students lost enthusiasm. We followed up with charades. 'A book? Yes. How many words? Eight, etc.' This lasted a week. With no paper and pen and no books, it was difficult. But it was really mental sloth. We were getting stupid. We would discuss at the start, but then they did not want to go on.

'Do you believe in God?'

'No,' I said firmly.

'Then how do you explain all this?' one of them would say, usually Brutus, as Pati was not happy to talk about religion. 'The world – how it was created.'

'We have learned a lot about that. Matter, atoms, the big bang. People believe when they don't know better.'

'Lots of more intelligent people than you believe in God,' was a frequent counter-attack by Brutus.

'If you believe in God, why do you behave the way you do, eh?' I queried nastily.

'Don't you want to pray to God?' he would ask. 'Don't you think that He can help us survive and get out?'

This recourse to prayer as the solution made me despair, but that was all we had and it must give many of us prisoners at least some comfort.

'No,' I answered firmly.

'I don't want to talk any more about this,' announced Pati. She was offended.

Then she and Brutus started to talk about how awful the Asians who came to the country were.

'They are dirty and their food is insanitary.'

I felt angry. I thought of my good Chinese friends. China was full of intelligent people and progressing as an industrial power and would be richer than Colombia. I stayed in my *caleta* and thought that it was just ignorance.

So we were different. It is said that a man and a woman cannot be friends, as there is always sex intruding. Pati was attractive. We lived in the world of imprisonment. The sentries were always watching us.

'You like her?' insinuated Bad Boy, later on, with a leer.

Many of the men had proposed to her. Meanwhile, we bathed in our underwear together, and asked how the other felt every morning. We talked and sang songs. She needed comforting at times, or was I being patronising? None of us could stick it out all alone. I needed to talk. I improved my understanding of Colombian politics. For each of us our families were the most important and what we missed most and thought of. We were totally dependent on them for our survival. And we had so little idea of what they were suffering and what progress they might be making. That is what we talked about.

We were in danger and hardship together. The companionship grew and has survived.

CHAPTER 40

The girls of the FARC

THE SITUATION OF FEMALES IN THE GUERRILLA is an unpaid prostitution. Girls are to satisfy the carnal needs of the men. There is no marriage, and no children, no family, no home, no stability. Making an electrical contact in Spanish is *haciendo masa* and the chosen girl is the *masa* of the man. Is there love? In time of war death is round the corner. It is the film *Brief Encounter* without the middle-class morals, Lili Marlene under the lamp-post, by the barrack square. The *comandantes* may allow a pair to stay together but more often from one moment to another one of the pair is posted off to active duty (*orden publico*).

Why do girls go off to join the guerrilla? What do their mothers think? What does society think of this debasement of girls of fourteen and fifteen years? In the year 2002, I had been at a dinner for a prominent politician, who had been appointed to represent the government of President Pastrana in the 'peace talks' in the distension zone. He wanted to tell us the following tale. He was a good storyteller and he was alive to the undercurrents of a peace process that failed totally. On one visit to San Vicente del Caguan, he had noticed the arrival of a mother with two daughters who were young, still of school age and very pretty. The mother had handed over the girls to the guerrilla and left. Why? He asked where she came from and was told. He remained with that image in his mind, so the next time he went to the zone, he had some time free and asked to be taken to the *pueblo* from which she had come. He found her and asked her why she had handed over her daughters?

'Doctor, you have seen my daughters? There is no secondary school (*colegio*) in our *pueblo*. If they go to the town, to go to *colegio*, I have no family where they can stay. I cannot afford to pay rent for them. It they stay here in the *campo*, the only work is on the land. If they go to the city to work, they will probably end up as prostitutes. They are pretty, as you see, so it is better that they go with young people of their age, to the guerrilla, where they will get clothes and food and companionship. I will be more at ease about them.'

A mother's anxiety for her daughters. An innocent vision of the guerrilla as a kind of Boy Scout gang. Perhaps in the remote countryside, for people who have never been in a big city and don't read or write, their contacts with the guerrilla have been that of a gaggle of young people who speak their same country language, walking into their land, eating, washing clothes, chatting and walking off again. But in the guerrilla, the girls are prostituted (without pay) anyway, and die miserably.

I told Brutus this tale. Typically he grunted, 'Why did they not just go and be prostitutes? *Hijo de puta*, what's wrong with that? Better than being an *hija de puta guerrillera*.'

Carolina, the fat girl, had appeared on the first day of the long march, attached to our *comision* and had marched with us and stayed with us. She had fallen behind for the first days, overweight and carrying a full backpack. She spoke city Spanish, with no obscenities. When we were settled down in the forest, she would often be voluble in the night-time sentry turns, to Pati, but open to me too. She had been born, the younger of two sisters, in a village near Sibate, above Fusagasuga, the cradle of rebels. Her father had left and lived with another woman, but in the same village. Her mother would fight with his new woman. The new man, with whom her mother had taken up, started to make advances to her when she was small. Her elder sister had left for the guerrilla. She herself was sent at the age of ten to work with the family of an uncle in Villavicencio in the llanos. No, she was not paid. She stopped going to school, but she had learned to read and write already. She looked after the children and cooked and cleaned. After three years, she came back home, and her mother found her a job as a maid in Bogotá. She worked for a rich lady, whose family had three cars and lived in an apartment near the Parque 93. This lady sent her to be the maid of her mother, who was 100 years old, and lived alone, in the old traditional *barrio* of Teusaquillo, in a house. She had no time off, but, after a year, asked permission to go to a school on Saturdays. She was paid a very small wage but she lived in the best areas of Bogotá and spoke to and lived with educated people.

Her sister wanted to leave the guerrilla, and was told that she could, if she sent a sister as a substitute. Carolina agreed to do that to help her sister. She met an organiser in the village she was born in and went to see what the FARC was like. She liked the company of the young people and stayed. The youngsters whom she had joined with had gone elsewhere and she thought that a lot of them were dead. Now she was with this commission, and then she would go back to active service. She was sixteen.

She had shacked up with Jaime, after a lot of men had paid court to her, for she was young and big-breasted. She would sit at night and talk and listen.

'Señora, I feel funny. My breasts itch, I feel sick,' she confided to Pati. Well, that wasn't toothache, was it? In theory, these girls took injections against pregnancy. She was on the road to an abortion in the forest.

Why was she here in the guerrilla? It was not easy to ask her, nor to see why not. Was the story of her sister true? These people are habitual liars.

'I bet she was an urban *miliciana*', said Pati. 'When she looked after the old lady.' These urban militia of the guerrilla, who are they? People who are attracted into the guerrilla while students or maids or employees of banks or supermarkets in the cities. We understood that if they are single, they are told to go into the fighting forces of the FARC in the forest. If they are married or have to support families, they might be allowed to stay in the city. They man safe houses and logistics. They are told to get jobs in certain places, probably. And so on and so on.

There is a famous story about a victim from the La Maria church mass kidnap in Cali, who moved to Bogotá and went to a Carrefour hypermarket to shop. When she arrived at the checkout, she looked at the cashier and recognised one of her captors. This girl put her finger to her lips and shushed and made a throat-slitting gesture. There are similar stories about maids, and no one wants a large balance in a bank account.

Some nights Carolina would be down and say that she was wasting her life. 'Why don't you go home?' we would urge. 'You will just die here.'

'Yes. But they don't let us go.' True. Even family visits were difficult, and kept to short periods. If you overstay, they come to look for you. We had heard on the radio a story of two boys who had deserted and gone back to their village in Boyaca. A FARC killer went and shot them dead in the marketplace of the village. Hernan had been dragged to a *Consejo de Guerra* after arriving back late from leave and given a punishment.

Carolina was in a pickle. She could regret her decision to join up (but what could she do?) or she could get her act together, identify with the cause, and smarten up and stop talking to us. She wobbled between these two extremes. She was always the bedfellow of one or other of the men. But what else? Nothing. A sixteen-year-old going to hell.

Sometimes she was not well. 'I have this pain when I pee,' she complained. 'Like razor blades.'

'You had better take that seriously,' warned Pati. 'Kidney infections are dangerous. Are you taking medicine?'

'Yes. Antibiotics.'

'You can't just take antibiotics,' I said. 'You have to be analyzed, and take the right antibiotics for the full course of treatment.'

'There is an *enfermero* who comes. He looked at me.'

'Christ. Be careful.' Was she pregnant and with kidney infection too? I dug my finger into her tummy and she yelped with pain.

We did not see her. And two days later, walking to the river to bathe, there was a *caleta* with a canvas wall around it, from which a continuous screaming rose. Pain.

In the evening we heard the canoe arrive. We asked about her. They did not answer or they said that she had gone away.

CHAPTER 41

Adriano's tale

A DRIANO WAS MOODY. If he was given responsibility, he got bossy. 'You can walk as far as that tree,' he pointed in the direction of the guerrilla camp, 'and to the *chontos* and no further. Get my meaning? We don't want any trouble, do we?'

'He speaks like a prison guard,' said Pati. 'I bet he has been in prison.'

Bit by bit, he told his story, when he was in the mood. 'I was born in the north of the province of Valle del Cauca, near Cartago.'

This was the northern end of the greatest sugar-growing area of the world. There are only two places on the earth where sugar cane is harvested all year round and not in a harvest season, followed by a resting season. One is in the Hawaiian Islands; the other is in Colombia, in the valley of the Cauca river, which flows north from the Andes up to the Caribbean. It has rich, black, volcanic soil and good rainfall and a hot climate all year round. There are great sugar mills, called *ingenios*, surrounded by flat fields of green cane. Cutting the cane for transport to the mills gives employment to hundreds of thousands of families. Those farmers who don't want to grow cane can plant sorghum, maize, flowers, practically anything.

Adriano worked as a labourer on the land. He moved into a flower nursery and did well, he said. Why did he not stay? 'I got bored.' He said that he decided to travel east to the llanos. There was work there, he had heard. He had no money. He probably drank his wages and saved nothing. So he walked and hitchhiked up the central cordillera, over the pass and down into Tolima.

'I hate those Tolimense people. We asked them for food and water. They might give us some water, but they are mean. We were starving.'

He and his companions reached Bogotá, but kept on down to Villavicencio. There, men like him could sleep in a hostel. They would go to a restaurant on the road out into the llanos, where meat was barbecued *à la llanera*, stretched on sticks over a wood fire. After the customers had all gone, the restaurant would give them the scrapings off the plates. The bums who hung out here talked of work possibilities. They could always go and pick *coca* leaves – *raspar coca* – in the forest, for the drug barons. A woman appeared who was recruiting men to go for at least a year into the forest of the Vichada to clear the trees and plant *coca* bushes. He went and lasted nearly a year, but it was isolated and grinding work, although the money was good. He collected his money and walked back. After a while in Villavo, he headed back to the sugar lands, which he knew well.

What then happened? He said that he had an argument in a tavern in the town of Santa Rosa de Cabal, in the heart of the coffee country, and pulled a knife to defend himself. The other man died. He went to prison for a long sentence, but got remission for good conduct. Perhaps prison suited his restless, undisciplined character. With us he displayed excellent conjuring tricks. He could carve in wood, something that prisoners learn. He played chess very well, and cards. He did really good card tricks, which amazed us. He had learned to read. He came out. Why did he end up here in the FARC? For lack of job opportunities? Because he had made contacts in prison? Because he was not willing to go back to hard agricultural work for low wages?

When he stood in front of us, we knew that we were in the hands of a convicted murderer. A sobering thought. In so many cases, it is the outlaws who become the manpower of the guerrilla. Back to Robin Hood and his Merry Men, on the run from the law. Should they be in prison? Should they be brought back into society by amnesties, retraining schemes, new identities?

There are prize-winning economists who study real-life problems, and calculate costs for the alternatives. Why do sportsmen fix matches, does gang warfare increase when drugs are illegal, are the penalties for drink driving sufficient, does the choice of a school have a relation with educational results, and so on. An interesting one is, if you prohibit abortion, are there then more criminals? Or, is it cheaper to have more prisons, or have more criminals?

Is it cheaper to fight a war or spend the equivalent money on rehabilitating dropouts and convicted criminals? Or if you must do both, what is the optimum distribution? Would a war which did not arrive at a final solution rapidly be a better solution to social violence than a huge social welfare expenditure? Is there a choice? The money for the first is not available for the second, perhaps?

I felt like trying some thoughts on my companions. 'Is the history of the welfare state since Bismarck in Germany at the end of the nineteenth century and Britain since 1911 up to now really a process of shovelling enough money to the failures of society to stop them being violent to the educated classes? No more Dick Turpin, the highway robber, or Fagin, the pickpocket?'

'No. That's not the way it is,' responded Pati. 'I am a politician. OK? The guerrilla may not like it, but I am not corrupt and I spend my time fighting for budget funds to spend on projects for the people in my area. Before I was taken, I had just got money for drainage and water for some villages above our town. I have to keep schools open. I have to make the health system work. Welfare is about the elected government taking the responsibility for managing monies to help ordinary people, instead of the poverty and charity of the past. They say politicians are corrupt. But I am not. I don't have money.'

'Pati, you have to believe that the people know this and the guerrilla will find it out and they will let you go, because you are a good person. It will damage the image of the guerrilla if they hurt you.'

Her eyes filled with tears, 'No, Meester, I shall die here. My children will never see me again.'

How do we 'innocent civilians' get ground up in the millstones of violence? How could fellow Colombians treat an elected politician like Pati with such cruelty?

A month or so after we had arrived in the river camp, the *guerrilleros* went out in the canoe, the one without a motor that was kept in the camp, and came back with loads of *guadua* cane. They were building a structure. We asked them what it was.

'An *aula* – a classroom,' they said. It stood behind the *rancho*, between the river and the *caleta* of Cat's Meat, and consisted of a row of benches, no roof, a lectern. Now, would they have done this on their own initiative? Was it a classroom for some scholastic purpose, such as teaching reading and writing, or mathematics, or geography, or English language? Did the FARC use the spare time of the boys and girls to complete their education? When the *aula* was ready, the guerrilla would be summoned to take their seats, and we could hear, by being silent and standing behind the bushes, what they did. One of them, one who could read, would read out articles from the magazine *Resistencia* or elsewhere aloud and then a discussion would follow, or a *comunicado* written by the *Secretariado* of the FARC would have arrived. At times there was a visiting big boss, who talked and joked.

Adriano told us that, apart from the 'squad' or military unit, there had to be a 'cell' of the Clandestine Communist Party of Colombia. This has a secretary (*commissar*?), who cannot be the military *comandante*. The secretary leads a session of criticism, including criticizing the *comandante*. The Party thus maintains a democracy 'from the base'.

What did they talk about? They would not tell us, except that there were complaints about slackers, lack of medicine, turns of sentry duty, and they discussed the behaviour of us, the prisoners.

It was noticeable that, after these sessions, the *guerrilleros* perked up and talked less to us and had better morale and discipline. The discussions about the war and their battles with the Army and their political objectives gave them what they called their 'convictions', the reason for their outlaw and ascetic lives – and eventual deaths. Well, Marxism is a kind of religion.

Carlos was a different person. He was polite and had a good vocabulary. He was very keen on music and sang in the evenings, when he was in a good mood. We could hear the others joining in on a good night. He liked *boleros* and *rancheros*. He went so far as to make a toy guitar of chipboard and wires, to twang. Someone told him to keep his voice down and he smashed the guitar and threw it into the river. He had a temper.

'I used to work in Bogotá. I had a variety of jobs – in restaurants, or in offices. I was the curator of a private school. But I could not stick to the routine. The money was not that good. I left and had no work. I had to stick up a lady in the street and rob her of her money. I was not proud of that. But I was hungry.'

He did not explain by what chain of acquaintances or circumstances he had ended up here. Was he on the run from the police?

If the country were rich and could afford to pay an unemployment benefit, would he be sitting in a café in Bogotá, watching Millonarios play football and humming *boleros*? Poverty creates criminals. Rich countries buy off the potential criminals (not very successfully in the USA and Europe).

'Why do you stay here? Why do you treat us like this?'

'We have convictions.'

'And if you stay here and die in battle?'

'We all have to die, Meester. All right for you. You have a home to go to.'

'You should have stuck at your job and got married and settled down.'

'*Que sera, sera.*'

I came to the conclusion that the essence of communism is that it enables the believers to blame society for their own failures. It is the fault of the oligarchy and the imperialists that they are poor. They can forget about personal responsibility and hard work and study and good behaviour. Whatever they try to do, it is no use, because society oppresses them. So violence is justified as a moral right against an immoral world. Nothing personal, Meester, that is the way the world is!

CHAPTER 42

The Nicaraguan comes

THE FIRST SENIOR PERSON TO VISIT US was a senior *comandante*, with a smart uniform and a beret and a moustache. He suddenly appeared down the path to the riverside, with Edwin, looked around and then walked to each of the *caletas* to meet us. We were the new boys, in his area of command. The first *caleta* was that of Pati. 'Are you all right? *Todo bien?*' He sounded sympathetic.

Then it was my turn – the foreigner. He joked, 'Welcome to Amazonas. Do you keep a diary? 'My days in the forest'. I suppose you will write a book when you are out?'

'But we don't have paper or pen. Can you get us that?'

'Sure,' he smiled and moved on. 'Make a list of the things that you need,' he said over his shoulder. He did not give his name. He walked to Brutus's *caleta* and asked his name.

When he had gone, we huddled up and whispered. 'Keep quiet,' said Pati. 'You talk so loud. They will hear.'

'Did you hear? He said that we are in Amazonas. We must be in Caqueta. Does this river flow south to the Amazon? Or east?' I questioned.

'I think we are in Meta province,' said Pati. 'Near Mesetas. I have been there years ago. It is on the way to la Sierra de la Macarena.'

'But that would be Meta, and not Caqueta, which is Amazonas. He said that we are in Amazonas.'

'They always tell you lies,' growled Brutus.

'This is not real rainforest,' I opined. 'These trees are not the deep forest trees. We know where we came from, when we got into the canoe, and the river we came down. How long was the trip? Four or five hours? The river is not wide or deep enough. We are on the edge of the deep forest.'

'How do we get home from here?' wondered Pati. 'Maybe we go south and west and come out by Neiva.'

That would mean that we would not have to get through the army front line on the way to Villavicencio. We could get west to the Magdalena river and round to the Panamerican highway from Cali. A long way? Probably the way that Ingrid Betancourt came into her captivity.

When Carolina was on sentry duty, especially at night, Pati could speak to her, as a woman. She asked who this visitor was. He was called Dario, but we were not supposed to know and should not use that name to anyone else. He had been the 'husband' of Carolina's sister. He was a good chap.

'Who is his superior?' The awkward question. Finally it came out that the boss here was 'El Negro Antonio', which was worrying. A huge negro, he had been the *comandante* in the La Mesa/Viota valley, where the Bogotá river flows down to the Magdalena valley, near Bogotá. He had therefore been transferred to the forest. His were not pleasant hands in which to place one's life. 'He's OK,' the *guerrilleros* said. In fact we never saw him, although he came to the camp several times. He was a soldier's man, and did not show himself to the prisoners.

But we had no doubt who the top man was. It was Romaña. His face with his famous beret was well known in Colombia. He had reigned over the road to Villavicencio and the llanos and the Sumapaz mountains for ages, and was a kidnap specialist. Was he nearby? It sounded as if he was. He had probably come down to the forest ahead of our group.

We never saw Dario again. He was not in the kidnap business. When we arrived, our particulars had been written down in his notebook by Edwin, or in fact by Sandra, because Edwin was not hot at writing. Edwin had a radio, which Sandra operated according to a schedule, once in the morning and once at about four in the afternoon. We strained our ears to hear it. Code words were used extensively. Even if the range of transmission would have been short, surely the overflying aeroplanes could pick up the transmissions. What were our code names? It was much later that we found out. Pati was just *la vieja* (the old lady). And I was *cucurutu*. What? That is the name for the owl. Why? My glasses? No. It was because *el meester no dice mucho, pero escucha todo* (Meester does not say much, but hears everything).

After three weeks, in the first week of October, our first real visitor came to deal with us. We heard the motor of the canoe coming down river, from the direction that we had taken. A young man strolled into our *condominio*, with Cat's Meat a pace behind. He was in full black uniform, with beret, and carrying some newspapers. He was jaunty and smiling.

'How are you all?'

'*Bien*,' we chorused.

'Here are some papers for you to read,' he said, and dumped them on Pati's bed, the nearest one. He sat on her bed, and opened a notebook.

'Now, who are you?' Oh, God, start again. He really does not know who we are? The notes that Cat's Meat had taken – what had happened to them?

He spent some time with Pati, and came over to me.

'What's your name?' I told him. 'Are you gringo?'

'No, I am English.'

'Ah, Tony Blair.' So he followed world news. He was educated. He read the international press? He had access to the Internet? He lived in a town? The questions bubbled up in my mind. This was a different class of revolutionary.

'I read Blair's speech to his party conference. *Hijo de puta*, he said that England is a socialist country. *Hijo de puta*, friend of the *Yanquis*. He does not know anything of socialism. Bloody imperialist oppressor.'

'Well, he is from the Labour Party who developed the welfare state and believe in social policies.'

'Crap. He is our enemy. Now how much are you going to pay us?' Did he not know? Had the files been lost? Were we starting again? I am not going to negotiate. He has to do that with my family.

'How about a hundred dollars? I am not rich. I am a pensioner.'

'Ha. Aren't you the one who worked for J. P. Morgan Chase?'

Oh, hell, he knows the names of international companies and he knows something about me, after all.

'No, I am not.'

'Are you married?'

'Yes.'

'We can talk to your wife. What is the telephone number for me to ring?' So he really did not have the number? Oh hell.

'She is not Colombiana. She is not in Colombia. You have to ring the negotiator. Do you have his number? I don't.'

'No.'

'What happened to the numbers?'

'I don't know. We were given nothing.'

'Ring this home number.'

'Where is your wife from?'

'The Philippines'

'Ah, *Gloria Arroyo*. You have some guerrilla there too?'

'Well, Muslim extremists.' So he knew about world affairs? Did he know about the Abu Sayyaf kidnap of the Burnhams, and how they were shot and only the wife survived? We would have to be careful with him.

'So how much are you going to give us?'

'I am here. How can I tell? I don't have much. You will have to ask the negotiator what the family can raise. Sell the car and the dog and the wife.'

'Ha, ha, don't pull my leg. You are rich. They pay and you can go.'

He got up and went to see Brutus. This was a tricky character, no country bumpkin. He had a sort of coast/Caribbean accent and brown skin. When he went, we tried to find out who he was. He was an assistant, under El Negro Antonio and his name was Lucas. Later, we learned that he was not Colombian. 'Either Nicaraguan or Cuban', more evidence that the FARC has foreigners with them.

We all felt that we were starting again – a new negotiating team, with no handover. Telephone calls would start from scratch. It was six months lost. How much longer?

After three weeks, Lucas appeared again, jaunty and smart. He came to me and said that the telephone number that I had given did not reply. Had my family changed it? How could he get it going? I had to suggest the Embassy or my lawyer, using directory enquiries. I remembered the second number at home. The effect of imprisonment meant that it was getting increasingly difficult to remember things, names, numbers. We were getting stupid.

'Meester, there is very little publicity in your case. That is good for you. Nice and quiet.'

Right. What is 'very little'? I had never heard anything. No *guerrillero* had said anything about news of me. Had there been a message on the broadcasts that I had not heard? The family must be playing a low profile game. Did Lucas expect that a captured Englishman would cause a storm of news in the press? Did he give a damn? I thought it was better like this.

He handed me a shopping bag, saying that it was from my family. I opened it and took out a jar of marmite, two AA electric batteries, two books and a letter from my son John. The letter said that Nanette and the whole family and friends were thinking of me, that I might have access to a radio, that the marmite might help since the food was probably pretty tasteless, that I should be home soon and he hoped that I would not have time to finish the books. I was moved. The thought of affection and family breaks the ice that surrounds one in prison and isolation and danger.

What two books would one choose in this situation? Long ones, great writing, non-political. In English. They were *Middlemarch* by George Eliot, about 1830 in England, and *The Adventures of Augie March* by Saul Bellow, the Canadian/American Jewish Nobel prizewinner, about 1930 (or thereabouts). Different, but each rich and deep. I read each one four times. I spotted typographic errors and I arrived at the conclusion that the first was by a woman, about women, and the second was by a man, about women. Oh dear! Can't get away from women.

I was lucky. I could escape into the Warwickshire of the early industrial revolution or the Great Crash of Chicago every day. Brutus and Pati could not. They never got a package from home. Edwin came and went silently. He materialised like an alien out of Star Wars, and made you jump. He was invariably polite and answered questions, but he never asked questions or started a conversation. One day, he stood there and I went up and greeted him.

'Have you got a brother?' he unexpectedly asked.

'No,' I stated, after a rapid bit of thinking. Better deny.

'Only child, eh?' he asked. I did not answer and he said nothing else and never mentioned the subject again.

The reason for this question could have been one of a variety of possibilities, most of them very disquieting. Had they tracked a Hutchinson through immigration at the airport? Had they seen a man in my home? Did they want to insist on another negotiator? He had said 'a brother', not 'brothers'. I was perturbed. The thought of them in the city spying on my family was unpleasant. But I shall never know why he asked me this.

The first things we had to read were the gifts of the Nicaraguan – a copy of *El Tiempo* newspaper, a copy of the magazine *Semana* (The Week) and a special edition of the magazine *Cromos*. This was of special interest. It was entirely dedicated to the first volume of Gabriel García Márquez's autobiography, called *Vivir para contarla* (Live to tell the tale). Senor García has achieved mythical status as the winner of the Nobel Prize for Literature and the inventor of magical realism. It would be a feeble remark to say that he is an excellent journalist first of all, a writer of clear nice Spanish, and an inventive novelist of great originality. When he was young he was deeply leftist, a correspondent for Cuba's *Prensa Latina*, was denied a US visa, and is a friend of Fidel Castro. So what? Not the kind of person to be *persona grata* in today's USA, nor in all of Latin America. He had written a brilliant book of journalism about a real kidnapping, *Memories of a Kidnap*, but a friend of mine who had been kidnapped told me that he found it 'superficial'.

The autobiography was eagerly awaited. The *Cromos* magazine editor had invited lots of people to write short reminiscences, and who would turn down being published alongside the Nobel Prize winner? There were contributions from Václav Havel, the Czech, a Polish writer living in Mexico, García's Spanish publisher, Fidel Castro himself, the Venezuelan politician Teodoro Petkoff, and Felipe Gonzalez, the socialist ex-president of Spain. We read the issue over and over. When it fell into a puddle in the night, I dried it on the bushes, page by page. The article by Petkoff was fascinating, as he referred to the mass defection of lefties from communism after the Soviet invasion of Czechoslovakia, how the left in much of Latin America shifted to positions from which they could fight elections – away from violence, unlike the mad violence of the Montoneros in Argentina and Allende's excesses in Chile, which provoked the Army into seizing power.

Castro referred to the famous 9 April 1948, when he was in Bogotá, as a student political organiser. Did he see García Márquez smashing a typewriter? Ten years later, Castro was on his way to power in Cuba. How much time and money and support has he put into helping the guerrilla get power by force in Colombia? Was it true that he had changed his mind and told the FARC to stop using force to get power? He certainly is fêted by the new left of Latin America, Kirchner of Argentina, Lula of Brazil, Chavez of Venezuela, and the USA rages.

As I read the magazine again, Hanibal wandered up. He was on sentry duty. 'What are you reading, Meester?'

I showed him. He cannot read but he looked at the photographs. He did not comment on Castro, whose beard was much the same as our own beards by now. I flipped the page and a good photo of Gabriel García Márquez came up.

'I know him,' he said.

'Well, good, he IS Colombian and perhaps the most famous one. After Juan Pablo Montoya!' I said idly.

'You know something? That *cucho* gives us money.'

'Oh, go on. He is a world famous man. How do you know he would do that?'

'Aha. Here in the guerrilla, we know a lot of things that you don't. And I can tell you that he does.'

'I don't believe you.'

'Well, I heard it from a *comandante*. Lots of important people give us money. You would be surprised.'

'I can believe that. But I don't believe the other.'

'Up to you, but we know.'

He wandered off. We had a number of magazines to read, which we circulated. The *comandante* asked for them to circulate among the guerrilla, but few of them could read. Slowly they disintegrated. The *Tiempo* had an article by Rudolf Hommes, an economist who had been Minister of Finance and Rector of the University of the Andes. I knew that the argument between free traders and protectionists had boiled up. Should trade be freed up or should Colombians grow their own food? Hommes argued that if the USA gave subsidies to their farmers, we should import their food, because we should be importing their subsidies, which would keep food prices down. Since farmers are not many, while shoppers in supermarkets are many, Colombians overall would gain a better standard of living for less cost.

'Does that make sense to you?'I asked Pati. 'We sit here with *campesinos* who complain that they cannot sell the food they grow. They don't agree with importing food from the USA, do they?'

'They would blame the rich and the oligarchy for the decision. Nice if you live in a city, to hell with the *campesinos*.'

'Well, the Europeans can't say anything. Europe has a Common Agricultural Policy just to pay the farmers to grow high-priced food which could be imported from here or Argentina. That is why we are poor.'

'And why the *campesinos* grow *coca* and poppies.'

'Our government has not got the money to give to the poor. And the poor cannot find other things to do.'

There are people whom you can talk to and people whom you can't and I was a foreigner and from a different background. I, being a foreigner, had to be careful not to say anything that could be interpreted as a criticism of Colombia. Colombia is a lovely country and the people are full of talent. How will it change direction and get out of this mess? If the question was, 'What alternative crops can be grown to replace *coca* and poppies?' then the answer had been sought energetically by the government with its plan 'Plante', and by the US/Colombian 'Plan Colombia' and by the United Nations Development Programme. The peasants should grow organic coffee, rubber, oilseeds, timber, cashew nuts. But it did not seem to be working. On a micro basis, friends of mine were doing something, without any government prompting – cardamom (which I am growing myself), leather ferns, orchids, herbs for cooking, trout, tilapia fish for Miami supermarkets, but as a government policy, it was getting nowhere.

Was I going to resolve in my mind the unresolvable problem of rich and poor? If the difference between the top 10 per cent and the bottom 10 per cent in Colombia is higher than in the USA or Germany, does this mean that the rich in Colombia are anti-social and don't pay tax, or does it just show that in developing countries, as we were a century ago ourselves in Europe, some people with initiative arise from the ranks of the poor? The top 1 per cent in Colombia can show you that they pay wodges of tax, and the cost of utilities and land tax are all cheaper for the poor. High taxes on the top 1 per cent would scarcely make the poor less poor. The whole economy has to get into a modern gearing up, as Korea did after the war, or China is doing now, using technology and knowledge-based industries. But for so many leftist thinkers in Europe it is too simple. The rich are responsible for the poverty. The FARC are justified in robbing. I was being robbed by the oppressed poor. My fault? What rubbish. No amount of frustration with the economy can justify criminal acts. A thief is a thief, even if he is poor and stands at the gates of Mr Gates's mansion. Morality is not subject to political consideration. If tax is to be paid, it is paid by legislation, not by robbery. Then the deluded Europeans have to respect the president and government of Colombia and let them apply the law of the country to bring peace. After all, the rebels can ask for a peace deal whenever they want. Why don't they want to live as law-abiding citizens? Ah, ha! Extortion and armed robbery are their professions. Brutus saw through their political balderdash and told them what they were. He after all had risen from poverty to a comfortable life. Not my kind of life, but he was fine, thank you. Why did they not do what he had done?

However, we were going to pay and walk home, or rot in hell. I tried not to think of poverty or death. Make the best of each day and keep busy and watch birds. It was the nights and the dreams that I could not keep at bay.

CHAPTER 43

The red-nosed reindeer

THE NICARAGUAN HAD COME BACK three weeks after the first visit. He sat on my bed and said, 'We cannot get through on the telephone number that you gave us.' Oh God, two weeks lost. Why did the telephone not work? And they did not have the number of the priest, whom I knew nothing of. Obviously in the march and the transfer from *Frente* 55 to *Frente* 40, all the papers (it would be ridiculous to call them 'my file') had been lost but maybe a new start could be a good thing?

Edwin never said anything. He was a sphinx. Pati said that he was a dangerous committed communist. We wondered why he and his 'wife' were so thin. Could it be Aids? If unprotected sex was the norm, the FARC should be wiped out by Aids, like Africans.

One day, some six weeks after our arrival, Edwin came with a new man. He stood there like a dummy and did not introduce us or the new man. This was a short, jolly fellow, who said he was called Rodolfo. Was he the new *comandante*? This was not clear. He asked us who we were and went away. The *guerrilleros* did not want to say whether he had taken over. It was confusing. I decided that he should have a code name, when we were talking. He turned out to be a great snooper, so he became Rudolf the Red-Nosed Reindeer, or Reindeer for short. *El venado.* If the *guerrilleros* talked to us, they were nervous about him hearing. They were not allowed to. He would give them punishments.

As a foreigner, I could be made fun of by him. 'Speak in English, Meester,' he would beg. And laugh like a clot, when I spoke.

The Nicaraguan (it was the Reindeer that called him that) came a third time, in fact the last time we saw him. He had walked over to talk to Brutus, and had only nodded at me. He did not bring any newspapers this time. I did not know whether I was pleased or not that he did not speak to me. After a long talk to Brutus he walked back past my *caleta*, so I asked this Lucas, '*Y que*? Did you manage to ring?'

'Yes, we spoke. It is moving.'

'Bring us some more newspapers.'

'Oh, damn, I had the *Tiempo*, but I forgot to bring it.'

He always gave the impression that he had been in a town. That was exciting.

Pati did not let him go, but got up and followed him on to the path. She had a long chinwag in the distance. It was a bad time for her. Was she political or economic?

197

The Reindeer was the opposite of Edwin. He came all the time to see us. He was fascinated. He would come in the night on sentry duty and sit on the bench and cough, until he woke us. Pati would say hello to him then. He came first thing and found me up first. He greeted me for a month with the word 'Tasty (*sabroso*)', a word that I had used once when Jaime had cooked a good stew. The joke palled after a hundred times. But I could talk to him. Brutus had given up being polite to the guerrilla. He probably was holding back an impulse to attack them. They knew it. Pati had to keep her distance as a woman.

I could discuss the war with him. 'Why do Colombians fight each other? Would it not be better to have peace?'

'Of course we want peace.'

'Then why don't you stop killing and kidnapping and talk to the government?'

'We want peace.' A pause followed and he remembered to say, 'But with social justice (*justicia social*).'

These were not Colombian peasants wanting a better deal. These were Communist idealists, extremists, not ready to compromise, and that is how it goes. When the government decides to talk peace, the enemy remember that they are revolutionaries who must ask for a communist world, so peace never comes. At the moment we are in war.

'My parents have a pharmacy in Ibague,' mused the Reindeer. 'But I was brought up in the llanos, in Puerto Gaitan, when they had a shop there. I used to work in an agricultural products business. That took me around the countryside. When I joined the guerrilla, they made me kidnap my uncle first. I remember a kidnap of an old man who lived on his *finca*. He came with a driver, who stayed on guard in front of the house. I crept up on him and put a pistol to his head and said, "*Quieto, quietico, viejo.*" Then we got the old man. We found out that he had money in Mexico and Miami. He had to pay a lot.

'I was stopped by the police, who asked for my military service book (*libreta militar*) and I had to do my service. I asked the guerrilla and they said, 'Do it.' I went straight back to the guerrilla, but I have my papers in order and can go anywhere. I served in the contra-guerrilla unit,' he laughed.

'I have a wife who is Venezuelan. She and my son live in Venezuela. I have not seen them for three years,' he said once. So this was a little bit of proof that the FARC did go in and out of Venezuela with ease. That became very clear in 2005, when Granda, the FARC's travelling 'foreign minister', was found in Venezuela.

'I'll tell you a story to show you that the "paras" work hand-in-hand with the Army. I was in my jeep, with my radio on. We were fighting the paras and giving them a hard time. They were surprised at our strength and were cursing. I heard them calling up the Army on their radio. "Send the birds," they called. "These *hijos de puta* have us pinned down. Send the birds and hose them down." I was

driving on the road and I bumped into a car with Red Cross people in it, and
foreigners. I pulled out my gun and made them drive to where the fighting was.
I made them listen to the paras. Then I said that they had to radio their people
and tell them what they had heard.'

'You kidnapped the Red Cross?'

'Too right. They have to know that the Army and the paras work together.
Then I let them go.'

This was his favourite story and he repeated it many times. When he ran out
of stories, then we had to swap jokes. Here is one.

'There were three friends who went out for a drink – a man from Cali, a man from
Medellin, and a man from Pasto (they have the reputation for being thick). They had
no money so they broke into a shop and stole some bottles and walked along the
street drinking. "If the cops arrive," said the Medellin man (the *paisa*), "we climb
into a tree each and make a noise." The cops arrived and they each shot up a tree.
The cop shone his light at the trees. The *Caleno* said, "Cock a doodle doo." The *paisa*
said, "Quack, quack." The *Pastuso* thought a minute and said, "Moo moo!"'

The Reindeer and any other *guerrillero* fell about laughing. I forced a cackle. I
told the joke about the Englishman, the Frenchman, the nun and the pretty girl
in the train in France as it goes through the tunnels.

'And the Englishman thought, "I can't wait for the next tunnel to give that
Frog a good slap!"' I ended up.

A total silence followed. 'You see the English and the French . . . oh why
bother?' It's a good joke, but it wasn't the right audience.

Anyway, that was a reasonable moment to press for permission to go and find
some howler monkeys, *araguatos*. 'Come on, *comandante*. Be a sport. I want to see
them. I won't run away.'

Next day, Hanibal and Colacho arrived. 'Come on, Meester. We are going to
find the *araguatos*.'

My two Colombian companions were not allowed to come. They did not want
to, but it was mean of the Reindeer. We walked along the path into the forest,
not far.

'Look,' whispered Colacho. And there high up in a tall tree were three brown
monkeys with dark manes of hair round their necks. They sat watching us. Then
we saw others. Having seen us, they would not howl. Slowly they got up and
walked along the branches on all fours with their tails held up – a different style
of walking than the other monkeys who swing from their arms and tails.

Then the Reindeer decided to reduce the service that we got from the
recepcionistas. They had brought our coffee and food to each *caleta*, as we lay inside
– breakfast in bed. He made Hanibal build a table by the entrance to our area.

'The *recepcionista* will put the food on the table and you have to go and get it
yourselves.'

A petty restriction. I marked the hotel down from two stars to one.

I am always asked whether I was badly treated by my captors. The questioner is anxious to know whether a captive is hurt. Are the FARC brutal? I was certainly in discomfort when I was bundled up in the boot of the car and when I was chained to a tree. I was in danger when we were on the march and when the Army was near. I would have been shot dead if things had gone wrong. Like Ken Bigley in Iraq? Well, not quite. If things went well, they would let me go home. It was not so clear in his case.

I was free to move. When we marched, we marched together. We slept on the ground side-by-side with the guerrilla. We ate the same food.

When Adam delved and Eve span,
Who was then the gentleman?

The rhyme of the peasant rebels of Old Europe came to mind. The FARC can only step backwards into history. They cannot cope with the modern industrial world. As the agricultural workers and hand-loom weavers of Europe threw their *sabots* into the machines to keep their jobs, the FARC blow up oil pipelines and bridges and dream of agricultural protection and the end of foreign investment into Colombia. While we were with them, we were reduced to medieval peasants ourselves. No electricity, no pens, no paper, no newspapers, no chairs, no tables, no roads, no screws, no wire, no houses, not much at all. How could we believe that they could run an industrial economy? No wonder they get no votes.

So are they peasant rebels, are they political rebels, are they just criminals?

Douglas Hurd, a former Home Secretary in Britain, summed it up in his autobiography. 'I repudiated the liberal tendency to excuse crime because of the circumstances of the criminal . . . we should reject the idea that crime is the inevitable result of unemployment or poverty. Family and the community of friends and neighbours are the key to an individual's development.' We, the prisoners, thought a lot about justice and injustice. It was totally unjust that an honest politician, an uneducated businessman and a foreign pensioner should be treated as we were. Nothing justified their injustice to us as individuals.

CHAPTER 44

The family gets a call

THE CONTACTS BETWEEN THE PADRÉ and the FARC had gone cold since late August. The telephone did not ring. Nanette was in Bogotá. My children were at their jobs in England. Was I still in the hills above Bogotá? The *Gaula* had lost the trail.

Martha and Pedro, old friends, had invited Nanette to their house for dinner – roast pork, followed by apple pie. They looked at the orchids flowering profusely in the patio of the house, under the Bogotá drizzle. Orchids grow at all longitudes and latitudes and heights and temperatures and are one of the biggest families of plants in the world. In Bogotá, the stars are *masdevallia*, little rock-hugging lithophytes of all colours; *oncydium*; *cymbidium*, huge with great multi-flowering spikes; *odontoglossum*, and *miltonia*. In early 2005, Kew Gardens in London was planning a show of Colombian orchids and had a wonderful book to publish of 1,870 watercolours by a collector.

'Our son knows someone who negotiates kidnaps for foreign companies. He has a case in Ecuador, but we think he is here now. Would you like to see him?'

'Of course. Thank you.'

'I shall get in touch and make an appointment.'

So Nanette met him at the same house after dark, in the second week in October. She told him the story. He said, 'They want money. They will call. You have to have all the telephone lines that your husband knows open and attended.'

Nanette replied, 'We unplugged the main number, because I don't want a call from these bastards. The priest is the one who does the calling.'

'But if contact has been lost, the only number that your husband knows is that number. It is vital that it be active all the time.'

'All right. I'll do it.'

'Don't worry. I shall help you. If ever you want to call me.'

There was another meeting with this man and the Padré was present. After that, he kept calling, but the effect was of 'too many cooks' and the relationship did not flourish. No one likes to share information about cases and contacts. Leaks can de dangerous, very dangerous.

He was right. The telephone was plugged in again. It was 21 October when this telephone rang in the flat in Bogotá and Ana picked it up. A woman was calling.

'Is that Carmen?'

201

'There is no Carmen here.' And she put the telephone down.

'Who was that?' asked Nanette.

'A woman, but she was rude.'

The telephone rang again. Ana picked it up. It was a man.

'*Alo*,' he called. '*Es la casa del señor* Hutchinson?'

'*Si, señor.*'

'So you don't want to talk to us? We have lost contact.'

'*Que?*' asked Ana, alarmed and confused.

'This is the FARC *Ejercito Popular*. Is that the house of *el señor* Hutchinson?'

'*Si, señor.*'

'I am Libardo,' the voice said, with a rich negro timbre. 'Is the *señora* there?'

'No, she is away,' stuttered Ana, her nerves beginning to overcome here again.

'I shall ring you again,' Libardo said, and he rang off. The recording machine had not been switched on for some time. Later the *Gaula* traced the call to a fixed telephone in the Meta province, in the llanos.

The game was afoot again. Why the delay?

When Ana reported the call, she was told to give the caller the mobile number of the Padré. And Libardo did ring and she did give the number. Then he rang again.

'That mobile phone does not answer. We can't get in touch with him. Has the phone been turned off? Ring him up and tell him to switch it on. I shall ring at one o'clock.'

It was a Monday and everyone was at work and busy in Bogotá. October is a busy month. The Padré was at the church. Nanette rang the church number and spoke to the wonderful secretary. The Padré was out on a visit, but she found him. He rang Nanette.

'*Ola*, Nanette. *Como estas?*'

'Ay, Padré, you have your mobile switched off. These people have just rung. They want to start to negotiate again. They want to speak to you at one o'clock.'

She was very excited. It was a breakthrough after a long silence. Could the process to get me back be on track again?

Libardo did ring him. The FARC wanted to negotiate, but the price was the high one.

'I am the only one here,' said the Padré patiently. 'The family are not here. I have been given the authority to talk. That figure is impossible, as we have told you before. You have to think about it, because that amount is out of the question.'

'Think about it, Padré,' replied the *guerrillero*. 'If you don't pay, you will get him back in a rubbish bag.'

'Fine, do it. Kill him. We don't have the money.'

'Think about it, Padré. We are not joking. I shall ring back.' He rang off.

The committee met. 'This is a new man,' they said. 'We start again. He is asking for pesos, not dollars. Is that a good thing? Can we talk turkey and get to a real figure?'

They authorised a figure for the Padré to mention in the next call. When Nanette spoke to the Red Cross, the idea of sending more parcels to me surfaced. The first parcel had been given to the Padré to give directly to the FARC. Had it got there? Red Cross parcels was the stuff of Stalag Luft VIII and Colditz Castle in 1943. Nanette should have knitted me socks, as in truth that was what I really needed. Our socks had holes like Gruyere cheese (and smelt like Gorgonzola in our rubber boots) and there was no way of darning them. Instead she chose books and filled in the Red Cross form, with a message to me. The Red Cross has people on the ground. They would try to deliver the parcel. It never got to me.

Nanette had got her friend Mercy to record a broadcast on the kidnap programme back in May, at the start. At that time she did not have the confidence to talk on the radio herself. She felt she would choke up in the middle. One rings the radio station and if one gets through, not always easy, they record the message over the telephone. Mercy did it, in Spanish. Now Nanette felt that she should send more messages. She had the telephone number. She wrote a message in English and rang and got through. The operator at Caracol told her to be brief and clear. She did it, and she did it three times, without any idea of whether it would get to me. Her friend, Doña Teresa, an insomniac, heard them. But the third time, Caracol warned her that it could not be sent in English. So she did it in Spanish. I never heard them.

Now that the guerrilla was talking to the Padré, they wanted to see him. They asked him to bring them presents. Once it was binoculars. Once it was bread. 'We are hungry,' they said. And prepaid cards for mobile telephones. In a moment of delirium, they asked for a satellite telephone. The Padré bypassed that one. They wanted him to go and see them, with these gifts, which Nanette had to provide. He would travel to Villavicencio and then hire a car to go into the country, meet a *guerrillero* and then walk for an hour up into the mountain. When he arrived at the trysting place, he would find the *guerrilleros* laughing at him.

'How do you make me walk so far? I am pooped.'

'Ha, ha. You will get better at it,' they riposted.

The amount of the payment never dropped and it was getting nowhere. The last time the Padré went himself to see them was late in December. This time, he had to take a car far to the south. He was picked up by a jeep and driven to a river and put in a canoe. When he got out, he was at a camp, where a large black *comandante* saw him. He was in uniform and carrying his rifle. The Padré was in his soutane. It was hot in the heavy clerical robe. The church stood before the armed revolution. Marxism is atheist, is it not?

'I am here to negotiate for the Englishman.'

'Well, you pay the amount we want and not a cent less. Then you can have him.'

'He does not have that money. We have told you. We have made an offer.'

'You have the money. Pay up or you won't see him again. That's it, eh?'

A long way for a short tough talk and no result. There was no disposition to negotiate. The Padré went back upriver in the canoe, and stayed at a local church for the night.

CHAPTER 45

The tale of the December 2000 sally

'WHAT DID YOU DO ALL THE TIME, in the forest?' asked my friend Jack, across the table in his house in Pimlico, when I was back in London. He lit a cigar. It was a wonderful warm summer in England in 2003. I had been swimming in the Channel, the day before, as if it were the Mediterranean. I thought back to only a few months before.

Before I could speak, he chuckled, 'I hear that you were teaching them English. Typical.'

'It's all about establishing routines. Disciplines.'

As we passed the months by the river, I thought often of my Uncle Ernest, who had been captured at Dunkirk and had spent five years in German prisoner-of-war camps. I thought of my father who had fought the war in the jungles of Burma. I had been born during the Battle of Donbaik. My godfather had been killed by a mortar bomb in the jungle. Maybe there had not been a World War since 1945 and the European Union had been formed to reconcile old enemies and Russia had given up its Marxist aggression, but this was war in the jungle, and I had inherited the family responsibility. I also thought that having all my children successfully out in the world meant that my death would be unimportant.

Meanwhile routine and discipline. Up early, eat something at every meal, walk ten kilometres in the morning, lunch, a bath in the river in the afternoon and wash clothes, play chess or another game, have a lesson or discussion or charades, supper, talk and sing songs and cheer each other up. Sleep.

Sleep, ah sleep, perchance to dream. Long nights, rich dreams. 'My regular dream, Doctor Freud, was one where I was in a self-service restaurant. I picked up a tray and filled it with plates of meat and vegetables and came to the pudding section and loaded on a chocolate cake and cream and stood in front of the cashier. I put my hand into my pocket and found no money and looked at the cashier and said, "I have no money," and woke up, realising that I was in the forest.'

'I deduce,' replied Dr Freud, 'that you are a greedy devil, who likes to eat a lot.' Maybe. Withdrawal pains from eating. I asked the others what we missed most in our prison. Food, sex, friends, beds to sleep on, sex, food, alcohol.

'Marihuana,' muttered Brutus.

'Food,' I moaned. 'What is the first meal that you will have when you go out? *Foie gras*, Dover sole, profiteroles, a glass of port?'

'Eh? *Carne* (beef), pasta, *vino*, cheese, ice cream.'

'Oooooh!'

'No,' said Pati, 'it is affection that I need. My children.' She was right.

I had another repeated dream. I was with friends and talking to them. Then I would lean forward and say, 'I can hear you, but you can't hear me, because I am not here, I am there in the forest, and you can't see me, but I can see you, and I must go back, because I am not free to stay and am there, not here, but one day I shall be with you and not have to go back, but not yet . . .'

I would wake up in the silent forest night in a fright. Maybe a sentry would walk past and flash his flashlight in each *caleta* to see whether we were still there or had escaped or died. It was the looking glass world. I was back behind the looking glass, in Colombia, but on another planet from my friends, invisible.

We were in a bad situation, enough to give us nightmares, but into one's dreams and thoughts float images of much worse historical abuses and crimes. Much worse. We had been force-marched into imprisonment. We could pay our way out, or we could die. We could become bargaining pawns in a political negotiation. Into my night hours came the visions of Jews packed into trains going eastwards across Germany, and the prisoners of the Gulags in Soviet Russia, the victims of the Cultural Revolution in China – gross crimes committed by men obsessed with dividing societies into us and them and eliminating 'them'. These horrible images reminded me of how bad Man can be. And all that was recent, in my lifetime. I did not bet that my captors were necessarily better.

Once the sentry was Ramiro, the bigger of the Indians, silent like most Indians. This time he talked.

'At the end of 2001, the *Estado Mayor* (of the FARC) ordered a column to march out of the *zona* and make contact with the north of Santander and strengthen our presence there. We marched north, along the east bank of the Magdalena river. But the route had not been prepared and there were not enough food caches. We were seen. The Air Force came after us. The Army came. We had to split up. I went eight days with no food. I got back, but of the 120 *guerrilleros*, thirty were killed, sixty deserted or were captured and only thirty of us got back. The local people did not support us. The route had not been prepared for us. There were organisational cock-ups at a high level. I hope those people paid for it. It was a major failure. Perhaps we are not good when we advance into the open.'

I remembered the story. The television news had shown pictures of aircraft dropping leaflets on the guerrilla, urging desertion. I remembered the news saying that there were about two hundred *guerrilleros*.

Ramiro told us another day how he arrived in the FARC.

'My family had a farm in the mountains. I had a walk of eight hours to the school, but I went every week and stayed the nights with a relation. We had a bad teacher, not a local man, from somewhere around Cali, I guess. A big man.

He used to shout at us and beat us, if we did something wrong. One day he beat me a lot. I went home and got a pistol. I came back and shot him in the classroom. I guess I did a wrong thing. Then I ran away. I was big enough. I worked in the countryside a bit, then I got a job as an armed guard in the emerald fields. Then I worked for Rodriguez Gacha (the drug baron) as an escort. When he got killed, I came here.'

I thought that he was destined to die in battle before he had ever had a chance to marry, or finish his education, or settle down. It was not convictions that had landed him here. He was a killer from his teens. Perhaps he could desert and the government could get him on the straight path again. Dreams.

Patas Chitas was another Indian, but he was fifteen and infantile. He had a craze for cutting bamboo into lengths with a knot at the bottom and open at the top. He would pour water in and add gasoline. This bomb would be hidden and at the right moment he would toss a match in. A satisfactory BOOM would make everyone jump. He would giggle. I am sure it was not sensible, in case the Army was around or the Air Force listening. This childish practical joking was stopped.

It was replaced with a scheme to catch our *guatin*. Patas made a superb trap, a little cage, whose door was open, and a noose attached to a bent branch, attached by a liana to a lever by the door. We put spare food in the cage, but with no result. Then one day there was a tremendous squawking and we found a wood rail – Brutus's 'chicken' – dangling up a tree by its foot. No *guatin* but this lively long-beaked bird.

At nightfall, the bats started to fly into the *caletas*, under the roof and scraping the mosquito net. You could actually hear their radar pinging. I hoped that they were scooping huge mouthfuls of mosquitoes (called *zancudos* in Colombia). Was there malaria here? Were these anopheles, and female anopheles at that. Or just harmless ones?

'*Buenas noches, Conde,*' Pati greeted the first one, and if there was a second '*y Condesa*'. They were Count Dracula and his countess wife. *El Conde and La Condesa.* We were careful not to have exposed flesh touching the net. In South America, there are vampire bats that suck blood from the neck of cattle and carry rabies. It was easy to fantasise about waking to two little pinpricks in a finger and a short step to rushing around the camp, frothing at the mouth and barking. Like a Russian muzhik, after an encounter of the biting sort with a Siberian wolf. Fantasy surely, and our visitors were on our side, reducing the infinite number of mosquitoes. What do mosquitoes do, when there are no humans to bite? Probably just mooch about, eating organisms off the leaves. When we appear, they get sex-mad and have to deposit their saliva in our blood, to carry their parasites. I did not know. Anyway, stay away from the netting, just in case.

'I shall sing first,' I announced.

I have often walked on this street before
But the ground has never moved beneath my feet before.
All at once am I several storeys high
Knowing I'm on the street where you live . . .

. . . ending with a strangled tenor finale, making my tonsils wobble.

'Jesus Christ, put a sock in it, Mister,' growled the Brute. 'You sing like a pig being slaughtered and I can't *hijo de puta* sleep.'

'It is against the rules of the old folks home to sleep before half past six. You'll wake up at two in the morning. Sing with us. Tell a joke.'

'I don't sing and I don't know any jokes,' he replied and settled down. A loud fart echoed.

'Hey, the gas delivery van has come. Ding a ding,' trilled Pati, like the vans that travel the country road, changing one's propane gas cylinders, on which we cook in the country. 'Natural gas, clean and cheap.'

I burst into lyrical expression again, thanks to Lerner and Lowe, and G. B. Shaw. The forest was transmogrified into the Drury Lane Theatre.

People stop and stare, they don't bother me
For there's nowhere else on earth that I would rather be,
All at once am I several storeys high
Knowing I'm on the street where you liiiiiiiiiiive!

No wonder I had to go for a career in an office rather than the stage. Like Mrs Worthington's daughter – or son, I mean. Diplomatically, Pati took over and sang *El barco de oro* and laughed at the end: 'When will our golden ship come?'

Our ears were tuned to the slightest sound of a canoe motoring down the river. Pati and Brutus had sharper ears than mine for that. Less years, more ears. Usually the canoe brought food. Often it took or brought *guerrilleros*, but they would very seldom tell us that. Sometimes a big chief came to inspect. Then it was obvious, as they put on their uniforms in the morning, carried their weapons, and looked like soldiers. There would always be a meeting in the *aula*, with a pep talk. A deep voice could sometimes be heard. Was it El Negro Antonio? Usually it ended in much laughter and usually there was a dividend, shared with us – bread rolls, or biscuits, or ice lollies. The ice lollies were exciting as they had been in a refrigerator some time before, which meant electricity, and possibly a town. Was there a town nearby?

Once the visitor brought copies of the FARC's magazine, *Resistencia*. Where was it published? It had articles by *guerrilleros* from all over Colombia, one of which argued that in the time of the *zona de distension*, the FARC rebuilt roads and bridges and set up schools and clinics. The most interesting article was by El Mono Jojoy, which was a morale-building piece about the successes of the FARC. It contained a list of:

enemies murdered
soldiers killed
rifles recuperated
helicopters brought down
military targets bombed
judges killed
municipal councillors killed

It looked like the game book of a Scottish sporting estate. 'We shot an exceptionally fat judge today, Angus.'
'Jolly good. Put it in the book, there's a good chap.'

The shamelessness of potting the judges and councillors was amazing. They were the agents of democracy, in the case of the councillors, elected by the people. This was the sign of dogmatic marxism. The servants of the State are the puppets of the oligarchy. The people must realise that 'People's Justice' comes only from the guerrilla. So what it is about is a fight about who owns the word 'democracy'. Colombia is well known as the oldest continuous democracy in Latin America. The constitution was changed in 1991. Elections have been extended down to mayors and town councillors. It also recognised the rights of all religions, not just the Roman Catholic. But since the Marxist left did not have the votes to be successful in 'our' democracy, then it was not a democracy. They insist on a monopoly over the ownership of 'democracy', and if you can't see that, so much the worse for you. Resign or die.

Pati was an example of a Colombian caught in the crossfire – democratically elected and in danger of being eliminated by the 'people's justice' or 'popular democracy'. *Resistencia* magazine perceived that it needed to justify its presence in the *zona* by its good works. The state is in the business of spending tax money on the public good, so the left attacks the state not for what it does but for what it can discover of corruption and loss of public monies.

We had not seen Lucas again but one day a new man, Ivan, came into the *condominio*, accompanied by the Reindeer. He was unprepossessing, a rough-looking peasant with a moustache, and blind in one eye. He was the kind of man who would say, 'You behave yourselves and nothing will happen to you. If you behave badly, you will have to be tied up.'

So he said it. Then he sat with each of us and asked 'Now, who are you? What is your name? What is your address and telephone?' Oh God, once again, we start afresh with a new negotiator. Can it be true?

He had just been released from prison after a five-year sentence. He said that we were better off than rotting in a jail. We could not let that pass.

'In jail,' retorted Pati, 'you get better food, exercise, visits from the family, opportunity to study, telephone calls. I have never been allowed to speak to my family.'

'And we are innocent. Why are we being robbed of money?' I added.

'The FARC needs money to fight the revolution. The State has money; so should we.'

It was not worth getting heated. This looked like a rough customer. He simmered down and chatted. He left and Reindeer dawdled. Then the Reindeer came to me and said quietly, 'Write a letter to your family.'

'Get me paper and pen, then.'

He got them and I started to write. 'Date . . . I am well but hope to see you soon. This is enough. I hope you are all well. I received the books and letter and marmite. Thanks. It helps relieve the boredom . . .'

'Put in that they must pay xxxxxx and you will go home,' whispered Reindeer.

'Must I?' The figure was the large one and had not come down. As always, I had to believe that the family would not take the amount at its face value, as I was under duress. The negotiation was up to them. Did it matter what I wrote? It made the guerrilla happy.

'Yes, that is the order.'

I signed it. Should I have done a false signature? I forget to do what we had jokingly discussed, squash a mosquito with my sweaty thumb on the paper. The idea was that the committee would whip out a magnifying glass and deduce that I was held in a hot tropical forest, with mosquitoes of the species yyyy, not too far away. They could check my thumbprint. They could narrow my position down to a million square kilometres of the Amazon and send a helicopter to rescue me. Elementary, my dear Watson. But I forgot to do it. It was a silly joke.

These letters allowed as 'proof of existence' are tricky. One assumes that the family has asked for them, and the negotiation is under way. The guerrilla will not allow you to say much. In fact, they will only want you to say, 'Love to Granny, pay up, I am alive and get me home.' You have to say that you are fighting fit and happy to stay for another year in captivity, or that you would like to go home. Which? Should money be mentioned? I should avoid talking money. But if they insist? Does it matter? Will they upset the family or reassure them? One thing is sure; no one is prepared or trained in what is best. It is all improvisation. What keeps one going is that one's friends and family are capable and tough, and they will take professional advice. But you don't know.

Later we asked the *guerrilleros* when Ivan would come back, given that he appeared to have restarted the negotiations from scratch again. They said that he had 'gone on a long journey'. Had he walked up to Sumapaz? Was he going to get nearer to our families? The canoes came and went, but we never saw the awful Ivan again.

'Probably better,' I opined. 'He was a very nasty-looking type.'

CHAPTER 46

We run in the night

MODERN WARFARE, WHAT IS IT? The rich country has the technology and controls the air space. It spies from the air by aeroplanes and satellites, looking and listening. The rebels creep along under the trees (if the infrared heat detectors don't spot them) and they can put on civilian clothes and walk around the cities and countryside and give the police headaches.

I felt that we, as their prisoners, lived in an 'Alice Through the Looking Glass' world. We were never far from the real world of our families, roads and houses, but we were invisible to them. They did not know where we were. We knew where they were. We walked on hidden paths and no one saw us. We were in Colombia, but a secret Colombia. One day we would jump through the looking glass and become visible. Like Doctor Who?

'At any moment, a satellite could magnify their downlooking images and spot us,' I joked to Brutus. 'They can read the number plate on a car. Wave to the blokes in Washington.'

'You mean that they can see us? *Hijos de puta*, why don't they come and rescue us, eh?'

'I did not say that they **can** see us.'

'Yes you f---ing did.'

'No, they **could** see us. If they knew where to look. But they don't, do they?'

'You said that we could wave at them. You bloody did.'

'Well, if you want a photograph of your house in Bogotá, you can buy one from a satellite company.'

'I can?'

'I know you can. If you give them your address.'

'Great. When I get out, I shall do it. But why don't they rescue us, eh?'

'They don't know where to look, do they? That is why the FARC keeps mobile phone and radio silence.'

'They don't keep radio silence, you berk. They talk on the radio.'

'You're right. Perhaps the transmission distance is so short and the power so low that it can't be picked up? The fact is that I know bugger all about radio waves. But they do talk in code.'

'You are not as damn clever as you think.'

'I know that if an Al Qaeda leader talks on the mobile phone, the USA can lob a Harpoon missile in his earhole before you can say antidisestablishmentarianism.'

'Why don't they lob a missile up Tirofijo's bum if they are so clever.'
'Obviously they never find out where he is?'
'So why can any CNN reporter go and have a chat with Tirofijo?'
'Checkmate.'
'I'll tell you why. The government has a deal with Tirofijo. And they have agreed not to kill him. They split the drug money with him.'
'Not Uribe, surely?'
'Well, Pastrana did.'
'You're nuts. You are a conspiracy theory person.'
'Well, tell me why they haven't killed these bastards, with all the technology that you seem to know about.'
'I bet they don't have a deal, and that the technology does not help them find the old man. He is a cunning old peasant, sitting under a tree. And they can't find us either.'

Nevertheless, the Air Force overflew the forest. And the sentries came running up to see that we did not have shiny pans out in the open or white clothes hanging out to dry. We had to go under the roofs of the *caleta*s and keep still. All the guerrilla switched off their radio receivers. As if hearing pop music would betray their position in the forest. If we were bathing in the river, we had to rush in and finish the bath later.

There were the high-flying spy planes, looking and listening. There were the 'pigs' flying low and quiet, with their machine guns and bombs. If we were seen, we would get the jets, with no warning, knowing where we were on their GPS and trying to kill us. And worst of all would be the Black Hawk helicopters, which could hover over us and shoot their heavy machine guns at us from close distance, or drop troops.

The spy planes were flying over almost every day. They must have seen something. We surely were surrounded by military camps. And every few days, usually at evening time, the pigs would come and we would hear bombs in the distance and the rattle of machine guns from the air, and sometimes back from the ground up at the planes.

One night, we were listening to the sound of the planes, and the *comandante* decided not to sit and risk it. Colacho ran up and said, 'Let's go. Quick. Quick.'
'What do we take?'
'A *carpa* to sit on and if it rains. The mosquito net. You'll be coming back. Hurry!'

So it was put on trousers and shirt, find boots in the dark, get backpack and stuff some things in, but it was too slow, once they had taken the decision to run.
'Come on!' Colacho ripped the nets from the uprights, breaking the guy ropes. A bunch of *guerrillero*s came along and we got into line and headed into the dark jungle.

'No lights. Keep silence.'

It was difficult in the pitch dark. I hung on to the shirt-tail of the man in front. The leader whispered, 'Tree!' and stepped over a fallen tree. The word was passed back. 'Tree!' I put my foot forward to feel for the tree.

'Can't you go quicker?' urged Olmedo, he of the parrot.

'No I f---ing can't. I can't see anything.' Crash, I tripped over a fallen branch and fell on my bum. My hands were bleeding from the unseen thorns and grasses.

I went faster. We did not have to go too far from the camp. Maybe two kilometres. We stopped as the ground rose a little and sat down. It was much hotter in the denser forest, away from the river. Maybe the planes followed the river and looked for camps and paths and canoes by the river.

Booooooooooommmmmmmmmm! A solid explosion. And a second later my eardrums hurt as the blast got to us even through the trees.

'Christ, where was that?'

'The other side of the river.'

'Damn near?'

'Not really.'

'Well, I felt it.'

'We'll wait a few hours and see. Sit down.'

I put down my *carpa* on the ground, and sat, with the mosquito net over my head. There were millions of large noisy mosquitoes. Brutus had not brought his net and sat in front alone. Pati huddled under a *carpa* with two girls. It was a black night and the sounds of the bombs was more distant. We sweated. Something crawled up my leg. And another. Pati yelped, 'Ants!' Of course, we were tourists in the territory of the ants. We were sitting on them. We leaped up and brushed them off, with little success. Better to stand than sit. And we could not see them.

'Let's go back,' suggested Olmedo. Would we find our camp bombed? We turned around and set off. It started to rain very heavily. We had to slosh through a clay stream. I fell over a tree trunk again. At least we were not in a hurry. Then I recognised the tree by the *chontos*, and we came into our camp. It was intact. We were wet through. The guys for the mosquito net had been torn off by Colacho and I could not get mine hung up again.

'Good night,' said Olmedo. 'We have to look after you, you know.'

The next morning I found the precious magazines in the mud under my *caleta*, where they had fallen in the rush. Soaked. I dried them page by page on the bushes for a week.

The *caleta* was filled with large, red, biting ants. They had got into my backpack in the forest and been transported back by me. Ants owned the rainforest. They were the undisputed kings in their millions. I spent days watching them when they transferred their cities from one place to another. The little ants made a plan and set off in the morning to form a long tunnel, with soldier ants on each side. Then others would bring out the eggs and rush them along the tunnel. Bigger predatory ants would try to steal the eggs but the tunnel of male ants would fight them off. And by night the city was somewhere else. The old city would be occupied by termites for a short rental. Termites in the forest would usually have their main nests up in the trees, because they knew that the river would rise and flood the forest.

The most impressive ants were the *ronda* ants, or Army Ants. They would appear in millions from somewhere and march in long lines. They went straight over everything, including our *caletas* and us, if we did not move, but they were welcome and did not bite us. They cleaned up the camp and the bushes and scavenged the other insects and beetles. There was a frantic leaping of grasshoppers and scurrying of beetles when the *ronda* came, so the *ronda* were accompanied by little black ant birds, who watched these refugees and ate them.

The king of the air was the wasp, which feeds on spiders. There was a small yellow and black wasp which dug a hole in the sand and then went to find a spider. The spider was stung and carted off to the hole and put in it. The wasp laid an egg in the spider and sealed the hole by stomping sand on top with its back legs. The wasp larva would wake up in its lunch, eat it, dig its way out and fly off to be the new generation of wasps. Those were the small wasps. Then there were the huge wasps which zoomed around. They probably ate monkeys! The spiders were thus at risk. They spun their webs each morning, delicate and lovely structures, and caught their flies, but they had to keep their eyes open!

The most impressive insects were the praying mantis. They wobbled along the branches, stopped and waited. In Spanish they are called *tembladoras* – tremblers – and when they are in waiting, they do shake gently.

I have been a butterfly addict since I was a small boy excited in England by a peacock or a brimstone. To be in the Colombian rainforest, was like a fisherman catching a dozen fifty-pound salmon. It is the best butterfly area of the world. I could see species of *Nymphalidae* in such vivid colours, and the huge blue Morpho floating in the open paths, the transparent Pierella, of the *Satyridae* family, in the shade, the ones disguised as leaves, and the ones that defecated drops of liquid on the leaves and ate them up again, the fast-flying yellow *Pieridae*. We had blue and red nymphalids that came everyday to sit on our warm *caletas* and spread their wings, and by the river the blue striped *Baeotus*.

The proof of existence letter arrives

In the second week of November, that 'proof of existence' letter that I had been asked to write was delivered to the Padré and he gave it to the committee. One of them rang John in London to tell him. They saw it as a 'cold affair' and took it calmly. They talked to a man in one of the security companies and all felt that the amount of money that the Reindeer had made me put in was irrelevant, as it was written 'with a gun to my head'. But was this the time to make a higher offer, from our side? The committee was not ready. The security company man was critical of the lack of planning. It was difficult for the committee, who could not afford to pay for the expensive help of the best people, and the negotiator was the Padré, who had to feel his way forward. He had to be tough on the amount we could offer, which was miles below the ridiculous demand.

Was I all right? Did I know that there were negotiations under way? In early December, the committee thought that a question and answer proof of identity letter would tell me that someone who knew me was asking the right questions, so the family and friends were in contact. My morale would be boosted. Was I under pressure to talk money? I should see that the negotiations were in good hands. John had confidence in the Padré and spoke to him before his next journey into the mountains. He did not have to risk his life, but if he did, the family would be eternally grateful. The Padré was made of tough stuff and confirmed that he would carry on to the end. He knew that the real proof of life had to come right at the end. No paying and getting a corpse, and no jumping up the offer too soon. Easy goes it.

At least one letter had arrived. And the contact was working. After the break from July to October, this was a relief.

I knew nothing of any of this.

CHAPTER 47

The broadcasts

SINCE THE DEATH OF THE SHORT WAVE RADIO, we had no radio of our own, despite always putting it on the lists of things that we wanted, when the visiting *comandantes* said that we could ask. Pati was the one who most wanted to listen to the radio, as she was aware of the special broadcasts for the kidnap victims. Caracol Radio had a programme from midnight every Saturday night until 4 a.m. on Sunday morning organised by the excellent Erwin Hoyos, and most days, at 5.30 a.m. and midday, RCN radio and *La Radiodifusora* accepted messages from our families. Could we find out who had radios and would they lend them to us? Hanibal did not. Adriano did. Carolina did. Jaime did. They all had problems getting new batteries.

Could Pati's feminine charms, and her situation as a mother, soften their hearts? Sometimes. Sometimes I asked. 'They do things for you, Meester,' she said often. Our *caleta*s were not so far apart, now. Brutus was not interested. 'A load of f---ing rubbish,' he opined. 'The *hijo de puta* guerrilla only allows us to hear the broadcasts to soften us up and make us give them more money.'

But in fact the attitude of the *comandantes* was unpredictable. Pedro had been very mean. Edwin was unhelpful. The Reindeer was extremely difficult, and required his permission to be sought, by any *guerrillero* willing to lend us his set. It is impossible for the families to know whether their radio message ever gets heard by us. I never heard a message. Pati was luckier.

The other thing was that we could not get reception of AM broadcast by the networks who broadcast over the whole of the country, as opposed to local radio, unless we had an aerial. This is a wire that can be stretched between the trees. The only way to get this was to get hold of (scrounge) a wire pot cleaner – a *Bombril* – and unravel it. It worked well. You tie one end to a bit of branch off a tree and hurl it up into a tree.

When we had persuaded Jaime or Carolina to lend us their radio, they promised to bring it at midnight on Saturday or early in the morning on weekdays. We went to bed at dark and tried to wake before midnight and ask a sentry for the time. Either the owners of the radios forgot or we got one. It stayed with Pati. She could not turn up the volume much, so I had to strain my ears to hear anything in the dark night, with the croaking of the frogs in the river bank and the voices from the 'real world'. And anguishing as it was, it gave us a tremendous perspective of the kidnap problem.

There were warrant officers and officers of the armed forces, who had been captured in battle and had been up to six years in captivity. Most of the private soldiers had been released in the successful swap for *guerrilleros* in the Pastrana presidency. They had a spokesman, a lady called Marlene Orjuela, who collected messages. Their families could also talk directly to the presenters of the programmes. They seemed to be given preference, and rightly so. What they suffered was much worse than our situation. There were the ones captured in the taking of Mitu, the capital of Vaupes province, a tiny town of wooden huts on the Brazilian river frontier, where the local police station had no chance against an attack, and the ones captured in the storming of Las Delicias in Putumayo. The messages would come from their wives and mothers.

'For my darling Fredy. I went to the school to talk to the teacher and she said that Juancito is doing fine. I have to buy some more notebooks, which I shall do tomorrow with Mami. I am thinking of redecorating the sitting room, so that it looks good when you come back. Don't weaken (*no te desfallescas*), eat well, take exercise, pray to the Holy Virgin every day. Her blessed cape will cover you and keep you safe. We pray for you and wait for you to come back. Our *saludo*s to Major Mejia and the Lieutenant.'

And so on – the appeal to God and the Virgin that comes from the desperation of the women at home who suffer for their husbands and children.

'Please, *señores de la guerrilla*, if you have our grandparents, who disappeared on the road to La Calera, in July of 2001, ring this number. We have heard nothing. Please speak to us. We are poor, but we want to talk to you and get them home. *Abuelos*, if you can hear, we pray for you every day. We are well, but Alicia had to go to the hospital, as she had pains. The grandchildren are all well and doing well at school. We hope to hear from you. Tell the *comandante* to telephone us.'

The horror of a man and wife in their seventies, not heard of for two years, shook us to the core, and made us forget our own plight. We would get out. Are the *abuelos* alive?

'We are the parents of Patricia Medina. No one has contacted us. Please ring the number . . . We have heard nothing for over a year. Patricia, we are thinking of you every day. Your grandmother prays for you. We just wait for the day of your return. Don't despair. We love you.'

'I am the mother of David Mejia, a boy of eleven years, who disappeared on the road from Villavo to Las Acacias on May the . . . If any one of you, *señores de la guerrilla*, has seen him, please telephone me, his mother, on . . .'

Heartbreaking and horrible. Like Goya's drawings of 'The disasters of the war' that painted the horrors of the Fench invasion of Spain at the beginning of the nineteenth century, but still real and surviving in the twenty-first century.

And the valiant and battling Jaime Mahuad, a Colombian of arab origin, whose son Mahmud had been kidnapped with fellow ecologists on a mountain trip in the Cocuy mountains north of Bogotá, and never heard of. He spoke in Arabic to his son and berated the guerrilla. A brave and angry man.

Amid all the injustice and danger and fear of the two thousand or so economic victims of kidnap, there stood out the fate of the political hostages, perhaps twenty in number, plus the soldiers and police who were hostages in truth, held for exchange of prisoners, held as political objectives, representatives of the State, which is corrupt and speaks for the oligarchy and oppresses the poor. Was Pati herself one of them?

There was Eduardo Getchen, the politician from Neiva. There was *la señora* Polanco, taken with her two young sons. There were the thirteen assemblymen from Cali (or was it twelve? Had one died?). There was Alan Jara, the former governor of Meta province. There was Fernando Araujo, the former head of National Planning, from Cartagena, who used to go jogging in the mornings with a friend of mine. And there were, since two weeks before my kidnapping, the outrageous cases of the Governor of Antioquia province, Guillermo Gaviria, together with his peace counsellor, Gilberto Echeverry. Gilberto was a marvellous man, the former Minister of Defence, and before that head of Cable and Wireless's mobile telephone venture, Occel, among other jobs. He was honest, jovial and capable, and he had a wonderful wife and a clever daughter, Lina, whom I knew. They led a peace march in the countryside outside Medellin, and were stopped by armed men and taken away. We knew from the broadcasts that they were in Antioquia and with some captured soldiers. Gilberto was probably near to seventy years old.

And there was Ingrid Betancourt, Presidential candidate in the 2002 elections, though she was unlikely to win. She was in the senate, with the highest number of votes in the 2000 senate elections. Young, slim, valiant, against corruption, she was a powerful speaker in the congress before moving to the senate, a hope for the future. She had gone to the distension zone, after it had been ended, to speak to Tirofijo, and been taken, with Clara Rojas, her assistant, like a fly in a spider's web. Was she ingenuous? Was she looking for trouble? But her courage was not in doubt. She had a second husband, Juan Carlos Lecompte, and children by her first husband, a French diplomat. She was educated in Paris, in the Ecole de Sciences Politiques, a 'grande ecole'. She is intelligent. She studied with the former foreign minister of France, Dominique de Villepin. She had published a book in France, *Le Rage au Coeur* (Rage in my Heart), which was and is a best seller. She was runner up in the competition for the woman of the year 2002 in France.

On 25 October 2003, the *Figaro* newspaper published a page which ran as follows:

> We are all women of today. Involved and violent, mothers, wives, mistresses, we fight, we make investments of ourselves, we try to be just, we want to be beautiful,

to seduce, we want peace in the world, to find in order to heal. We want Liberty and Equality. However there is one woman that I should choose – INGRID BETANCOURT. French-Colombian, born in Bogotá, she went to the lycée français in Bogotá. During all her childhood, she heard the future of Colombia debated by her father, her mother, Gabriel García Márquez, Pablo Neruda, Botero ... She goes back to France (her father was an ambassador in Paris), studies in France, and gets a degree at the Sciences-Po. She marries in France and has two children. A horrified spectator of what is happening in Colombia, she goes back to Bogotá, with her children and stands for the parliamentary elections. She wants to fight the corruption of the politicians sold out to drug money. Then a terrible thing happened to her. Kidnapped by the Colombian rebels since February 2002, nobody has really heard anything of her (despite petitions). She is beautiful, young, moving, superb. TODAY'S WOMAN.'

For many in Colombia, she was irresponsible to go to the heartland of the guerrilla, as a presidential candidate, to talk to them. But the problem of the armed insurgency needs solving, needs understanding. Or as Brutus would say, 'Just bomb the s--t out of them and kill the *hijos de puta*.' She underestimated their cynical lack of consideration for human lives and hatred of the political class and the oligarchy. Did she think that she was not one of the political class? She certainly is not a communist. She probably is a genuine crusader against corruption.

Her mother used to send messages regularly. She is Yolanda Pulecio, who was a senator of the republic herself once and had access to President Uribe. She told of the progress of the negotiations to exchange FARC prisoners for kidnap victims – the meetings, the efforts of the French government to help. Ingrid's first husband was a career diplomat in the service of France. The FARC had let a video be made of Ingrid in May 2002 and it had been widely shown.

Was she near us? She had been captured in the mid-south of Colombia and would have entered the distension zone from there and not from the north as we had. She would be kept apart from us. Was Clara Rojas, her companion, still with her?

It was the Red-nosed Reindeer who let on. He said that he had been guarding her, before he came to us.

'She is in high spirits. She has a radio and in the morning puts on music and dances for exercise. *Es fuerte la vieja* – a tough bird.'

I remembered seeing her, thin and lively, with Clara, in the airport in Bogotá after her election victory for the Senate, on her way to Cartagena, in jeans and a white tee-shirt.

But he would not say any more. Had he left her for us, because she had been moved far away? Was she dead?

In November, a canoe came up river and three new *guerrilleros* appeared. They were a strange trio. One was a young black man whose face was recognisable.

'He looks just like er-hem-er, that member of the *Secretariado*, you know,' Pati said.

'Christ, don't say anything,' I said.

He was recuperating from severe wounding. He pulled up his shirt and showed us the huge scar. 'I was attacked by an infiltrated spy,' he confided. 'This man joined up and one day pulled out a knife and attacked me.' A mile or two of his intestines had been cut out and replaced by some hosepipe. He could not digest grains or pasta and had special food, not that we saw it.

'What happened to the spy?' asked Brutus.

'He was executed,' was the answer. We ended up calling this amusing, wild young man *El Principito*, the Little Prince. He was the aristocracy of the FARC, an untouchable. He had a minder, a nurse, a cook called Amelia, a capable strong girl, looking older than her age. She was careful about talking to us. It was impossible to guess what had brought her into the guerrilla. She had a pet peccary, a little wild pig, called 'Pipo'.

There was a third man with them, called *Perro* – Dog, who had a busted leg with a metal plate in it, and he limped. They came from down river. We guessed that their commission had been wound up and the kidnapped victims sent home. They said 'No, we were not guarding anyone. We were on a special mission.' We did not believe that.

Pipo the peccary followed Amelia everywhere and slept under her bed. He liked to be tickled under his chin and liked to rub his ears between your legs. But if you scratched him on the top of his head, he tried to bite you. I liked him but Brutus loathed him and threw sticks at him and shouted, 'Go away.' The pig took a hostile attitude to Brutus. What made the pig more *simpatico* was that he disliked the Reindeer. He would stand still, then rush at him, chomping his teeth and trying to bite the Reindeer's legs. What good taste this piggy had. He could sniff out the bad boys.

CHAPTER 48

The volley ball and Christmas

A T THE ENTRANCE TO OUR *condominio* Brutus had made a bench. That involved using a living tree as one end, and ramming a forked branch (*una horqueta*) into the ground as the other end. That itself meant that he had to beg for a machete, to trim the fork. When he asked brusquely for the machete, from Hanibal or another, the look they gave him spoke volumes, but he usually got it. He still had the penknife that he had got from Grandpa so he could lash some poles with lianas between the uprights. That left two front legs – forked sticks again – to be rammed into the ground, and the seat to be made of poles lashed with lianas. Brutus got down to the job with energy and it turned out well and was somewhere to sit, off the ground. A luxury. The guerrilla does not run to chairs and there is little space to sit on the edge of the beds, so this was somewhere to play chess and to eat.

Hanibal came to see.

'To sit on that will cost you,' joked the Brute. 'A million pesos in advance. A million dollars for *el Mister*, ha ha.'

Always the mention of money was uncomfortable, especially when Brutus seemed to be on the other side.

'Oh! Then we shall have to charge you for the food,' riposted Hanibal.

'If it was food, *hijo de puta*,' cursed Brutus. 'That pasta is full of *hijo de puta* weevils (*gorgojos*).'

'Shut up. They don't charge for the weevils. Good protein. Kentucky fried weevils, *que mas quiere?*'

Hanibal pushed off, having collected the machete. We two men sat on the bench, Pati in her *caleta*.

'Let's play chess? *Echemos un chiquito?*' said Brutus. 'It's the only thing that keeps me sane. Come on do me a favour. *Ale, pues*, Meester. I am going crazy'

If I played more than two games of chess a day with him, I felt myself going mad. I could spin out each game to about one and a quarter hours. I was under orders from Pati to let him win as much as possible. Fair enough. But when he won, he opened his huge mouth and roared and slapped his thighs and cried, '*Hijo de puta*, Mister, I shit on you. *Te cago encima*, not so clever as you think. This bruto, he eats your king. You think you are very clever, but *los colombianos*, we shit on you.' Etc, etc.

The guerrilla had to pass the time and combat boredom. So did we. I remembered the *tejo* court that we had made in the cold country and playing with

Grandpa. I made another on the path going to the *chontos*, with the target stones under a tree at each end. We could pick up flat stones when we went to bathe in the river but they did not last long as they were compacted sand rather than granite or quartz. Pati would sometimes play, but Brutus refused.

'I don't like it,' he growled. 'It's a stupid game.'

The *guerrilleros* liked it and challenged us. It was a pleasure to beat Colacho who was good. Patas Chitas was not so good, but Adriano was a champion. So they built a court at their camp, to the right of the *rancho*. They built it as a mini-*tejo*, with a wooden box and a tube sunk into the middle, and much smaller stones. It became a craze. When we went to bathe, they would invite us to play. I played Carolina and Yasmin and Colacho and Patas Chitas and the Reindeer, sometimes doing well.

But like all crazes, it lost its appeal and they gave up playing. The next craze was much better. They decided to make a volley-ball court. This was just behind our *caletas*, next to the *chontos* of the first week. There was a lot of merry chopping at the banana plants and clearing of the ground. A net was stitched together from old potato sacks, a football was sent down from the big camp and the court was inaugurated. The enthusiasts were Bad Boy, Reindeer, Jaime, Colacho, Yasmin and Edwin. Bad Boy was distinctly good at it. Patas Chitas was hopeless. Dog played well, with his broken leg, which occasionally seemed to bend backwards and almost snap. It was four-a-side as there were not enough of them, and it was a good idea to invite us. So they did. The prisoners made up to six-a-side. Pati was a good player but Brutus was useless. I had the broken wrist but used my hands joined together as a club. It was very enjoyable. Reindeer was a great clown and fell dramatically whenever he could.

It made one sweat furiously. We rotated the players. If I came off court, I was asked to referee. This caused great hilarity.

'An international referee,' they cried.

'And you had better obey the rules or you'll see,' I shouted. 'No Colombian tricks. Or I'll send you off.'

'Eh Meester, tough man, eh?'

The main argument was about applying the rule of rotation of servers. One player could not do all the serves. But this did not suit them, so I called fouls and they laughed. And when Bad Boy did one of his smashes and touched the net, I had to give the change-over to the other side. He swore and protested. Obeying the rules was not their way of playing. Jaime got upset when his plays were called out, and retired in a fit of pique. It became difficult to get teams together. They lost interest or became offended.

One day it was over. What had happened?

'Hanibal got angry and cut the ball in half with his machete,' reported Bad Boy.

'Get another ball. It's such fun,' I appealed.

'Ah, I don't know.'

It was over. That is how they are. What to do? We had the walking, which Pati and I did every morning. She started to run instead of walk. I had not run for years. Too old, too overweight, too lazy. She made me and I started and, by God, I could do it and increased the number of circuits that I did running. There was not enough room on the track and Brutus had to stay out of the way of Pati. She did gymnastics after the run, while I lay on my back in the *caleta*, recovering. What I got good at, with the weight loss and the exercise, was knee bends. I could crouch and stand up easily. But I could not do press-ups. My left arm had healed all crooked and useless.

We also had swimming in the river. At the start, I could splash Brutus and get him to play childish water games. When relations broke down, he washed silently. The guerrilla had rigged up a swing in the big rubber tree by the river bank and would swing out on it and land in the river. I could not do that because of my wrist but if it had rained up river, the water came down full of clay from landslides higher, such as we had seen on the long march. Indeed it was the same river, was it not? They would not tell us. Then we came out of the water dirtier than when we went in. Less sweaty, more clayey. If the canoe was heard, we had to jump out and go to our camp quickly. We could not see the visitors. They did not want to know about us either.

The walk to and from the river took us through the *guerrilleros'* own *caleta*s, where they were sleeping, sewing, listening to the radio and, in the case of old Polo, mending radios or, in the case of Carlos, singing. Then they started making straps, by weaving polyester thread. They had a contract from the military command and individual quotas. Did we want to do this? It was voluntary and in principle not a good idea for us to work for the FARC, but Pati decided to learn to take her mind off her anguish. She made several straps for backpacks. I suggested that she adopt the strategy of Penelope, the wife of Odysseus, and undo them at night, to spin it out for longer without losing the activity.

So we saw the *guerrilleros* weaving away. The radio would be on somewhere and often tuned to the FARC FM programme. Once I heard a voice saying a prayer to Ché Guevara, as if he were in heaven. 'We look up to you and admire you even in death, as your great life is a guide to our own fight for democracy . . .' etc etc. 'Oh, Ché, help us in our lives and guide our actions according to your beliefs and principles.' Otherwise the radio would insult the government and the oligarchy and *Yanqui* imperialism. It would invite people to join up, while saying that girls had to be fifteen years old.

'Why don't they have a cooking programme?' I suggested to Pati. 'They ruin all the ingredients.'

'I shall suggest to Edwin that they turn the carrots into juice. When they chop them up small and boil them in the soup, they lose all their vitamins.'

'Go on. Offer to write a guerrilla cookery book. Why don't they have eggs?'

What were we going to do for Christmas?

In the forest the prospect of mince pies was less than zero. We pestered Reindeer. 'What are we going to do for Christmas?' At least he could let the lads go and shoot a *pavo* (turkey) or, better a *paujuil*. He could make a clay oven to roast it. We would help. On and on we went, pestering him, miserable devil. The *guerrilleros* looked uncomfortable when we told them.

So Christmas night fell. Nothing. This had to be the stupidest Christmas ever. The FARC were unable to cope with the idea of a religious holiday, a family holiday and were more than ever like the 'lost children' without Wendy. Marx said that religion is the opium of the people. The FARC had to be the people with the religion of the opium and of the *coca*.

And to make it worse, the turkeys were roosting every night in the trees over our heads. Ha, bloody, ha.

CHAPTER 49

Waiting in the forest

THE MORNING STARTS BEFORE LIGHT. The bed is hard and my hips ache. I have to sleep with my broken wrist on top of my body. All the time in the forest, trees or branches fall crashing to the ground, with a big noise. It is the dying and renovation of the greatest rainforest of the world. I need to let out air from my stomach. Who is on sentry duty? Did the aeroplanes come over? Are we going to move?

I get up and walk to the *chonto* in the dark. When you eat so little, you suffer from a kind of reverse constipation. If by constipation you mean that you have something inside you and it won't come out for days, then this must be 'prostipation'. You go every day and nothing is there to come out. It takes days to accumulate waste food inside one. The carbohydrates have burned themselves off by exercise. There is nothing else. I come back feeling better, and stand or walk. The sentry may come by and say hello. Brutus was the one who said first that there must be other prisoners the other side of the camp. I pooh-poohed the idea. How could he tell? We went through the camp to the river and never heard or saw anyone. But he was right. The guerrilla sometimes called Pati 'Miriam' by mistake. Why did the sentries walk through our *condominio* and go off round the back, leaving us alone? The canoe came often and never took us home. Why was it difficult to get them to lend us a radio?

Then Pati put two and two together. In the broadcasts to the kidnapped, messages were sent to a Miriam by her daughters. And then we heard messages for Laureano. Was that my friend? Had he not gone home? Where was he held? Then we heard that Laureano's wife sent regards to him and to his companion Miriam. So we tied the loose ends together. We had neighbours.

One day we were in the river and we saw a short lady, with long black hair, fetching water from the river further downstream. Then we saw a stocky man, with receding hair. That was not Laureano, so we had to whisper in the night to the sentries. 'How many are there? Has anyone gone home?' The most believable of the boys said that we had had up to sixteen in the camp and eight had been released. We could not verify this at all.

Pati recounted one morning that in the night she had been told that on the other side of the camp there was an old man with white hair, who said that he knew 'el Meester'. My God. Was this the luckless Papa Noel? Had he not gone home? Poor old chap.

We could sometimes hear radio news. However little, we had raw material to fill our imagination. Passenger aircraft would fly over to the south-west.

'That is James LeMoyne and his United Nations team coming to negotiate the exchange of prisoners,' I used to tell Pati. 'You will be home for Christmas. And we shall rot here.'

'Not with this president,' she shook her head.

'You will be home soon,' said Hanibal.

'You said that I should be home for Christmas,' retorted Pati. 'You are a liar.'

'Well, by the end of the month.'

'Don't you hear the broadcasts? The families have lost hope. I tell you with this president, I shall die here. He does not care for us and our lives.'

'Why would you be here with us, if you were not going to go for money, eh?'

'Maybe. But I don't think so.'

'Why not? Admit it, it is logical. You are not political after all.'

'But I don't have money. It would be better that I was political. I shall write a letter to Romaña, asking him to tell me which category I am.'

'My God, I should not do that, if I were you.'

'At least I might know. Brutus hates me because he thinks he is being kept until I go first. He told me. If I am political, they can take me away to another camp and let you go. I should prefer to be alone.'

She was on the verge of tears. The thought of being on her own for years more must have been terrifying.

'I might be put with other political prisoners. Or soldiers?' she remarked. 'I am sorry if I am a nuisance to you.'

Was the United Nations able to be a peace negotiator in Colombia? It had been active in the time of the *Zona de Distension*. When Alvaro Uribe launched his campaign, he had said that the UN would be the intermediary. But the FARC had become difficult. They objected to the level of envoys that the UN sent to see the scene. Tirofijo is the kind of person who wants to be invited to see Kofi Annan, and nobody junior to him. Did the FARC want to negotiate at all? Their demands were dramatic. Their politics was extreme. They were 'safe' in the forest or what they called 'Las Montañas de Colombia'.

So there we spent our days, Pati tortured with not knowing whether she was political and detained indefinitely, like Ingrid Betancourt, because of the stubbornness of Alvaro Uribe and his legal advisers over the humanitarian exchange of prisoners, and Brutus and I wondering if the money would ever be raised to pay the ransoms.

From what we heard on the radio, Colombians were divided about swapping the FARC prisoners for us. A tough speech was made by a senator, German Vargas Lleras, whose grandfather had been president of Colombia. No swap. Fight the FARC. In December he opened his mail one morning and a parcel bomb exploded, damaging his right hand and arm. He was rushed off to hospital and patched up. That's what you get for talking tough. We as the merchandise in this trade had mixed emotions. There was no doubt that the FARC wanted the swap and that the government preferred to keep us rotting in the forest than let out a few FARC condemned rebels.

'He was a hothead. Why did he open his mouth?' mused Pati. 'They don't have any conception of what we are going through.'

We got up and looked at the little space where we were confined. Our only outlet was the bathing in the river, which was a great plus. We kept cleaner than in the cold mountain and we could swim, a form of exercise – up river, against the current, crawl and backstroke, hard exercise, good feeling. Mind you, we only had half an hour. A sentry came to fetch us and stood watching us, along with any other *guerrilleros* who wanted to be there looking. Brutus and I wore underpants, after having been warned not to go naked, as we had done on the march. Poor Pati had to bathe in her underwear, in front of all the men, including us. This must have been humiliating and shaming. When we arrived, perhaps the camp had not been there for long. The water was less disturbed, which meant that the sting rays, which abound in these tropical waters, were close to where we stepped into the river. The first week, I saw a fishing line attached to the big rubber tree, at the river edge, where the canoes unloaded. It was jerking, so I told Olmedo. He pulled in a ray, twitching its sting. If you are stung, it hurts like hell. The antidote is to find a woman with the curse, and sit her on the place where you were stung.

'I hope I am stung on the nose,' roared Brutus.

'I am not swimming here,' announced Pati. It took her some days to get up the courage to enter the water.

There were little baby fish that tugged at the hairs on one's leg. The guerrilla caught them with a hook baited with dough, as I did at school, fishing for roach in the Marlborough House pond. These were the bait for the big fish, out in the deep water. There were catfish (*bagres*) that took two strong men to pull out, *cachamas*, round fish like carp, which were good eating, *sardinas*, and *capaz*, which were the best.

In the oxbow lakes and *caños* and still water, there are always piranhas, called *piranha* in the Amazon area, a Brazilian word, or *caribe* in the north and middle of Colombia. They are not as voracious as Hollywood would like to have us believe and you can perfectly well swim in waters with piranha and fish them out at the same time. So once or twice we ate fried piranha, but not often because it is a poor fish with little flesh and plenty of bones.

So every morning, the *saludo* was, 'How did the fishing go?' Of course days passed without any catch, as is the way, but it was good to have a bit of fish on top of the rice, from time to time.

Once there was a sound of a burst of AK-47 fire from down river. Colacho told us that they had taken the canoe and paddled into a canal (a *caño*) leading into an oxbow lake. When the river is high, it floods. When it goes down, as it was now, in the dry season, there were narrow *caños* into the flooded lakes, at the sides of the main river. Then even they dried up and you had to walk. They had paddled into a lake, where typically there were high reed beds before the lake surface opened out.

'Watch out,' shouted Hernan. The folklore is that you can tell when an anaconda is after you. These huge twenty metre long constrictor snakes lie waiting in the reeds. They emit a sweet fetid breath which drugs the prey and stops it running away. Hernan fired a burst in the direction of the snake. It rushed under the canoe. It could absorb a burst of ammunition without slowing down. The canoe was turned around, and Colacho fell into the water. He was hoicked in and they paddled like fury back to the river and home. You don't argue with an anaconda when you are on the water. That is their element.

'Do anacondas (*guios*) come across the land? Would they come into this camp?' asked Pati nervously. The thought of being strangled in the night and swallowed was not pleasant.

'No, they stay by the water. Don't worry. It is only the crocodiles that come along and get you.'

Pati looked pale.

'Just joking.'

'It is all very well for you men. You can pee over the sides of your *caleta*s in the night. We girls have to get up and walk into the bushes.'

When we first arrived in the rainforest, sleeping in the forest was scary. Rustling noises in the bushes when you are only protected by a mosquito net are unsettling. We were careful not to touch the net with any part of our body, thinking of the vampire bats that suck your blood at night. But my nemesis was a small grey animal – a mouse. I used to keep food in my *caleta*, old *cancharinas* or bits of *panela*. I would hear a scrabbling noise on the roof or on the bed itself. The legs of the bed were covered in athlete's foot powder to stop the termites (*gorgojos*) climbing up. It is disgusting to find a million termites under one's sleeping bag. The mouse probably did a Tarzan swing to the bed. In Spanish folklore, the tooth fairy is called Perez the Mouse (*el raton Perez*). My little Perez found out that he could eat holes in the mosquito net and get in to steal my food. I would wake up to the feeling that I was not alone in my bed.

'Darling,' I cooed, and reached for the voluptuous . . .

Hell, it was no bride, but Perez. A fight ensued, involving flying mouse, ripping net, cursing man. At times the sentry would come and flash his light and help. I started to hang the food in a shopping bag from the cross pole. The mouse gave up.

Every night, we had the space between bedtime and sleep, which we had to fill. Brutus was no companion and did not want to talk, so my relationship with Pati grew. There is not so much that you can say when there are sentries spying on you, but we could talk of family, our children, and some politics. But best of all was singing, not talk.

So she sang Colombian *boleros* and I fell asleep first – well, Brutus was first – and I was up before dawn to go to the *chontos*. The operation of *chontear* involved lowering one's trousers and exposing the flesh. One could do one's thing and simultaneously wave one's hands around one's bum. This risked losing one's balance in the dark and possibly falling into the *chonto*, which was not a good idea, but, if not, the mosquitoes, and any other insect passing, zoomed in and bit mercilessly. In the afternoon, one day, we were in the river, in underpants, bathing. I saw a red bite on my right upper thigh. All the next days I saw it. It did not go away. I squeezed it and juice came out. It was not unlike the leaking of my knee, when I had bashed it up in the mountains. I was not worried. It would dry out.

It did not dry out. It formed a scab of a sort, but stayed red all around. It leaked and in the morning was stuck to my trouser. It got bigger. Pati saw it, when we were bathing and called Yasmin, the nurse, to have a look.

'That is leishmaniasis,' she pronounced. We had seen leishmaniasis on *guerrilleros* when we had arrived at the river, No wonder that many of the guerrilla say that they prefer to serve in the cold mountain and not in the hot forest, where tropical diseases abound. Leishmaniasis is carried by a sandfly. It deposits parasites in your body, when it bites you. The flies abound when the rivers fall in the dry season and there is sand for them to breed in. The parasites breed in your flesh and you have no defence. They either spread out along and under the skin, making a wide patch, like a fried egg, or go inside and migrate around the body. In the end they cause your ears and nose to fall off, and you can die of heart collapse.

There is a drug, called Glucantime, made by Rhone Poulenc of France, which kills the parasites. In Colombia, the drug is controlled by the state and not available through pharmacies. Yasmin consulted with Cat's Meat and collected some ampoules of it. The labels showed that it was made in Brazil and distributed in Venezuela, from where it has obviously been smuggled across the Orinoco into the forest. It could be injected into the muscle or the needle could be pushed into the infected hole from the side, as if a direct attack on the parasites would kill them better. So she got four ampoules and drilled into the hole from each side. She put a plaster on top, not that that would do much, except keep it clean. After a few days, we looked at it and it did seem to be drier. She found three more ampoules and I was given them. And then there were no more. The FARC was not going to get this drug easily, if the Army tightened its blockade around us.

Even the Army is said to have twice as many casualties from leishmaniasis as from wounds.

It was not enough. The infection got bigger. Hanibal had a look at it. He made a suggestion.

'Meester, you do what I do. I get clay and put it around the thing, leaving the hole uncovered. Then I pour alcohol into it and set fire. It burns the flesh away, and cures it. I have done it before.'

'Cripes, I don't have alcohol. Do you?'

'I have a little. There is another way that some people do it, if they don't have alcohol. You get a machete and heat it up in the fire and press it on the infection. It burns it away.'

'Hanibal, if you think that I am going to do that, you can think again. I should rather wait.'

'Up to you.'

'Well, don't you think that I am going home?'

'Of course, but better cure it now, than wait and let it get worse.'

I had to believe that I should be released at some time, and could go to a proper doctor. The disease would grow slowly and my nose would not fall off, before I could be in good hands. I was not going to press a red hot machete to my thigh. Hanibal did not insist.

'See,' I said to Brutus, 'they are not worried, and that shows that they think I will go home.'

'Balls. You are dreaming. They don't care a fig for you, Meester. They are *hijos de puta* and would kill us all at the drop of a hat.'

Brutus had other health problems. He had boils, known as *nacidos*, an unromantic schoolboy complaint. These boils, which the guerrilla suffered from, usually erupted under the armpits. They swelled and hurt like hell and grew huge under the skin and tender. You saw *guerrilleros* walking about with their arms held up, as to let them touch the boil was too painful. The solution was to cut them and squeeze them to get the 'head' out from inside, after which they healed quickly. This was very painful, unless the guerrilla had some xylocaine anaesthetic to inject locally. Pedro had that in the hills, but here there was none. If you did not cure the first boil quickly, then six others grew around it.

Yasmin told Brutus that she would cut open the boils. He refused. Bad Boy came and told him to be a man.

'*Hijo de puta*, it hurts,' he complained.

'Be a man,' Bad Boy said. 'I'll do it.'

So Yasmin cut, and Bad Boy squeezed. 'Ayyyyyyyyyyyy!!!' yelled Brutus, and wept hot tears of pain and rage.

'These bullies are always the worst cowards,' whispered Pati.

Boils are attributed to 'bad blood', whatever that means. So the guerrilla gives you the usual box of antibiotics to take. I felt that it could be due to blocking the pores and accumulating sweat and dirt under the skin. Whatever it was, not everyone got boils. I did not. Bad luck for Brutus, who got them twice.

Pati had to catch something, and she did, and then Brutus did too. But I did not. It was *nuches*. These were disgusting worms under the skin. They were laid in the bite of a big greenbottle fly, and they flew around everywhere. You see one morning a red lump on your skin and if you feel it, it has a hard centre and, if you look very carefully, there is a tiny hole. That is the air hole of the worm, or rather 'larva' of the fly. It has to breathe. It grows fast and wriggles. Ugh. It has hairs which point outward and stop you from squeezing it out. I know about it because my dogs get them, and so do horses, and cows, and now we humans. Horrible.

The guerrilla have an easy cure. You puff energetically at a cigarette and spit the nicotine juice on to the place, covering the breathing hole, stick a plaster on top and wait. The worm is killed by the nicotine and then you squeeze it out dead. If you are lucky, the hole cures itself nicely, or else you are marked for life with a red scar. Pati got one on her shoulder. It wriggled. But the nicotine worked and it was got out when it was still small. I remembered how big the ones on my dogs grew, before we spotted them. Like caterpillars.

The other fears were malaria and yellow fever. There were a trillion mosquitoes. Were any of them female anopheles and carriers of malaria? My companions and the guerrilla were confused about how one got malaria. They thought the carriers were 'the big yellow' mosquitoes. Or was it the red ones? I did not see evidence that there was malaria around. The FARC took no prophylactics, such as the traditional weekly Maloprim. If you got it, then you got a massive dose of pills to cure you. But yellow fever is there in the Brazilian/Colombian jungle and it kills you. I had had the vaccination, anyway. So the mosquitoes bit us merrily. We called the river camp 'Mosquito National Park'. What worried us most were the big green bluebottles. We felt that they would lay eggs in our flesh. So we pursued them.

Caracol's end of year show

Given the failure of Christmas to happen and doubts as to whether New Year would be an event either, we were keen to hear the last Sunday messages transmission of the year. It had been advertised on the radio and the presenter of the programme, Erwin Hoyos, was keen to get a big presence of family and friends, well any good Colombian, on the Plaza de Bolivar, in the old centre of Bogotá, on that last Saturday night. The idea was to have the families in the centre of Bogotá and transmit the programme from there, with the presence or at least the voices of the top people. The morale of the prisoners deserved to be raised,

as the end of the year had come and they were still not free. Of course, this
laudable aim was going to get mixed with the messy politics of the 'exchange of
prisoners' project.

So Saturday night, 28 December, was the night that we wanted to be lent one
of the radios.

'Meester, you ask for it,' said Pati. 'They always give you what you ask for.'

'You are the lady and Colombian. You know how to speak to them.'

'Sometimes I just don't want to ask for anything. It is so humiliating.'

'All right, if you don't, I shall.'

We did get a radio. Would our families send messages to us? I had never heard
one for me. Either they were being very discreet or I was just unlucky with the
timing. But Pati had regularly heard her daughter's words or her friends' messages
read out by the presenters. I had not heard a message for Brutus.

'I have no friends and have not spoken to my family for twenty years. The
people in the Sanandresito must be hoping that I am dead. They hate me,' was
the opinion of Brutus. Did he care?

The presenter of the programme had apparently invited the Minister of Defence
and her military commanders to take part in the event, but they had declined. But
General Campo, the General of the National Police, had agreed. He was splendid.
He knew that he was speaking to his men, some of them over five years behind
barbed wire in the forest.

'Sergeant Ruiz, keep your spirits up, man. I was with your wife and your
mother recently. They are well and send regards. Corporal Gonzalez, your
companions send you Christmas greetings and are awaiting your return. Constable
Dominguez, we know you are behaving like a true soldier and are proud of you.
Courage.' And so on. It was inspiring stuff and just what the doctor ordered when
you are a prisoner, and needing the support of your friends. You feel that you
would die for the Fatherland.

Then, the programme telephoned the President in the Palacio de Narino and
Alvaro Uribe answered the call and spoke on the programme. Would he also give
us hope? His calm voice filled the silence of the forest. But he spoke of the
difficulties of negotiating with the guerrilla, of the impossiblity of releasing the
guerrilleros serving prison sentences, of bringing about an interchange. Our spirits
fell. We were to be the sacrificed, ground to pulp between the millstones of
heartless processes. Did they not value human lives?

After this, the voices of the families, who had worked so hard to promote the
interchange sounded sad and depressed and hopeless. The two sides were
intransigent. No intervention by the UN, by anyone, had any effect on the
stubborn players in a 'war against terrorism'.

What did the family of Ingrid Betancourt think? And how to keep up the
morale of poor Pati?

'This is what Uribe meant by "there will have to be sacrifices",' I said to Pati.
'He did not say that.'

'I heard it on the radio. We will be sacrificed. That is the nature of warfare when dialogue breaks down.'

'As flies to wanton boys are we to the Gods . . .'

CHAPTER 50

A new *comandante*

THE REINDEER DID NOT COME to see us one morning, nor the next. Had he been posted away? Who was in command? A new face appeared, a tall, strong young man, in uniform with a beret, a smart, ambitious man. One had to be careful about these ones. He was 'Jaime'.

'How are you?' he asked. But he was not the sort to get us anything that we wanted, newspapers or a radio. He might get us clothes, and indeed he came the next day, and opened up some bags, containing shirts and trousers. This was as depressing as ever. It showed that he knew that we were not leaving for home soon. The guerrilla did not give us tracksuit bottoms any more, just uniforms.

'It's a new rule. You can only wear camouflage,' he said. And then he said that there was a new *comandante*, and he wanted to see us, and would call us one by one, later. He did not come to see us. Why? Because he had a bad leg – another war-wounded posted to a Stalag. 'Alvirio' was his *nom de guerre*.

The first person he wanted to see was Pati. He told her that all was going well and she would be home soon. He liked to chat. He said that he had a farm in the civilian world and he had a family, whom he saw every now and then. His daughter was going to go to university. Could Pati help this girl get into university, please? How could one refuse? He could call on her, when he was out. Er, hem.

His leg had been badly broken, when he fell on a march. It had been operated on and had plates put in, but they had worked loose. His leg was swollen and painful. He wanted to have an operation in the civilian world. The FARC would pay for half and he had to pay the rest. It was a lot of money. Perhaps someone could help him with that? Sorry about the kidnapping, but you understand, the FARC needs money. Anyway, we should be out back with our families soon. 'This gringo, what is he like?' he asked her, referring to me.

When it was my turn, I went to him as he sat on a tree trunk with his leg up on another log and a walking stick in his hand. He was reading. He was most amiable. He talked of his daughter. Is it easy to learn English? Yes, did he want some lessons? Maybe, but for his daughter. She could get a job in the USA, if she spoke English. They did not teach it in the school where she was. 'Will he ask me for a British Council scholarship?' I began to wonder in a delirious state. Did I play chess? Maybe I could play with him. Yes.

'What about me?' I asked.

'Don't worry, it is going well. Patience. You will be home soon.'

'And *la señora?*'

'Going well too. But that other man. What do you know of him? That could take longer. He is difficult.'

'Oh, go on. He really does not have money. He spends it all on riotous living. His house is worth very little, as he has mucked up the legal side. Let him go, *pobrecito.*'

'Ha! Don't say anything. I shall see him at some time.'

I went back, and the lunch had come. I asked Pati and she explained that this chap had asked for her help. I said that he had talked of English lessons. What a nightmare to think that such a man could imagine that he could see us afterwards, as if nothing was wrong.

'What's the difficulty about Brutus?'

'Well, one of the guerrilla said that his so-called woman had said that he was a vagabond, only slept at home from time to time, did not tell her about his financial affairs. She had no signature on his accounts, so why should she pay anything? What would she live on when she got old? He could stay with them for ever for all she cared.'

'Oh, my God. He is reaping the harvest of his misspent life.'

'Oh, they will let him go. The woman will pay something. The guerrilla and he understand each other. We are the ones who suffer unjustly. Not his sort.'

But the new *comandante* was a change, older and more worldly. Was he important? Was he involved in our cases or just convalescing? In fact a few days later, the Reindeer wandered into the *condominio.* Back again. Why? Where had he been? Scouting around? Seeing if the road was clear for us to go home? Who knows?

One night, we had gone to bed when a giant hand seemed to shake our *caleta*s from side to side violently. The trees were not moving, so it was not a wind but an earth tremor. Exciting. Reindeer came up to see how we were. He said that the epicentre was close. An hour later the radio news said that it was about 160 kilometres away, in the llanos lowlands. That did not sound normal. These tremors were mostly in the central cordillera. Colombia is on the meeting of the Nazca tectonic plate and the one under the Pacific. They slip one under the other, and get stuck and jump. One day in a thousand million years Bogotá will be destroyed. Will I still be negotiating my ransom then?

'Before a tremor, you can feel that it gets hot,' he said. 'Did you feel it?'

'Not actually.'

'I did,' he claimed. What an imagination!

Carlos, the musical one, suddenly came one afternoon and said goodbye to each of us, which was rather polite and well-mannered of him He was in uniform and smart. He was going. Whither?

'Oh, a bit by canoe, then walk in the forest, then by road, then by the river again, a long trip.'

'*Adios*, Meester, *suerte*.'

He left. Unexpectedly, an older man walked up the path. It was *Comandante* Milton. He smiled and sat on the bench. It is disquieting to be in the presence of a senior *comandante*, someone who sees the chiefs on the *Estado Mayor* like Mono Jojoy, Romaña, a fighting *comandante*. Our lives in his hands?

'Still here?' he asked Pati. What could she say to such a painful question? What did he mean? Should she be out? Was he on her side? She did not cry or even look shaken.

I walked away to my *caleta*. She should be left alone with him. Brutus had never come out, or greeted the big chief. They talked and I tried not to listen. I had a book to read.

When he had gone, Pati said, 'Did you notice all the thousands of *garrapata* bites?'

'Well, yes, I did.'

'I asked him. He said that they had to run off suddenly into the bushes and spend all night there. There were millions of *garrapatas*. He came to take Carlos. They are off on a long trip and Carlos knows the way.'

This was the life of the guerrilla, hidden in the forest, going to meetings, hearing Tirofijo discuss the future. Not, I assume, a future of talking to this president, or of anything resembling peace.

We were not just kidnapped, we were participants in a guerrilla war. How often this thought popped up.

'Do you think that Uribe can win this war?' I asked, of no one in particular, at supper.

Brutus had reverted to his caveman mood. 'Don't be a tit. We have to kill all these *hijos de puta*. Bomb the shit out of them. Hey, Meester do you think they are nice chaps. *Mierda*, they would kill us. Wake up.'

'No, what have we learned about war? CAN we win? What do the guerrilla say? The Army advances, we retreat. The Army retreats, we advance. The bombing – does it kill them? It has not killed us. What is war about? Why does it end? Should we not offer them pardon and a huge Swiss bank account?'

'Your money, Meester. You are rich.'

'*Por Dios*. Let's talk. What else have we got to do? *En serio*. Can the government win? It does not have enough troops. They never get here where we are, do they?'

'With this president, we shall win.'

'Look, I am not a Colombian, but it is Colombians who have said that until every Colombian does his military service, the whole country will not really do anything about finishing off the war. We have had this discussion before. The war is just left to the Army. They have generous retirement benefits. It is not I that say this, it is you Colombians.'

Pati was quiet for a few days. Then, one morning when the coffee had arrived and she was getting up, she said quietly that Milton had said that he had asked for her to be released for money and was genuinely surprised that she had not been released, but he was not in charge of that. He would do something about it, when he got back from his travel.

'But you must be really happy?' I asked her.

'I don't want to be optimistic. You always say "Keep calm and don't risk disappointments." Well I don't want to be disappointed, but I am almost sure that I will get out if my family pays. I am not a political after all.'

'Congratulations. The United Nations were getting nowhere. You were right and I was wrong. You will be home first.'

'That is what he said.'

'Hurrah!'

The fact that Pati was in a mood to believe that she would get to see her home and children was very good news. She ran the greatest risk of any of us. I was worried about Blair's attitudes and the war against terrorism. Just calling everyone a terrorist was a gross simplification and a justification of fighting them. The radio made it clear that the anti-terror countries were giving Iraq an ultimatum. I did not want to be in captivity when Iraq was attacked. That would complicate things. Or was I being paranoid? Was the war in Colombia a 'Colombian matter' as Tirofijo often said? Or were all the terrorists of the world in a kind of alliance? Were we both political and only Brutus economic? Or none of us? The FARC seemed to be against any kind of intervention of foreign countries, United Nations, the Pope, Red Cross or NGOs in the conflict. They were in a very Colombian mood.

In a full moon night of December, after Christmas, old Polo came down and said that he had been authorised to take us for a walk along the river bank in the moon. We went through the camp and down to the river and downstream, where we had never been, only looked from where we bathed. The water was low and the exposed sandbanks were vast, with whole drift trees embedded in them. We walked for a while and the whole river opened up and revealed a large sky and moon and stars. It was a change from being shut up in the forest.

We did this once. Neither Pati nor Brutus wanted to do it again. I don't know why not. They were both 'humiliated' by the treatment as prisoners of these people. It may have been more humiliating for the Colombians. They did not like receiving favours or talking to the guerrilla. It was perhaps easier for a foreigner.

I was given another walk one day, like the previous one to see the *araguatos*. Hanibal and Colacho took me along the path, which we took when we ran from the bombs. We arrived at the same end point and crept around in the bushes. They saw two huge white *paujuil* birds but were slow to shoot them. I suspect that they were not allowed to. We found the skeleton of a tiger and a tortoise nearby. They went to a stream and pointed out a path made by tapirs. On the way back we saw *araguato* monkeys and watched them. I don't know why they were told to take this walk, but I enjoyed the variation to our routine and the chance to see animals. They knew that I liked that.

CHAPTER 51

A chance meeting in Bogotá

AMONG OUR FRIENDS, THERE IS AN architect, Gregorio, married to a European. They have a small son and a large dog called Otto, which bays mournfully like the Hound of the Baskervilles when left alone. Gregorio is ebullient, emotional, a wonderful friend. One day he was visited in his office by a young girl, an architect too, but more dedicated to decoration. During the meeting, she revealed that her mother was a kidnap victim and that the family was negotiating with guerrilla and had had to pay something, without getting her mother released. She had been in contact with the kidnapping support group *Pais Libre* (Free Country), set up by Francisco Santos, of the family that own the *El Tiempo* daily newspaper, who had been kidnapped himself, in the days of Pablo Escobar. She had learned that her mother was held with an Englishman (this was information from Grandpa, surely), so our friend was able to understand that I was with her mother and that was Pati.

Before Christmas, Gregorio rushed over the street and came in to the flat. He told this story and Nanette got excited. It was a breakthrough.

'I want to meet her,' she cried.

'I will speak to her and get a day when she can come and see you here.' And he rushed off.

He rang her and this young girl came to the flat after work. She said that her aunt was negotiating, in Fusa, and these people would go and visit her. She was a brave woman, for all this was unpleasant and frightening. A price was agreed and the first amounts were paid.

'We think that they take the money, but they also want to treat it as a *secuestro politico*, so they won't release her. Can you help us?'

Nanette's heart opened to her. 'We can try.' Now she knew that we were together. Could both of us be got out? How?

'If it is *politico*, your husband might come out first, and my mother might get left behind. Maybe we can help each other? Can you find out about my mother?'

This reflects so well the anguish of Pati and the uncertainty and the difficulty of interpreting the messages, or lack of them, in the broadcasts. Pati had felt that the family was not offering hope.

Then Nanette discovered that the Padré had met a powerful woman who had asked him to help with Pati too. The Padré had met Pati's sister and the daughter, and they knew that I was with her and the Padré learned this and the circle of information was complete. He was juggling two balls.

The FARC asked him to go to see them, on Christmas Day, of all days for a priest.

'Padré, you can't go at Christmas time. You are needed in your church. Tell them "no",' said Nanette.

'I must go,' insisted the Padré. He was afraid of breaking the contact. It was a terrible commitment. What if they got offended and stopped calling?

When he got to the agreed place, they did not show up. He wasted his trip.

John had come to Colombia for Christmas, and he and Nanette were invited to Medellin for New Year. This is a special pleasure, as our friends there are the most warm-hearted and supportive people in the world. Even among *paisas*, who are marvellous people, they are exceptional. Their farm is the most beautiful mountain retreat, with views of volcanoes, birds, flowers, and it is surrounded by vast coffee plantations, on vertiginous slopes. When you are there, you really believe that Colombia is the most beautiful country with the best climate and most exuberant vegetation in the world, let alone the best coffee, and rum, and the loveliest, smartest women. Down, boy! The two of them danced the New Year in, to rum and coke and cigars and salsa. Perhaps with the odd thought for me?

And so on 9 January, our family met with Pati's daughter at *Pais Libre*, who had rung. It was an emotional meeting. My family compared notes. Pati had been in captivity for seven months. She had been with us in Sumapaz. She had been kept separate, but had later got to speak to me. The negotiations for the two had proceeded very similarly. The first negotiator had been Leonidas, for the *Frente* 55. He seemed to be serious, which in Spanish means 'a man of his word'. Old Grandpa had been liberated in the end near to the town of La Uribe, Meta. Both Pati and I had been moved from *Frente* 55 to *Frente* 53, more under the wing of Romaña. Libardo had restarted the talks for both of us, from Meta, down below. They had got a letter from Pati in October too. Libardo was replaced by Andres. There was an Ivan. Was he the same as Andres? The FARC insisted on speaking to Pati's sister and not a priest. If they wanted a letter of proof of survival, it would take two weeks (we were far away). Pati's family had paid 70 per cent of the amount and held out for the balance on release. Andres wanted the balance now. He seems unreliable.

So January was hell for both families. Both Pati and I were stuck, far far away. Andres was a nasty type. Pati had paid and they had welshed on her release. They still asked for a huge amount with nine zeros in pesos for me. The communications between President Uribe and the FARC were nil. Was the Padré the right man for us? He was only human and showing signs of losing his patience with the FARC. They had him dashing down to the llanos all the time. It was exhausting and time-consuming. They showed no signs of understanding the realities of money. Should he give up? Who could replace him? He was an exceptional man. But there was no result.

This discovery of the existence of a woman in the proximity of me, of a mysterious 'Pati', was too much for Nanette's friends, Gustavo, Maria Elvira, Raimundo. They roared with laughter. 'So David has fallen in love in the forest. Watch out, Nanette. Romance with a dark beauty. He must be teaching her English – nudge, nudge!'

'Ha!' muttered Nanette to herself. 'Who is this woman? David is bound to be in love. He is a soft touch. I shall raise hell!'

Gustavo could not contain his laughter.

The Club El Nogal bomb

On 7 February 2003, just after eight in the evening of a Friday, a very busy social day in the week, an employee's car (so it appeared) pulled up to the barrier at the entrance to the staff parking of the Club El Nogal, on the 7th Street (*Carrera la septima* (or *la se'tima* as a good Bogotáno would pronounce it). The Club El Nogal is (or was) a substantial building, on the main north/south avenue of the city, in the centre of the new financial district. It is a town club, like the London clubs that line Pall Mall, but it has a large swimming pool at the top, squash courts, a golf driving area, saunas. The first floors are parking areas. The members are business people, as well as families looking for sporting facilities in the centre of the city. There are rooms for business meetings and office/secretarial support. El Club El Nogal has correspondent relationships with clubs in New York, London and other major cities. One of the moving forces, and at one time chairman, was Fernando Londoño Hoyos, a brilliant lawyer, with a silver tongue and widely read. In August 2002, the new president Alvaro Uribe appointed him Interior Minister, with responsibility for justice as well as home affairs. It was clear that he was to be a hard man, and someone to manage the tricky relationship with congressmen and senators, to get their votes for legislation and the fight for security.

John Fredy Arellan was a squash coach. He had parking rights, and his own Renault Megane car had entered the parking earlier and been parked next to a concrete column. The new car was driven in by his uncle Osvaldo, and was a Toyota jeep. The papers had been fiddled, so this car entered with a nod from the guard. The Toyota was packed with 330 pounds of anfo explosive, and a timer. Osvaldo drove it up to the third floor, and got out, walked a few paces and activated the automatic lock, by a radio pulse.

At 8.30 in the evening, people – ordinary people, families, men back from work, foreign visitors to Colombia – were playing games, swimming, having dinner. A children's party was in full fling. A huge explosion tore the centre out of the building. Was it the gas to heat the swimming pool? Was it a bomb? It was a bomb. In the car parked by Osvaldo, the pack of explosives had been set off by the radio pulse. The bomb-makers had told him that it was set to explode at ten o'clock, but they had set it for this locking act and wanted him dead too. The centre of the building collapsed and diners and children from the party cascaded into the hole made by the bomb in the centre of the building. The roof fell in on the cars parked in the car park on the first two floors of the club. Thirty-six people died, and four times as many were wounded.

It was Adriano, who had a radio, who told us that there had been an explosion in Bogotá. He brought his radio over and we fixed up the aerial. There had been an explosion in the Club el Nogal, but it was not known who was responsible. The Avenida Septima was closed, as fire engines arrived to rescue the dead and wounded. Reactions from the government were repudiation of violence, sadness for the death of innocent women and children, worry that peace talks were broken off.

'This is a message with a name and address on the envelope. Fernando Londono has been the president of the club and it was lent to Uribe's presidential campaign as their headquarters,' said Pati.

'He is screwing up the exchange of prisoners process, so this is the message, you mean?'

'No, it is against Uribe's policy, too. If they can't kill Uribe, this is how they get at him.'

'Hey,' said Adriano, ' I don't think that it was we, the FARC, that did it. It could be the paramilitary, or the common criminals.'

And in fact, no communiqué came out subsequently from the FARC, claiming responsibility, not a great vote-winner.

'Do you think that this shows that the FARC can step up an urban terror campaign? When do we get bombs in the shopping centres?' I said when Adriano had gone and taken his radio.

'Huh, who knows? Maybe not,' said Pati. 'Keep your voice down.'

The night fell and we retired to bed and the mosquito net, thinking of the deaths, and remembering the club and the many meetings and lunches I had had there with friends.

At about eight o'clock, in the pitch darkness, we heard the aeroplanes come, the Pig and then the KFIR attack planes. They flew right over us. The bombs fell on the other side of the river, not far away. We put our boots on and packed our backpacks, and lay and waited. Would we have to run into the night? Thump, thump, echoed the bombs.

'*Hijo de puta* hard pounding,' murmured the Brute.

But no one came and the planes flew away and we stayed in the camp. The violence of the guerrilla had met the counter violence of the State. Tit for tat. Are we going anywhere towards peace?

On the next Tuesday, as the scale of the attack had sunk in, and the trucks and bulldozers, which closed the Septima to traffic, were carting away the debris, the

Minister of Defence, the efficient Marta Lucia Ramirez, was in Washington, seeing Donald Rumsfeld, the US Defence Secretary. She said to the correspondents that the El Nogal bomb was a sophisticated operation, needing assistance from foreign terrorist groups. She mentioned the IRA and the ETA. The FARC had always been a forest army, without explosive skills. A comparison has been made with the bombs in 1992 and 1994 in Buenos Aires, Argentina, against Jewish targets, where the security services of that country had clues that the material and know-how came through the Iranian Embassy. She linked the FARC to drugs.

'Every time that drugs are consumed, terrorist groups are being financed,' she said.

At the same time that the El Nogal attack was underway, there had been a dramatic appearance in a court of law by a deserter from the FARC. Edwin Giovanni Rodriguez testified that he had seen the three IRA men giving classes in February 2001 inside the distension zone. Rodriguez had been driving for Jorge Suarez Bricenio, 'El Mono Jojoy'. He had had to take the Irishmen from the zone to a village called La Y. Mono Jojoy had said that they had finished their instructing and were 'on their own'.

A year later, investigations had arrived at the conclusion that the Arellan family had a brother, Herminsul, in the guerrilla. He had put out lots of money to persuade his stupid and greedy nephew, John Fredy, to do this suicidal bombing. The investigation had been helped by a deserter in August 2003 from the *Columna Teofilo Forero* (who had taken me?) called Vladimir. Oh really? That was a name that I knew.

PART 5

Negotiations

CHAPTER 52

Deeper into the forest

IN THE THIRD WEEK IN JANUARY, the bombing had become more constant, although the guerrilla shrugged off the danger. We did not run into the forest in the night, but the bombs sounded close. The summer continued and the river was falling. The *yarumo* trees had fewer leaves. Were we more exposed to the eyes of the pilots observing from the aeroplanes? There was no indication of release and no visitors. Alvirio seemed positive about the negotiations, but sat in front of his *caleta*, with his swollen leg on a log. Rodolfo appeared again one day. Why? Was he number one or number two?

But one day, Jaime came and walked up to me. He handed me a piece of paper and a biro and asked me to write down the answers to some questions.

'What is the name of the suburb in Australia where you lived? And what is the name of the pub near your mother's house?'

My God! This is the 'proof of existence' process. It has happened. My family have asked for proof that I am alive. They are negotiating. Will I be out in days? Grandpa was out in two days after his questions. At the end of August, so long ago, in the hills. I felt excited.

What was the suburb? Easy. Toorak. What is the name of the pub? Oh hell, I cannot remember. It is not the Merry Harriers. What is it? My mind went blank. That is what happens after confinement in the forest prison. The mind is derailed.

'I can't remember,' I bleated to Jaime.

'Don't worry. Take your time,' he said. 'But everyone get packed! We may leave today or tomorrow.'

I walked around the tree and banged my head with my fist and tried to think of the walk to the pub on a summer's evening and the inn sign hanging outside. Blank. Then it came. The Horse and Groom. How stupid was I? So many pints of Harvey's bitter and good meals in the Horse and Groom. I wrote the answers down, elated. Was my capture coming to an end?

Suddenly Rodolfo came up. 'Ready? We are off.' So the three of us walked for the last time to the river and there was the canoe, with the Indian boatman, and a second canoe. What of the 'others'? It looked as if we were to go first. The canoes were loaded with plantains, dry food, a gas cylinder, the cooker, our bags. Up the river we went. The water was low and frequently the guerrilla had to get out and push, standing in the river. We were on the move and our hearts rose. We could see fish in the water, and birds on the bank – kingfishers, ibis, cormorants, hawks.

'Take off your camouflage jacket,' said Rodolfo. 'If they fly over and see it, we are in trouble.'

Did he think we could be taken for locals out fishing or travelling by river? It was pleasant to be in the sun with a bare chest, listening to the sound of the water and the outboard motor, to move in a direction, after four months of walking around the tree, like mice in a cage. This must be back in the direction we had come from in September. The river bank was high to the left, going upstream. At times great horizontal rock slices ran along, parallel to the water. There were some big high trees and, on the other lower side, masses of heliconias, with red 'bird of paradise' flower spikes drooping over the river. Once on the right, two men, with some blue PVC barrels, sat on the bank. This must be the point where we pulled into the bank in the darkness in September. Was that the way to the field hospital? Were they pulling out too?

It was only an hour, and we suddenly headed for the sandy bank on the left and stopped. 'All out,' they cried, and we went ashore, along the sand and up the bank, into the bushes and into a small clearing. There were two lemon trees and some guavas. A bit further in, the clearing continued and bent right and a tree-trunk bridge crossed a stream. We ate some cold rice, and sucked lemons (for the vitamin C). The afternoon passed. All the stuff brought up in the canoes was dragged up. Soon after it fell dark, we were taken uphill, across a field, where the grass had been burned – probably on purpose to get fresh shoots for cattle to eat – and there was a house, of planks, with a balcony, a kitchen at the back, rooms with doors, a real farm, the last farm before the forest, but abandoned. There was no livestock. We were given a room for the three of us, with a wooden bed, but no mattress.

'Who wants the bed? You, Pati?'

'No, not me. I'll take the floor.'

'No, go on, take it.'

'You have it.'

With a curse, Brutus hurled his pack on the bed and it was his. There were planks missing from the floor, and a heap of barbed wire stuffed underneath. But there were shelves. A room, what a luxury! We laid out our sleeping bags, in the pitch dark, and stepped out on to the balcony. A near-full moon rose.

'No noise at all,' warned Rodolfo, who went into the field with his rifle. Our pans came with rice and lentils. There was a bench to sit on. Brutus was on the bed inside. A bird sang a two-note phrase in the bushes on the other side of the field. I imitated it. It answered.

'*Que es eso*? What's that?' said Colacho.

'It is I, chatting to the bird'.

'Well, don't.'

Rodolfo came up. He listened. The bird sang its two notes. Rodolfo put a bullet into the breech of the rifle and said that he would go and investigate. Good heavens, was he nervous? Were we nearer civilisation and the Army? We sat on the bench without going in to bed. It was a luxurious feeling, reminiscent of our real lives.

'Why don't you go to sleep?' said Colacho out of the darkness of the house. The guerrilla was inside and bedded down, so we went in to sleep on the dusty hard floor.

Before dawn, the guerrilla moved about and then came the handclaps, 'Up, up!' I went out for a pee. Brutus awoke and let off a tremendous fart. I stood on the balcony and coffee came around, followed by breakfast of soup and *cancharina*. We packed and marched back down the path into the trees, across the tree-trunk bridge and stopped. Ahead, a cleared pathway went north. The river was just on the right. This is where we were to stop. We asked if we were to go a long way. 'No, not today.'

'They are probably bringing the others,' whispered Pati.

The guerrilla came and started to make *caleta*s for us. It was dry and hot. Why put up the tent? What if it rained?

'It won't,' said Pati. 'I shall sleep without the tent.' This was to be a night on the ground.

Hanibal came by. 'Don't walk far from the path, up at the end. I saw the nests of snakes.'

'Four noses?' asked Brutus.

'Probably,' was the reply.

'Let's see,' I said. And we went up the path.

'That's where a snake lies,' said Hanibal. There was a patch of flattened grass. Was he telling a story to stop us walking about? The sides of the path were all heliconias, and wonderful ones – yellow, red, bird of paradise, hanging ones, and inside the trees I saw two superb ones, with round clusters of balls, red and blue, growing from the roots. Any botanical garden would be thrilled to have such beautiful plants.

'Can we go to the river and bathe?' I asked. Hanibal looked nervous. The wide sandy beach of the river offered no protection against overflying aircraft.

'Wait,' he said. We stood looking out onto the river. Little sandpipers scurried on the sand. Swallows swooped over and landed on the big beached tree trunks, washed down in the floods. In the sand at the start of a dry stream entering from further up, we saw hoof prints. This is where they bring the mules with the provisions and load them on the canoes. There to the north is civilisation, towns, roads, food markets.

We went back. Brutus had his radio on, and was listening to a news programme. That is when we heard of the journalists kidnapped in Arauca. On 21 January, two journalists who had gone to the province of Arauca had disappeared. Arauca is the northernmost province of the llanos, up against the frontier with Venezuela. The Arauca river flows slow and wide east into the Orinoco, and under this province is oil. Occidental Petroleum, 'Oxy', of Bakersfield, California is the operator, in an association contract with Ecopetrol, the state oil company, and the oil goes to the terminal in the Caribbean for loading into tankers, down the Caño Limon pipeline. This is blown up frequently by the ELN – *Ejercito de Liberacion Nacional*. This of course deprives Colombia of millions of dollars, and is highly off-putting to potential investors into Colombia. But the ELN must think that the oil is Colombian, it stays in the ground, it should not be pumped up by the vile Yankees, etc., which is not so clear to the local government of Arauca, who earn huge royalties from their oil, and spend them on hospitals, roads, schools (indeed Olympic swimming pools in schools, the rumour goes). And there is huge leakage to the ELN of this money. What a confusion!

I was, I remember, visiting a chamber of commerce, not long before, when a journalist from Canada came for an interview. She wanted to talk about oil and foreign investment. Why? Because, after 11 September 2001, the North American newspaper owners realised that there was a story behind the businessmen working abroad in US companies, making and selling things, drilling for oil, running factories, promoting US medicines, cosmetics, household cleaning products. These people had been forgotten. They deserved to be known. They deserved to be protected by their country. The USA is the biggest trading nation of the world. Go and find it out again. The forgotten heroes? Hollywood made films about them in the 1960s – the Berlin Wall, Africa, Madama Butterfly (well, that was another time), Doris Day and Gregory Peck. What can the USA do to keep the oil flowing down the Caño Limon pipeline, and to back up the Colombian armed forces?

The two journalists were from the *Los Angeles Times* (I think) or writing for it. There was a story in Arauca about the conflict around an American-run oil field. Was Al Gore not involved in Oxy? Or was it another US politician? Scott Dalton was an American photographer. The writer was Ruth Morris. After some days, it was reported that she was British. They had disappeared, probably travelling on a road and caught in a roadblock and marched into the hills, sleeping like us on the ground and eating rice. The difference is the fuss. Oh my God, two journalists kidnapped. What a terrible thing! Journalists are usually able to get to the guerrilla camps and film television interviews with the *comandantes*. They pass on the message of the rebellion to the world, but the Army cannot get to the same leaders, to capture them, so the radio echoed protests, approaches to the Colombian government to get them released. A few days later we heard the early radio programme for the kidnap victims, and a reassuring American voice said, 'Hi, Scott and Ruth, hang on. We are doing all we can to get you out.'

'They will be out soon, you'll see,' I said to Pati. 'The government will do a deal with the ELN leaders, who are in prison. The ELN needs the press.'

'What about us?' she said bleakly.

A very similar ELN kidnap of foreigners was to take place in late 2003 when backpackers in the Santa Marta area were taken, including the Englishmen Matthew Scott and Mark Henderson. Their leaders decided that the kidnap was a mistake and had to be reversed. The ELN is different to the FARC.

In the afternoon we were allowed to go to the river and bathe and it was delightful to lie, in underpants, in the shallow cold water. Birds flew across the sky over the river and there was a sense of space and air and sky, which we had been deprived of while we were shut up under the trees. The sandpipers scurried along the sand. Swifts flew over at speed.

'I am not going to put up my tent,' said Brutus, when we got back. He slept inside the mosquito net only. The supper was just rice, as not enough food had been brought with us. We were on the move. The reason for the short move from the hut to here must have been that another bunch of prisoners were coming behind us and had taken the hut.

The next day we walked parallel to the river, upstream, into the forest edge. The path rose. We turned a corner. Pati made a movement with her head and I looked right. Over the river below and the treetops, we could see in the distance a mountain range, not a big one, sticking up out of the forest.

'La Macarena,' she mouthed, and shushed me. It was a clue to where we were, and that was dangerous knowledge.

The Serrania de la Macarena is a natural paradise, one of those rocky outcrops in the Amazon, like the 'Lost World' of Sir Arthur Conan Doyle, in the south of Venezuela. Adventurous young people working in Bogotá still go there for holidays, but it is highly dangerous, as the FARC is considered to roam around. It is a treasure-house of birds and insects and waterfalls and rocky heights. It was to the east and so we were between it and the eastern cordillera, in the south of Meta department.

The path wound up and down, along the river bank. It was hot and we sweated as we carried the backpacks. The floor was uneven and roots stuck up. The Reindeer charged up behind, with a pack and a can of gasoline in one hand, and his rifle, in good form. Crash! He tripped over a root and fell flat on his face, with can and rifle flying into the forest. I roared with laughter, and so did he. We got to a fork in the path, the left going at ninety degrees into the forest and the other straight ahead.

'Wait here.' We sat. Some people went on ahead. It appeared that there was a house ahead. 'We don't want anyone to see you.'

After an hour of waiting, we were told to take the left fork and almost immediately we turned into the forest and were told to make camp there. It had been a short walk. The forest was dense and the floor was uncomfortable. The number of ants was huge and so were the ants, as long as a finger joint, swarming along the branches and lianas. This was their forest, their home, but they did not bite.

'Stay here. People go along the path,' Reindeer said. This was exciting. Real people. Civilians. We had to remain the invisible ones, behind the looking glass. After a night on the ground, we arose before dawn and were urged to get going quickly, with Polo in front. The path debouched into an open field, with chopped down trees, but no crops planted nor cattle, and then we were back into the forest, through the trees. Little Jonhatan was carrying the red Honda generator set on his shoulder, in addition to his pack. Someone carried his rifle. He looked unhappy. It was hot. The path dipped down to a stream and up a steep path again and again. It was hard going, with the packs on our backs. But it was before midday that we stopped beyond a stream and set up camp to the left in the trees. We stayed for two nights here. I suppose that the advance guard had lost contact, not come back, not reported, and it was too dangerous to go on, or maybe the way was not known. We spent the days watching little fish in the small stream and the huge blue Morpho butterflies. We could bathe in the stream, although it was shallow. I could read my book.

On the third day, we went on up the path. At the top were some huge trees, with buttress roots. One of them had little yellow fruit all over the forest floor underneath.

'The monkeys eat these,' said Reindeer. They must have been worthless as wood, or they would have been cut by lumberjacks years ago. It was open and beautiful here. We stopped to prepare water from the stream, and drank copiously. The path wandered on and split into two. We believed that Jaime and the Prince had gone ahead to open the road. They should have cut and marked it, by cutting a slash in the tree trunks. Sometimes they had.

'This used to be a clear path in the time of the *Zona*,' commented Reindeer. It had had a year to grow over and had become dense. The advance guard had slashed on each side with their machetes, but the path was no longer visible. We went left and got into thicker and thicker forest. We stopped and sat on a tree trunk, soaking in sweat. We were lost. An argument started up. Two of them went back to retrace our steps. We were not going to get to our destination before dark. The two of them came back and we backed and found a path to the right. After a while, it ended at a clearing. There was a noise of a motor saw and trees were crashing down.

'Stay back in the trees,' said Reindeer. Colacho went across the clearing. We waited. Trees crashed. This was a typical 'slash and burn' farming job. The trees would be burned. A crop like papayas or bananas would be planted, to grow high. Under this cover, *coca* would be planted. Invisible from the air? There is no better cash crop than illegal drugs. Then we were marched around the edge of the clearing, and back into the forest. We came to a stream and boggy ground. It was late now. We had not got the time to go on before dark, so a camp was made in the foul boggy ground. We could see an indian hut, no, three of them, at the edge of the forest, and a field beyond.

'Keep your voices down,' said the Reindeer. 'There are people living there.'

It was an itinerant indian community. They wander through the forest and find a site to slash and burn and cultivate yucca, banana, maize, for a couple of years. They make platforms of poles and a grass roof on top. Maybe there are three or four families, or perhaps only one, with dogs, pigs, chickens. The guerrilla wandered down to beg food off them and cook on their fire. We saw an indian woman and a couple of men, coppery bronzed, with straight black hair, short and strong – like Patas Chitas and Ramiro. We ate a rice and plantain meal and slept on the very uncomfortable earth, with the big black ants of this forest.

Before dawn we rose, and marched into the forest. We walked through a patch of white anthuriums, beautiful and wild, and thick groves of bird of paradise heliconias, and along stream beds, dry in this summer. It was hot and close and we poured with sweat. Uphill the ground dried out and the trees were bigger and the forest more spacious. Then we walked down a hill, stopped and waited. Who was that coming along? Hanibal and the Prince. We had arrived.

The destination was this forest of tall trees and plenty of light. This was 'deeper into the forest', as Hanibal had said, but 'easy to get home from', as Bad Boy had said. It was February and well into the next year, 2003. Would we ever get home? We had walked through a kind of bog to get to our new home. Where was the *chonto*? It was dug out through the trees on dry ground, hard to dig out because of the dense tree roots. Where was the water for washing? That was back in the direction where we had come from. There was no running water, no stream, no river. This had worried all of the guerrilla. They had made us carry water on the journey. Now they had to dig deep holes in the boggy ground and wait for them to fill up. The water was milky clay-coloured, not clean. The waterholes were set in a mono-species natural grove of palm trees of many types. It was very interesting and lovely. I called it the 'Palm Court'. The branches die all the time and fall crashing on the ground. They make a noise in the wind. The monkeys are able to leap on to the spiny branches and scurry up them. Interesting birds liked the hidden inside parts of the leaves near the trunks – the large white-throated toucan; a pair of cream-coloured woodpeckers, which afterwards I read in the Hilty and Brown bird book are 'uncommon'.

The day that we arrived, early, we had to clear the area for our *caleta*s, which were quickly put up. Logs were laid one across the other for the bed, and bamboo poles placed on top. The canvas roof was strung up, the mosquito net (*toldillo*) extended. The sky grew dark. It rained heavily and the water ran down the roof. I stripped off my clothes, seized my soap and showered in the rainshower cascading off the canvas, clean water, which suddenly switched itself off. Jaime came along and asked '*Se bañaron*? Did you bathe? All the guerrilla did.'

'Si, señor, nice and clean, thanks.' He brought new clothes, camouflage. It was always depressing to get new clothes. How much longer did HE think that we would be staying? A clue to our fate. Where did this issue of uniform come from? Was there a big fighting camp nearby?

I looked around for an exercise circuit. There was a huge tree, nearby. I walked around the back of it and measured a thousand paces through the undergrowth. On the way was a lesser but tall tree with green seed pods, which kept cracking open and dropping a pair of nuts on the ground with a thump. Later I could see the *choyo* monkeys eating the nuts, if they could get them before they fell.

I asked Jaime the next time that he came, whether we could make a walking track, and would he lend me a machete. He agreed. On this track, there were often hummingbirds. Bird of paradise plants grew in profusion. A little bit off the track, I found a wild pineapple plant, or cousin of the pineapple. The pineapple is a bromeliad, which usually grow on trees, as epiphytes, in company with orchids. I saw no orchids. This plant grew on the ground and out of the centre came a flower, like a pineapple in shape. The leaves were long and thin and spiky.

At the far end of the circuit, we could see further very tall trees not far off. At times there was a tremendous cackling and it was obvious that large macaws had flown in. We looked and looked and at last saw them, mostly the red-and-green ones, huge, walking up and down the branches, often as married couples and happily screeching away.

Colacho came up behind me as I watched. 'Don't walk any further in that direction,' he said. 'It is mined. Dangerous.'

At the entrance to our *condominio*, whence the *guerrilleros* came to see us, there was a pale-barked tree, not very tall. 'Interesting,' said Hanibal. He cut a diagonal slash in the bark with his machete. Later in the day, a yellow sap oozed out of the slash. He came back and sniffed it. 'Yes, that is the *cariaño* tree. That sap is a good medicine.' All the other guerrilla came to look.' Patas Chitas said that it was so. Polo came and touched it and sniffed and said, 'No, it is the *loro bobo* tree.'

'Ah, *Viejo bobo*. Old fool. It is *cariaño*.'

The old man looked sceptical. He was older by far and more experienced. But Hanibal had leishmaniasis, as I had. He came and collected the sap to apply to his infections.

'And I? Should I do the same?'

'If you want, Meester.'

'Get me some sticking plaster.'

So I collected some of the sweet-smelling sap and spread it on my putrid hole and put a plaster on top.

'That will cure it,' said Jaime. 'I knew someone with a much worse one than you, and it went away completely.'

I was left with two thoughts. (1) Natural medicines are of some use, but in the old days where you died in your forties anyway (hurrah for chemistry), and (2) why worry if I am to return to the real world and real doctors. So I shut up.

When we were on our own, it got quiet. The rift between Brutus and Pati was wide and unbridgeable. My *caleta* was, as ever, the one in the middle. He would play his radio very quietly so that she could not hear. She could ask the guerrilla to lend her a radio, so that she could listen to the messages. If he went to wash at the waterholes, he would take all his clothes off and prance around naked, so she had to go at a different time.

'He thinks that I am the cause of him being here so long. You economic prisoners have to stay until I go first. You can't go, because you may say that I am here and the government will have to rescue me. It is nonsense. But he hates me.'

She had a point. So did he. What did I know? But afterwards, it became clear, when I saw what was going on on the other side of the looking glass, after I had come out.

One quiet evening, Pati said, 'Shush, listen to that?' There was a noise. It could have been a truck.

'It is a truck. We are near a road. Very near a road.'

This was exciting. Very exciting. This was our way out? The next day, the guerrilla carried into the *condominio* a lot of planks. They replaced the bamboo on our beds with planks. I had mixed feelings. Sleeping on planks is not the most comfortable thing in the world. The guerrilla thought it as good as 'Sleepeezie', the springiest bed in the world (available from your local furniture stores). But it meant that there was a source of planks not far off and a means of transporting them.

The guerrilla went off to have their teeth looked at by a dentist. They went in a dump truck, we were told. By road. The dentist's drills were powered by a generator. The generator was in a guerrilla camp. There was a big camp nearby. We knew this from Jaime, who went there for a couple of days. The Prince told us that a FM broadcasting station was nearby. Milton had a separate camp. He had a regular spot on the radio, *la Far'eana*, as it was called. Romaña was in another camp not far off. Jaime had been in one of the camps and had met Simon Trinidad. That was exciting. Simon Trinidad was a member of the *Estado Mayor*, the General Staff of the FARC. He was passing through. What did he say?

'Simon Trinidad says that there will be an exchange of prisoners,' confided Jaime.

'When?' asked poor Pati.

'Patience,' the usual response of the FARC.

Why did Simon Trinidad feel that there would be an exchange? The only explanation is that the FARC wanted an exchange and would be the gainers from one. They may have felt that the civil society would not want their kidnap victims to die and would give in. But we felt that, at least in the short term, President Uribe and Fernando Londoño would not want the captured *guerrilleros* to return to be a nuisance to the country, nor would they want to set a precedent. 'If we do it once, then they will just go on kidnapping,' is the argument of many Colombians. Would Pati die after years in the forest or go home?

'As flies to wanton boys are we to the Gods. They mock us for their sport', as Shakespeare wrote. Our lives are worthless in some greater struggle of Good against Evil. I have heard even friends argue, 'Your life is of no importance, David, in this war. We have to win it.' Beyond mere brigandry, it is a total war, and thousands must die. Well, I am not so sure. And the thousands of families who want their husbands and sons back alive are not likely to feel the same way. Is it right to pay a ransom? What is the value of a life? In fact, quite a lot, my friend. Everything! Life is everything or the only thing. There is no life after death, so cling on to life, chum.

'Simon Trinidad' may be a *nom de guerre*, but he is a real person. His name is Ricardo Palmera. His family comes from the northern city of Valledupar, a hot, whitewashed tropical city, near the Caribbean, famous for being the home of *vallenato* music. Its folkloric words and accordion accompaniment are the standard party music for the young of today and its stars are Carlos Vives and the scandalous Diomedes Diaz. 'Vallenato is for listening to, not for dancing,' I was told, by friends at our table at a party, when I asked why the young were not dancing. Pity, and dull compared to the hip-swaying skills of the Cali people, when the salsa bands are in full swing.

Ricardo Palmera's father, Ovidio, was a prosperous lawyer and was appointed Vice-Minister of Agriculture in the government of Mariano Ospina, the kind of appointment that presidents make to reward provincial big-wigs, in presidential systems. Ricardo was educated at the Swiss school in Bogotá and one of the Bogotá universities. He became a banker. The land around Valledupar was good for cotton and cattle. Ricardo married and had two children, but in 1986 he upped and headed for the Sierra Nevada de Santa Marta, the mountains, where he joined the FARC. Why?

The Sierra Nevada mountains were where the hidden fields of marijuana and then of opium poppies were. The mafias of Barranquilla contracted the FARC to protect these fields, and the cattle of the farmers began to be robbed and there were kidnaps. The state was unable to guarantee security. Decent people had to hire bodyguards. And out of this grew the self-defence forces or 'paramilitary', who took on the guerrilla and provided security to the farmers. A friend of Ricardo's, Rodrigo Tovar Pupo, took this course after his family was the object of kidnaps. He is now known as 'Jorge Cuarenta' – George Forty, the 'para' leader. So now the government, because in the past it was unable to guarantee security and catch the criminals, has to negotiate the demobilisation of both these groups, and the former *guerrilleros* and former self-defence forces have to find legal work as drivers, cowboys, waiters and carpenters – in an economy of over 13 per cent unemployed, on top.

So there was the infamous Simon Trinidad, uncaptured since 1986, so near to us.

The Colombian Air Force flew over every night. We felt secure. But we knew that we were surrounded by guerrilla military units and they were not just guarding us, but rather these top FARC leaders and their communication equipment and radio stations and files. Was it easy for us to get out of here to go home? Why the minefields? Was the Army going to attack? Would we have to run into the forest deeper?

My leishmaniasis was not getting better. It oozed liquid and in the morning my leg was stuck to my trousers. There were no medicines. The food was down to rice and beans – no meat, no fish, no plantains. Dog was in a bad way and he said it was malaria. The water level was falling, it being dry season, and the wells only had some milky, dirty water at the bottom.

The boys caught a *guatin* by finding her hole and digging her out. She was pregnant and when they cut her open, the baby was alive. This was a challenge to these country boys who wanted to save the baby, but they could not. So it was cooked and eaten.

At evening there were bats, but high up, and they did not fly into our *caleta*s. Macaws flew over the treetops. One day, I watched what I now think was a Crane Hawk, an amazing blue-grey hawk, with a barred tail. It was walking down the big rubber tree and over a huge termites' nest, hanging upside down, and picking at the crumbly nest and its holes with a strong beak. I had no idea what it was. A blue parrot? A cuckoo? A *potoo*? Most unhawk-like behaviour! Why did the FARC not give up being naughty and run ornithological holidays? Get money by working not stealing!

CHAPTER 53

Negotiations get sticky

I F I THOUGHT ABOUT IT, which I did not, I should have felt that I was managing well enough. I had never lost hope that my family would find a solution. The worry that I should become a political hostage, because of the Blair/Bush firm stance against terrorism, never went away, and I could not discuss it with my fellows at all but it was not a big worry. I was saved the horrors of the prisoners in Beirut of a decade ago or in Baghdad today. I could last a few years here, if I did not fall ill or lose interest in birds and insects. I could read my books another five times, slowly, or translate them in my mind into Spanish or Latin. I don't think I could play much more chess, without a brainstorm. It was a blessing that I had company, even though we were so different. The company of a woman could be complicated but Pati was a good sort. How she managed the fear of being taken away as a political prisoner, I don't know. She did not weep. She knew that we had a better chance. Her children must have been in her mind all the time. Brutus was impossible to talk sensibly to, so it had to be chess. We were of course like animals in a zoo, to the guerrilla, whose eyes we could never be hidden from.

Relations between Pati and Brutus were at a low point. He was as far as he could from us. He switched on his radio early in the morning and turned down the volume, so that we could not hear the news. The Little Prince came several times to berate him.

'*No seas hijo de puta.* Don't be a bastard. I shall take the radio away. Let your companions hear the news. Don't play *hijo de puta musica* all the time. The radio is for the news.'

'He pees all around the *chonto* and makes a mess,' complained Pati. 'He does the other thing and does not throw earth over it. It stinks. He is a pig.'

Brutus would bathe in the rain, but cavort naked in full view. Was that the way that a macho treated women? Or was it aimed at her?

'He thinks he is here only because they have not let me go,' Pati said. The old story. The economic prisoners cannot go until the political have been released. 'He hates me.'

He was not keen on me. He had stopped even asking to play chess. He made a private path to the *chontos*. When we walked, he stayed in his *caleta*. When he walked, we stayed in. I called 'Good morning' first thing and he did not answer. Pati and I ate together and he stayed alone. We had so little in common anyway and the long imprisonment was getting us all down. Why did she not go? What did they want with me? Could his women raise any money for him? It was ages since Grandpa had gone. The relations between the government and the FARC were zero, only insults. There was more warfare and danger of getting caught up in it.

Jaime came with fresh clothes, all camouflage, and new towels. This was depressing.

For the family in Bogotá, it was a bad period too. The New Year had started and the demand was ridiculously high. Padré Rodrigo was getting worn out. What to do?

I would wake up before dawn and find my way to the *chontos*, sometimes losing my way in the pitch blackness. It would be about half past four in the morning and we had been in bed for too long. The bed was hard on the hips. Back in the *caleta*, I waited for morning sounds from the camp and, with luck, a morning coffee. I got up and stood up. The dawn started in the east, long before the sun itself was visible.

I thought often of the Odyssey, and of the years in college in Oxford, reading the classical texts. Odysseus, the great wanderer.

'*Imos d'erigeneia fani rhododactulos Eos.*'

'When early rising Dawn appeared with its rosy fingers . . .'

Odysseus and his sailors must have slept on the ground, wrapped in sheep skins. They rose, dirty, with matted and greasy hair. No soap to wash with? Just what they could get from plants. What food could they have carried? Dry grain. Just a sharp sword or a spear or a bow and arrows. What did they do for illness or a toothache? What indeed would we do for that?

The *araguatos* might start their howling, or the *titis* charge over the treetops. Birds would fly over. We would be brought a coffee, with luck. Time to brush teeth. '*Buenos dias*, Pati. *Buenos dias, hombre*,' to Brutus. His radio would come on.

One day, the news was that a small plane had been brought down, coming in to land at a military strip to the south of where we were. It contained employees of a company, contracted by the US government, to monitor fumigation of drug crops. A 'spy plane'? The army was rushing out to find it before the FARC got to it. The Reindeer would bring his receiver set, so that I could translate the English broadcasts, if there were. Once I heard a US voice saying 'Moving from sector 154 to sector 163, roger?' Well, it might have been a pilot of any nationality, including Colombian, trained in the USA, using American English as a lingua franca.

Then the news was that two bodies had been found in the plane, one Colombian and one American, with bullet wounds.

'We don't kill people,' said Hanibal. 'If they had fired at us, then we should shoot at them.'

The other three Americans had disappeared. 'Hey, perhaps you will meet your gringo friends,' joked Hanibal. The Army must have been urgently seeking them.

I imagined them walking up the jungle paths, as we had. Maybe injured from the crash. Or dead?

No, they were alive and were valuable prisoners for the FARC. We heard on the radio that Tirofijo had decided to have them as political prisoners, for exchange. On 21 February, the FARC issued a communiqué. 'The general secretariat of the FARC-EP states that the life and physical well-being of the three gringo officials in our hands can only be guaranteed if the Colombian Army immediately suspends its military operations, and the overflights, in the area between Santana de la Hermosas, San Antonio de Atenas, San Pacho, San Guillermo, Ano Nuevo, La Esperanza, el Para and Norcasia.'

On 2 March, a further communiqué was issued 'from the mountains of Colombia', the famous address with fifty years of pedigree. 'The three gringo prisoners of war in our hands will be released, together with the prisoners of war of the Colombian State, once the exchange is carried out in an ample demilitarised area, between the government of Uribe Velez and the FARC-EP. To sign an agreement and release all of the prisoners of war on each side, it may be agreed that authorised representatives of some governments and personalities be present . . . The causes and consequences of our country's internal conflict will be resolved between Colombians.'

Well, yes, but a headache for George W. Bush and for the Southern Command of the US Army.

CHAPTER 54

Further into the forest

WHEN WE ASKED DIRTY DOG IF WE could get home easily from the 'palm court', he had always said 'yes', but he began to say 'The roads are blocked.'
'Is there a long way round?' asked Pati. Could we go east to the Sierra de la Macarena and then north? Could we go up the hills to the west?
'You might have to go all the way back,' said Hernan.
'Oh God, we would never make it. All that way uphill,' we groaned. And indeed the prospect was frightening. Had the Army really advanced and blocked the roads? Why were we stuck and not going home?

The radio broadcasts for the victims had become pessimistic and sad, after the end-of-year broadcast. Ingrid's mother was not heard. But the *guerrilleros* were saying that many people had gone home before Christmas. There had been other people not far from us. Laureano's family spoke to him regularly to keep up his spirit.

The Air Force overflew a lot. But we did not hear bombs. Polo and Jonhatan walked to the old camp by the river to bring back food. Was the road in from the north closed by the Army? The Army should be running a strategy of strangling the lines of supply. Were they? When the two of them came back, we found out that the old camp had been bombed. We had escaped in time.

It was ruled that no smoke could be let rise into the sky. Maybe gas canisters were running out. It was decided (by order from the big bosses nearby) that underground ovens be built. This is a mud chamber with an escape channel underground and coming out far away. The smoke was distributed over a large area and became invisible. Otherwise the pots were cooked on the top like any stove. We may have been near to a road. The Air Force probably followed the rivers and the roads to look for entries into the forest and signs of traffic.

One day the *guerrilleros* went en masse into the forest, carrying things. It was depressing to think that we were not going home but deeper in to the forest. The next day, we packed up and marched, back along the path we had come by, then right into the forest. Luckily it was not too far, but the forest was thick. We stopped at the top of a slope and made a camp. The ground was uneven and full of roots and stumps. There were ants everywhere. We slept on the ground. When I got up, I picked up the sleeping bag and underneath it was covered in termite columns, heaving masses. I made a little path to walk on and found a *cattleya* orchid on a fallen branch. It was a rare occurrence to find orchids. Should I rescue it and

261

take it home to Nanette? If I had to spend a long time more as a prisoner, it would die. I left it and there it is.

The camp of the guerrilla was lower down and by a stream. We only spent one night on the ground with the termites. They made us a camp further down, and built three good *caletas*. We swept the ground clear around. Termites crept along all the branches of the trees and aimed at the *caletas*, along the guy ropes. We were fed up with the new move and the worsening of the conditions. I told Hanibal to go back and collect more *cariaño* sap for our leishmaniasis.

The aeroplanes flew over but went on past and did not see us in the thick forest. There was at least running water nearby, in theory. The summer meant that the water had dried up. There were just brown-coloured pools. The water had to be scooped out in buckets and put into a big plastic barrel.

'Very healthy clean water,' said Jaime. 'You can drink it.' It was brown, and green weeds grew around the pools. We had to bathe with it and the towels turned brown AFTER we had washed with it. Lack of water is no good for forest people, but it was better than the fetid wells of the previous camp.

Now there was no pretence that we had no company. Across this stream, we could hear the voices of other prisoners. A visitor came to see us and said without thinking, 'Where is the other *muchacho*?' Was it Laureano?

It was my sixtieth birthday. I did not say anything to anyone. I should have been giving a jolly party at home but I was in the forest. In the afternoon, Jaime came up to our *condominio*, with a messenger, whom I had not seen before. He stood by my *caleta*.

'Write a letter to your family,' he said.

'Give me paper and a pen,' I said. 'Dear everyone. This is the wrong place to spend my 60th birthday (this pinpointed the date and that it was me), but enough is enough and I hope to see you soon (this was more or less what I could deduce from the guerrilla's remarks). I am well. (I can stick it out.) Much love to all.'

At least, there was no insistence on mentioning money. On the rule that it is not what is said, but what is not said that matters, maybe the money was resolved?

The messenger went off. The FARC was off radio and on messengers with forked sticks. The letter would go to the big camp and be approved by a big boss and carried by road transport to Bogotá, I supposed. In fact, I learned later that it was never delivered.

I felt that I might get out. I calmed my excitement. Keep your emotions on a level keel. I imagined being driven on a road which led to the city. I asked Hanibal, 'Do I get my identity document back to go home?'

'Of course, Meester. You get all your things back. What did you keep when you were taken?'

'Absolutely nothing,' I replied.

One morning La India was on sentry duty. I approached her. She never spoke unless spoken to.

'*Ola, Buenos dias*,' I warbled.

'*Buenos dias*, Mister,' she replied. So far, so good.

'Do you remember when I came in, the first day?'

'Ah, si, I remember,' she seemed to be on the edge of becoming voluble. 'That was above Sibate.'

For the first time, I had a clue about where I had been taken on the night of 1 May last year. If you drive south and west out of Bogotá, on the road to Cali, before the toll on the main road west, where the road plunges down to the Magdalena river, there is a fork to the left. It goes to the village of Sibate, famous for its mental hospital. Then it goes over the edge of the Sabana, down the 'old road' to Fusagasuga and the river, the stamping ground of Grandpa. It has a fearsome reputation for hold-ups and bandits. So we had taken that fork and then turned left and south to climb the hills. The lights I had seen were those of the Autopista del Sur. But hang on! How did I cross the Autopista, when I went into the Sumapaz. So I was south of the Autopista? I was above Usme? I am still confused.

'I wanted to ask you if, when I leave, I get back my documents?'

'Don't you have them?'

'No, you chaps took everything?'

'Oh.'

'That *comandante*, when he handed me over to the next guerrilla, did he give them my things? Could they have got here?'

'I don't know. It could be a bit difficult to find out.'

'Why?'

'After you left, on 20 May, the Army caught up with us. You remember that black girl?'

'No, I don't.'

'Well, she and I are the only ones alive now. The rest were killed.'

'Christ. The *comandante*?'

'Yes.'

'The two *negros*?'

'Yes.'

'You mean they are all dead?'

'Yes. They sent me and the *negra* ahead and stayed to fight it out. We went back the next day and saw the bodies.'

'So, my documents? Not much chance of finding them?'

'Not much.'

I thought about the chance of the Army finding my papers. In fact they did not, as I could deduce afterwards. So all those young *guerrilleros* were dead, uselessly gone in their youth. The Army had proved itself effective. It was so near to Bogotá. It was difficult to prolong the conversation. Amazing that the silent girl had said so much. It must have affected her. She wandered off.

Meanwhile, the family was in a pickle and worrying. They spoke to Pati's daughter, who said that her aunt had said to Andres that the family had done what was agreed and had paid, so he must release Pati. The bastard replied, 'We can think about it.'

The Padré talked to Andres. He did not say much.

'These bastards play so dirty,' complained Nanette in an email to Victoria. She had become involved in raising money for the Padré's Foundation to run schools for poor children and was organising a golf tournament and seeing how our friends abroad could make donations.

Father Antonio, an assistant to the Padré, was in La Julia, sitting it out and talking to William, said to be the boss of the awful Andres. Antonio had asked for the letter of proof of existence. William was asking for less money but still a huge, impossible amount. He had said several times that if it was not paid by the end of February, it would go up.

Victoria asked the experts why the journalists had been released by the ELN after only eleven days. Had we done it all wrong? No, we had not. The ELN is conscious of their ideological position and political image. They would hope that the press would speak well of them in the US and European media. No fools, there are many left-wing thinkers ready to believe in their cause. The FARC is another kettle of fish, and the game is pay or die. To hell with image! We had to stick it out and be tough. There is no more money. Repeat the mantra.

What if we were taken for two payments?

El Tiempo newspaper reported on 30 January that the Army had liberated six victims in the Ariare area of Meta. Was I in Meta? Yes. The embassy said that they were all Colombians.

Andres was also speaking to the Padré, which was creating confusion. William seemed more reliable. Andres was a crook. Andres had seen the Padré near Villavicencio before, but now said that he was 'much further away'. Was the Army closing in? Yes.

On 13 February, the committee had talked of 'if' the military bombed the FARC and we were used as human shields. They did not know that we were being bombed. The situation was not good. There were plenty of tears, and large rum and cokes to warm the cockles of the heart, a specialty of the committee.

Antonio had his neck in the noose. He was in a village where the comandantes of the guerrilla wandered around like Peter in his house (as one says in Spanish). He was standing up to William. The church was carrying out its religious duties. The school next door was teaching its children. The shops were selling their food and household goods. The bars were blaring music and selling beer at night. The

Army was nowhere near. The big tropical sky glittered with stars and the river below flowed south into the forest, where the FARC was hidden.

He rang the Padré when the telephones worked. The reduction was insufficient. A time limit was being put on us by William. What the hell was Andres doing, in another part of the country, interfering? Who was in charge?

Why was Pati not released? A brainwave came to the Padré. He told Antonio to tell William, 'We are fed up. We can't trust you. How can we talk of the Meester if you don't release la señora? You are liars.'

The mousetrap sprang.

'OK, we shall release la señora. Tomorrow.'

CHAPTER 55

The last camp

I T WAS THE LAST SUNDAY IN February and the second day in the new camp. Pati was changing the planks in her *caleta*, to make it more comfortable. We were sweeping the jungle floor. Jaime walked in and told Pati that she was wanted down in the guerrilla camp. There was electricity in the air immediately.

'You're going home,' pronounced Brutus decidedly, with his usually sharp instinct for the way the guerrilla worked.

She walked out of the *condominio*. Brutus was happy. His theory was that she was the cause of us being kept so long.

'It's good that that *vieja h.p.* is going. She is responsible for me not going home. Now we shall see.'

After a while, Pati appeared. She looked anxiously about. She picked up a few things from her bed and said, 'Where is my cap? Where is my cap?'

She came over to my bed and scrabbled around. She put her head next to mine and whisperered, '*Te vas en una semana*. You are going in a week.' Then she left and waved and was gone. Later in Bogotá, she told me that she had been told to go home and asked, 'What about el Meester?'

The Reindeer said 'Don't worry. He will be out in a week.' So she did the friendly thing for me and thought how to get back up to tell me. What a chum.

Now it was el Meester and Brutus, the two of us. Ugh. But better than Brutus and Pati, an impossible and dangerous mixture. He switched up his radio *fullo blasto* to *vallenato* music.

'We are better without that old bag,' he opined.

Well, good for her, thank heavens. But I could have thought of a better partner.

'Let's play chess, eh, Meester?'

'My dear fellow, what a pleasure. Set it up.'

I was reminded of the Evelyn Waugh novel *A Handful of Dust*, where Last, the Englishman, living up the Amazon in an indian village, has to read stories every day to the chief, Mr Todd. One day his friends arrive in a boat to find him but he is given a sleeping draught and wakes up the next day to be told that his friends had come and gone. 'Now read that story again!' asked Mr Todd. Not really, because the likelihood of the end being near was much more real. But how could I really know? Not at all.

Behind the *caleta*s was thick forest, with tall trees. If you walked forward too far and turned round, you had no clue where you were and had problems returning to the *caletas*. So I made clear paths with my feet, and developed a technique of noticing a certain tree each fifty paces and retracing my steps to each marker tree. From the *chonto*, a wide ant trail went into the forest and under a fallen tree. There were millions of red ants. Some days we could put up a pair of Great Tinamou birds scurrying along the forest floor. The *choyo* monkeys would pass during the day, and this was the backyard for Pipo the Pig.

I was sitting in my *caleta* rereading *Middlemarch*, when there was a high-pitched scream. Brutus came into sight at full speed. Behind him Pipo was doing the hundred metres like Linford Christie. Brutus caught his foot in a root and crashed to the (soft) earth, leaped up, and climbed a tree without one boot.

'Leave the little bugger alone, can't you?'

'I like to throw thing at the little *hijo de puta*. He does not like me.'

'For someone born in the country, you know damn all about animals.'

'*Callese*, Meester. Shut up. Play some chess?'

'Right.'

And we set it up in the middle *caleta*, left empty by Pati's departure.

'I bet you miss her, eh? Just me to get on with.'

Difficult to disagree with that.

'Hey, look at this. Come.' He pulled out from a bush a coil of liana.

'This is the noose for when I hang myself.' He meant it. 'If I am left here, I shall kill myself.'

'Shut up. Don't be pathetic. Of course you'll get out. You'll be home before me. They know you don't have much money and are a simple chap like them. Why do you say such tripe?'

In fact he had the radio on all day, playing *vallenatos*, and the annoying presence of the Woman had been removed. He was talkative, even cheerful.

Jaime and Dog liked to go out hunting at night. They explained that at night you can hear the big herds of peccary crashing through the dry leaves. It had not rained for ages. It was a dry summer. The trick with the dangerous peccary is to let them all pass, while you stand still, and shoot the last one. One evening, I was going to bed, when they arrived in an excited hurry and dropped a heavy object on the ground.

'Meester, meester, look.'

It was a *tigre*, a golden and black striped large cat, not as big as a jaguar, but not small. It was alive, and had been shot in the jaw, which opened slack and smashed. It was in shock. A thing of beauty.

'Why did you shoot it? You can't eat it.'

'Yes, it was a mistake. We were standing there silent, and it came into the clearing. I just shot at it,' said Jaime.

'What will you do with it? Sell the skin?' In the past, there had been a market for tiger skins. Perhaps there still is, but it is illegal.

'No, we'll let it go.' They took it away.

'Thanks for showing it.' They knew that I should be fascinated.

Hanibal would come in and look at me. He showed that he knew that I was on the way out, but could not say so. The Prince and Dog disappeared for three days, but came back. They had probably been out on advance guard, scouting for the Army, to see if the exit were clear.

Hanibal was chatty.

'Once I was looking after a foreigner, with whiter hair even than you . . .'

I have dark brown hair – but to Colombians we are all blondes (*monos*). Joke: 'What were the first words that Columbus heard when he arrived in America?' Answer 'Can I keep an eye on your boat, blondie?' (*Te cuido el barco, mono?*).

'What nationality was he, Hanibal?'

'I don't remember.'

'What language did he speak?'

'Not Spanish. But I can't remember.'

'Well, where did he come from? Sweden? Holland? Europe? Asia? China?'

'I can't remember. But he was taller than you and blonder.'

'Was he Japanese?'

'Maybe . . .'

'Just joking, *viejo*,' I laughed.

'We took him and it was a problem. He had no family here, apart from one brother, but the brother had been kidnapped already, in another part. They had a business together. He did not speak much Spanish, and there was no one to speak to. We had to get messages to his family in his country. It took over two years to negotiate. He cut off the bottoms of his trousers and made shorts, and went around without a shirt on or shoes. He liked to accompany us on hunting trips. He was left on his own and we let him come and live with us in the camp. He was a good cook. You know that when we told him that he could go home, he said that he did not want to. Could he stay? Well, that's against the rules, so we told him he had to go. But he was happy in the forest, all alone. He did not speak to us much. We had to take him to a road and send him home.'

Difficult to say whether Hanibal was a compulsive tale-teller and romancer. It sounded like a total pack of lies.

But when he came again and said, 'Eh Meester, when you go back, live in the country, and not in the city. It will be safer. Take my word for it. We shall take the war to the cities, you will see,' then I listened. They had, after all, done the Club El Nogal massacre.

It is not easy to protect the cities, anywhere! A year later, I was in Spain when the Madrid train bombing happened and 190 'innocent' Spaniards were murdered by a cellphone-activated chain explosion, like the attack on President Uribe on 7 August 2002 in Bogotá.

The Air Force flew over every night, the Pigs, quartering the skies. The captured Americans were not far away, but the forest was very thick here. The *guerrilleros* hinted that we would have to move deeper into the forest. Not a happy idea.

'Why don't you just release me to the Red Cross?' I asked Hanibal. 'They can get me home, if the Army had blocked the roads out.'

'Oh, no. We have thought of that. But the *Secretariado* has forbidden that. It makes too much scandal (*agranda el asunto demasiado*).'

So having an international fuss about me, in the papers and with the NGOs, was bad for the image of the FARC. Ha ha! How cynical. Just a quiet robbery and keep the image of a people's political movement? Or kill me and bury me under a tree in the forest, in an unknown grave? It would not be the first time.

CHAPTER 56

How to pay

Pati had gone home by bus from La Julia. She slept in a hut where the bus crews slept and had to borrow money from a shopkeeper to pay the bus fare. She promised to send the money from Bogotá. When she arrived at her home to the joy and surprise of her children and sisters and mother, her daughter telephoned Nanette. Nanette had been in hospital for an operation for a cyst on an ovary. At such a moment, it had blown up. Pati was having a check-up at a hospital. The next day, they could meet. But the next day, Nanette's condition went wrong and she had to be readmitted for a follow-up operation. She sat in the admission area. A nurse came up and asked who she was and she started to cry.

'Are you with anyone? Is your husband here?'

'No, I am alone.' And the tears fell. The nurse put her in a wheel chair and pushed her into the emergency room. Nanette's doctor, Manuel, entered and saw her distress.

'What's the matter?'

'I am all alone,' she blubbed.

'Don't worry. I shall look after you,' he comforted her, whipping out a large knife. Or was it a stethoscope?

Nanette was put on a drip and patched up and the next day when she was recovering, Pati's daughter rang again and said that her mother wanted to see Nanette and had a message from me. So Nanette called the doctor and insisted on going home, despite her pains. He understood and gave her painkillers. Our loyal friend Susan drove her to the flat in her car, where the committee was called to come and hear Pati at nine at night. The committee members came on time and Pati was late as she did not know the way. This made everyone anxious. My situation was still in the air and the committee was highly nervous.

'You don't look too bad for someone who has been in captivity for nine months!' joked the Padré.

She smiled and sat down awkwardly. Ana gave her an orange juice. The questions flowed. She told them about the day she left and her worry about wearing the rubber boots, which could be her death warrant if the Army thought she was a *guerrillera*. But she was lent shoes in La Julia, where she got the bus. She said that I wanted to go home and it was the right time for the family to negotiate, as the FARC wanted to let me go.

270

This was an electric shock for the committee. They all felt that it was time to strike a bargain and get me out. But the risk of paying and then being made to pay twice was still there.

'What to do so that they let him out and don't cheat us? We have got the woman out. Now what?'

'What if we agree to pay what we said NOW and the extra we pay when he is back here? We end up paying much more than we can afford, but he comes out alive. If we don't, we may lose the chance and God knows what will happen. Does he mean it that he wants to go home?'

'He is all right,' said Pati. 'He is a strong man. But he has leishmaniasis.'

'The most important thing is not to lose the chance. If they do want to let him go, we must not cock it up.'

So the Padré made a telephone call and sent his colleague Antonio down to the llanos to meet William. It worked. William bought the deal. For the first time the figure was down from the impossibly stratospheric and became merely outrageously huge. But everyone had to move fast.

'He will be out in a week,' William had said.

Pati felt that the guerrilla had expected more. The Americans had been taken, upping the stakes in the kidnapping game. The guerrilla started to refuse to meet families, much less hand over victims, in Villavicencio. It had to be done down in the forest.

John met a secretive man in a hotel near the Parque 93. 'It is unusual for the handover to be so difficult and so far away,' he said, after opening the door and squinting down the corridor. 'But it always turns out all right. Don't worry.'

As John turned into the corridor, a phrase followed him from this wise man. 'Don't worry, you'll be all right. You're British.'

So Sandy Arbuthnot and Richard Hannay comforted themselves in the face of the dastardly enemy in 1916. 'My name is Bond, James ... Bond.' Thanks a bundle. But well meant and quite right.

Now that William had agreed on the money, the first instalment had to be got together. Andres was coming and going, but we had a deal with William. Andres was a total bastard. He had asked for mobile phones and radios and binoculars and once even for 'a woman'. Antonio had been in La Julia. He had seen them face to face. William was good for his word. Andres was out of the picture.

John's view was and is that the first half of the ransom went to the FARC and the rest was pocketed by the negotiators.

How did the team arrive at so bizarre a deal, with such untrustworthy people? It had to be a win-win deal. Everyone does better than they thought and everyone feels that the time is right and nothing will be gained by delaying. But would I be delivered alive?

Antonio came back to town. The money was in Europe. The guerrilla wanted to see Antonio with the money on the Friday in La Julia. I would be released the same day.

'Don't forget,' said Antonio. 'The *muchachos* are so ignorant, that they have to count all the money, and they are not good at counting. It takes ages.'

The committee thought. 'Nine hundred and ninety-seven. Nine hundred and ninety-eight. Nine hundred and ninety er ... er ... er ... er ... Oops. Start again. One. Two. Three ...'

Father Rodrigo reacted differently. He was furious. 'You gave them a day and a time for the handover of the money? Are you crazy?'

He told Antonio to cancel it all. What if a band of the boys took the initiative to go and hold up the car and nick the ransom? I would be left in the forest and the money would have gone.

Antonio felt sick in the stomach. If he cancelled the deal, the FARC could kill him. He told the committee. Go on or not. A solution was reached that the first car would go for the scheduled meeting, without the money. The message was passed. A second car would go, unannounced, with money later. There is only one road to La Julia.

So the bank in Europe had to be told. Lend us the money and wing it in dollars through the US correspondent bank to the Colombian bank, broken into small amounts in different names. This has to be the most tricky route in the world, watched by the US Department of Justice for possible money laundering, and subject to an exchange control registration when it arrives in Colombia for the same reason – and the money going to criminals to save an innocent life.

On the third day, the bank in Bogotá rang. The money had come. There would be a truck. It would take down a nurse and pick up some sick children to be put into a home in Bogotá. The next day the truck was ready and, after dark, it was driven into the underground parking of the bank. The cash was brought down from the strong room in black plastic bags and piled into the back, which drove on to the street, and nervously to the church, where the big gates were closed. What to do with the money for the journey through the countryside? Sometimes it is put into the spare tyre or behind the back seat or hidden in the clothes of the passengers.

John noticed a panel which was fixed by rivets, above the front seats. If it could be opened and riveted again, it would be safe from roadside checkpoints. Where could it be done, at this hour? One of the committee thought of a repair garage in the 7 de Agosto *barrio*, full of workshops. But the money had to be broken down into parcels. A heap of plastic bags had been bought before and into these the team stuffed the money, like filling sausage skins.

'Stop,' said Nanette. 'Let me look at this a minute. I shall never see so much cash again in my life.' Her eyes goggled. Goodbye, all our savings.

The truck was driven out in the dark and to the workshop. They agreed to drill out the rivets and remove the panels. While the mechanics went away into a corner, the bags were stuffed into the space. They fitted. The panel was slotted back on and the mechanics came back to rivet them in. A lick of paint and the hiding place was not visible. Who knew? Antonio, who was not going on the first trip, and the driver, a young novice priest. The nurse would not know. The truck was driven back to the church. The journey had to start.

'Oh hell,' thought John. ' How do they open it up the other end? We shall have to buy a hand-held drill and a rivet gun to seal it up afterwards. Where can we go?'

It was after nine o'clock. The team drove a car to Carrefour hypermarket at full speed. It was open late. They found the tools and rushed back. The truck set off. It could only get to Villavicencio, because there was a curfew on the roads south. The team went to bed, unable to sleep well, for nerves. At one thirty the telephone rang and Nanette answered it.

'Alo, señora Nanette? We arrived in Villavo.'

'Hurrah.'

'But we have a problem. Where are we supposed to go?'

'Oh my God,' she shuffled among her papers by the bed. 'I forgot to give you the map. Just go south to La Julia, through Granada. And go to the church.'

In the nervous rush, the vital instructions had not been given to them. The next day, Friday, they were supposed to arrive in La Julia, meet William the *guerrillero*, hand over the money, and pick me up. The family stayed at home, biting their nails. The telephone did not ring. Sleep did not come easily.

On Saturday, the long silence was dragged out. The money was out there. No news of me. In the evening the telephone rang. It was Antonio. There had been no line. La Julia is a place which is not connected to the main electricity. There is a generator, which comes on at seven in the evening and is switched off at 11 at night, enough to power the juke boxes at the local taverns, which blare into the dark, to accompany the beer drinking. The reception for mobile telephones varies a lot.

'Yes, they took the money. They spent all yesterday and today counting it. No, no news of Don David.'

The worst possible situation!

CHAPTER 57

I walk to freedom

IT WAS BEFORE DAWN ON SUNDAY 3 March. The Brute was in bed. The Reindeer came to the *condominio* and looked at me, and went away without a word. I brushed my teeth and dressed and stood watching the dawn come up. Someone walked up. It was Jaime, no coffee in hand.

'Come down to the camp.' A minute later, I was among them as they were getting up.

'You are going home,' said Jaime. So this was it.

'What about breakfast?'

'Have breakfast and go. You have to get to the river. Tonight you will be with your family.'

'Can I go and get my things?'

'What do you need? You are going.'

I packed my backpack with my two books, a towel, my civilian clothes, my raincape.

The Brute was getting up. 'Are you going?' he said.

'I suppose so.'

A silence. I could not take messages, nor help him. He was the last one left. Had his hopes risen, or was he thinking of his noose to end his life? I don't think so. Is he alive and out in the world of free men?

I went down to the camp. 'Who is taking me?' I asked.

'I am,' said *el paisa* Adriano, and the new young man, Carlos, grinned and seemed to be the other. Two girls were doing the *cocina*. Hanibal was cutting up the pig. '*Venga*, meester, eat.' And I had a pan of rice and pork crackling and a jar of chocolate.

'When you get home, you won't tell the aircraft to come and bomb us, will you? Eh? We know where you are.'

'Well, I don't know where you are, do I?'

'*Adios.* Remember us. And think well of us, eh?'

'Hurry up,' said Adriano. 'We have got to get to the river, and we have a seven-hour walk.'

So we were going to walk in one day what had taken us six days to do on the way here. We left at eight o'clock, Carlos ahead, then me, and Adriano behind – my last march. But I felt too cautious to be exhilarated. I climbed the path and turned to look back. There was the camp and the *guerrilleros*, moving around. A squalid place. Misguided people lost in the forest.

274

I marched on, with Adriano close behind. I did my best. 'Hurry up. We must get to the river, or the canoe will go without us. If we miss it, we shall have to come back and God knows when you will go home.'

That was a good argument to go as fast as I could. Home. Could it be? We stopped for a drink and biscuits and, and marvellous, a sausage. It tasted of horse. I remembered how the horses in the area of my farm got stolen for meat for sausages. Well, beggars can't be choosers. I wanted to keep going. 'Wait a bit,' said the two *guerrilleros*. On we went. The path had been cleared by slashing, since we had come this way.

Across the path strutted a pair of huge birds. They were large curassows (*paujuiles*), leisurely and unfrightened. I pointed them out.

'Stop here.'

Adriano and the young chap unslung their rifles and crept forward. The birds walked into the forest and I watched one hop over a fallen tree. The *guerrilleros* hunted them, but they did not see them. I could. This went on for twenty minutes, until they admitted defeat. What a meal that would have made. Several times we saw the rootling grounds of herds of peccaries. The woods were full of them. But that was nocturnal hunting.

'This is a highway,' joked Adriano. 'Get a move on, Meester. We are late.' Indeed, he had started over an hour later than he had said in the camp. After a while the path split. It was where we had got lost before. On the left it went down to a clearing, on the right into the forest. We found the way and had to wade a stream and the way started to get more up and down. I slowed down on the steep climbs.

'Come on, Meester. If we don't go faster, I shall have to take you back.' At the top of one climb, before the place where we had slept on the way here, I had to stop and sit down.

'Hurry up, Meester.'

'Let me rest.'

'We are late. If you can't go on, I shall have to take you back.'

Despite the impossibility of contemplating not going home, I could not even stand up. My body was on strike, a strange feeling that I had never had in my life. Total weakness.

'Adriano, pull me up.'

He heaved me up. I balanced. I could not move one leg before the other. My brain did not send messages to my legs. Oh God. I took out a piece of *panela* and sucked it. I had a swallow of water. One step, yes. Another. The body returned to action. Was it the *panela*, or the rest? It was a very slow progress. Adriano complained desperately.

'It's not my fault. Ten months of prison. I am weak.'

'If we don't make the rendezvous, you will have to go back.'

'No, I am going home.'

The other man had gone ahead. I staggered on. We were getting to the open field that I remembered. Then the other man appeared leading a mare. I was pushed on to its back. Marvellous. The branches were low. I ducked, but one branch caught me and swept me off the saddle and crashing to the ground. Thorns had pierced my skin on my broken arm and blood gushed out but I climbed back on the saddle. Soon we were on the path again and going past our campsite. The T-junction appeared and we turned left and crossed the stream and stopped. I slumped on a tree trunk.

'Wait here. We shall get water. Don't move.' The big river, the Duda, flowed in front of me. They went to the farm to find the boatman (*barquero*) and came back with sugar-water and biscuits. I relaxed. The boatman had not gone. In fact he was lunching. So, after a while, the canoe appeared, with the boatman and his deputy. I got in. The boatman had been frying fish and he offered me fish and rice. He started the Yamaha outboard motor and we moved up the river, seeing the same panorama of birds and alligators. The canoe touched bottom often and the *guerrilleros* jumped out and pushed.

We saw a bunch of women washing dishes on the left bank and we pulled in. A *guerrillero* walked down from above and called out. He jumped in. I recognised him.

'Going home? You will speak well of us, eh? We treated you well? When you go on television, tell them about us.'

I was on the way home now. The sun sank in the west to the tree level. Skeins of ibis flew over. Parrots rocketed over. We pulled over to the bank again. There was a hut and some women and a few men. Adriano got out and then came down with a *guerrillero*, carrying between them a heavy sack. They heaved it into the canoe, then repeated the trip. The sacks showed a number of strange heavy objects like small metal milk churns with handles, the colour of lead. They were offloaded further up the river, as the night fell, not before I had realised that they were mines. Months later I saw them in a photograph in a newspaper. The weight must have been not just the explosive, but the metal ball-bearings or whatever is the anti-personnel munition they use. I suppose that the mines were to be sown where the Army might tread as it advanced, especially around the FARC camps.

Just before dark and after the mines operation we came into the left bank and ran the canoe on to the muddy bank.

'This is where the journey ends, Meester. Change your clothes here. Have a bathe in the river.'

So I opened my backpack and fished out what was left of the clothes that I was wearing at dinner with my friends on 1 May 2002 in Bogotá — a pair of gabardine trousers, my cotton shirt, my filthy grey sweater. The jacket had been eaten by the Pig. The shoes had gone the first day. The socks had lost themselves. I did not swim in the river. I left any camouflage gear and my towel. I had to wear the welly boots.

There was a *tienda* – a country store and bar – with horses tied up outside, and a few jeeps, so a road must end here. A long pole flew a white flag, which I had been told was a sign to the Air Force not to bomb the folks. A four-by-four Nissan with a shattered windscreen drove past the store and up to us by the river.

'*Adios*, Meester.'

It was the farewell. I got in the cab, next to the driver, a civilian farmer. A normal Colombian? Or a guerrilla sympathiser? The *guerrilleros* got in the back. I started to talk to the driver. He said that farmers made no money. The government allowed the import of dumped agricultural commodities, ruining the farmers. The cost of transporting plantains to the markets made them uncompetitive, and so on. I was back in the real world! The night had fallen and he switched on his lights. I was travelling in a car. The countryside, with barbed wire fences and cattle fields, flashed past. It took more than an hour to get from the river, but finally the lights of a town appeared – a dirty high street, houses, bars, electric light (exciting for me to see electricity!) and music blaring. The jeep stopped. What do I do? The driver indicated a church with a grass lawn in front.

'Go through that gate and walk into the church. They are waiting for you.'

'*Gracias. Adios.*'

I walked slowly across the grass and stopped inside the church. It was full of women and some children. Mass was being celebrated, with bright lights and church music. At the altar were two priests and two monks in brown habits. A bearded dirty figure with a walking stick sat down in a pew and waited. It was I. This was a moment of transition. There was a pause in the mass and a priest walked down the aisle and came to me.

'It is you? David? We were expecting you days ago.' And he gave me a huge embracing hug. '*Gracias a Dios.* You are welcome, David.' Tears came to my eyes and the anxiety of these long months slid away.

One of the priests led me to the rectory where they lived. There was a sister in the kitchen. She came and embraced me.

'Sit down, sit down, my dear. Have a drink of orange juice.'

It was dark. The faithful filed out of the church service. All the priests came in and embraced me in the way that Latinos have, when they express deep emotions.

'Nanette is waiting for you at home. And John.'

I did not know that Victoria was on an aeroplane from England to join them. They put a huge plate of food in front of me. Meat, rice, salad, cheese.

'Let's have a drink to celebrate. We are so relieved to see you. We have been waiting for you for two days. When did you set out?'

'This morning. I have been walking all day. I nearly could not make it. But here I am.'

'Eat up.'

'I have not had a decent meal like this since May last year.'

They opened a bottle of communion wine. It was a wonderful taste, followed by lots more wonderful taste, as the second bottle was opened.

'So I have you to thank?' It was Antonio that they signalled. Antonio was a small, smiling priest. I had never seen him, but he was my saviour. He was not a resident, but a visitor. He took great risks to drive into the far forests and bring the money. One of the smiling faces drove the truck that had come from Bogotá. I was not going immediately, but had to spend one night here. La Julia, where I was, was far from the capital.

Who were these wonderful people who knew all about me, and yet I had no idea of who they were? There was absolute badness in the world and I was now in the presence of absolute goodness.

'You are not home yet,' they warned. 'There is a long journey and lots of roadblocks.'

'I have no documents.'

'Ah. That is not good. But we have thought of a way of getting you through. Tomorrow we tell you. We start at six. Don't worry. Relax and enjoy this evening.'

We talked about my months with the FARC. They saw the guerrilla walking about in the village. There were shops and bars, the nearest ones to the guerrilla camps. The Army was not here. La Julia is a new village, not on the maps of a few years ago. It is on a bluff overlooking the Duda river. On the other side, an unsurfaced road starts and the bus leaves for the capital.

This was a political frontier zone. 'We provide the teachers at the school,' the elder priest said. 'If the State sends teachers, the guerrilla kills them. They cannot accept anything from the State.' The church had won some sort of confidence from the rebels, the same rebels who killed many priests each year, and the Bishop of Cali, and had tried to kidnap a monsignor.

We talked about the *guerrilleros*, who they are, their youth, their ignorance. They are a social problem for society. They seem to have no families to go back to.

'Yes, the breakdown of family life is indisputable. People don't get married in church any more. Women change partners. Children grow up without fathers. You know, we have had to change our religious language. We cannot any longer refer to 'God the Father' (*Dios el Padré*). They don't have an idea of what a father is, at least not a good idea.'

'So what do you call Him?'

'God the all-mighty.'

I remembered Adriano saying much the same. It was Peter Pan and the lost children. I started to form a theory. The essential difference of Christianity from 'gods' two thousand years before was to place 'God' in a family. The 'Son of God' was invented, as a break with the Jewish yahweh. God lived in a family, with a mother (tricky – the virgin birth was invented) and father, Joseph, and a birthplace and life on earth. This was successful. Christmas replaced the winter festival in Europe and the Nativity was the main story. A baby and mother. But human society was on a different evolution. The end of family values in the modern world had taken us back to 'God the All-mighty', the Watchmaker, and the waifs and strays of the broken family are either cared for by a good social system or drift into vagrancy. No morals, nor family values. They had been my keepers.

I slept my first night in a bed under the protection of Mother Church. The next morning was Monday. I was free. I was free! I was up before dawn and had a long cold shower. I left the beard and put on my civilian clothes, but with the underwear and shirt and socks from home that Nanette had sent me. The church was empty. My rubber boots stood in a corner, finished with. My toenails could grow again. I looked out on to the courtyard of the school next door. Pupils began to walk in. Chickens scratched in the dust. Dogs wandered around.

'Come and have breakfast,' said the sister. I sat at the table where there was coffee, bread and cheese, eggs, oranges. The priests came in, cheerful and merry. This was too good to be true.

Six o'clock came and went. We were late. One of the priests came in. 'You can't go like that. I'll get you some clothes.'

He came back with a clerical collar and grey shirt and grey trousers. In a minute, I was a bearded priest.

'You are a foreign priest, doing a project with the church here. You don't speak Spanish and you forgot to bring your passport. Don't open your mouth, if there is a roadblock. Sometimes the soldiers ask to be blessed. Do you know how to do the sign of the cross?'

'No.'

So I had a lesson. Then we got into the truck, with the nurse and a girl with measles and a mentally deficient boy, and I went home as a priest. God had the last laugh. How Brutus would have guffawed.

The truck crossed the river, splashing through the water, and went past the bus station and up the other bank and north along the terrible dirt road. We passed a few farms. I saw lots of children trudging miles and hours to school, the girls looking clean and smart in kilts and white shirts. There were some men on horses. On and on we bumped, until the turning to La Uribe, west. A filling station appeared, selling gasoline at outrageous prices – take it or leave it. There were rolling green meadows and white zebu cattle. We reached the town of Granada, and the first army roadblock. Now I was inside the real Colombia. The road turned into an asphalt highway and the noise of the tyres softened. We lunched before Villavicencio, in a motel with a swimming pool and a restaurant. I ate chicken and drank Coca-Cola. Antonio took photographs of us next to the truck. He had won. Before, I had been a name. Now the name had become this ragged man in his hands.

It became dark as we drove into the modern middle-class buildings and shopping centres of the north of Bogotá. I recognised the streets. We turned right at the Pepe Sierra, crossed the *calle novena* and headed for Usaquen. Not home? Where were we going? We pulled into a doorway and stopped. Everyone got out. I was the last. And there were my wife, my son, my best friends and colleagues. What did they see? A thin, bearded man, with a walking stick and a dazed look.

Dressed as a priest.

Epilogue

I HAD LOST SEVENTEEN KILOS WEIGHT, and my leishmaniasis had to be cured and my wrist was bent and useless, but I was alive. I went to see my doctor, which the Embassy kindly arranged, and he put me through all the tests imaginable. There was no sign of malnutrition. It was no bad thing that I had lost weight. I could do knee-bends easily, showing that my power to weight ratio was much better than before. I could fit into clothes that I wore when I was 27 years old. The psychiatrist found me able to talk coherently and prescribed me sleeping pills, knowing that my dreams would be disturbing. My toenails began to grow again, or perhaps they had never stopped.

What did I feel about being back in the real world and with my family? People asked me that in a kindly way. I had lost almost a year of my life. I should never be the same person again. You cannot forget such experiences but I just wanted to take up things where I had dropped them. The Ambassador asked if I wanted to stay at the Embassy, nice man. Did he think I might be afraid? Of course I was afraid of noises and people and strange cars and the telephone calls. I did not want to die or even be hurt again. Would I get my confidence back? There are nasty people in the world and they knew me. But how nice it was to be enveloped in the family and friends and food and a chair and a bed and a hot shower. The visitors poured in and I did not want to move, much less go out.

To my surprise, it was not easy to step back into normal life. I could not answer the telephone, or if I did once, I could not do it again for several hours. Odd! If an aeroplane flew over from the Eldorado airport, I felt frightened and wanted to creep under the bed. I walked to the bank, and had to cross a road with traffic. I could not, but stood frozen on the curb and started to weep. I looked for other pedestrians and crossed with them. When visitors came with flowers and champagne, I talked non-stop. I had to eat chocolate cake, lots of it. My brain was slowed down and confused but my stomach recognised the pleasures of chocolate and alcohol. Oh yes!

Had I grown to sympathise with my captors – the Stockholm syndrome? In Colombia, your captors are not of other races which need independence or other religions which need respect. This is not Ireland nor the Basque country nor Chechnya nor the Sudan nor the Palestine/Israel conflict. These are Colombians who cannot compete and have decided to break the law to live. Failures and the occasional communist fanatics, as you have seen in my story. They have no right

281

to run the country their way any more than anyone else, but they behave badly. That does not mean that I could not wish that society could absorb them, pay them social benefits, make their access to health and pensions easier. Is this not what Europeans have done in our own countries with our losers and misfits? But he who commits a crime must pay for it. We have to get to him before he commits the crime. Bad Boy, Hanibal, Pancake, Jaime the musician – could they not have been Good Boys? I don't believe in their 'convictions'. So is it perhaps not a war but a social problem, with a dash of good policing, so people do not 'get away with it'?

I got permission from the *Instituto Nacional de Salud* to be given the medicine Glucantime (free) to cure the leishmaniasis. It required 20 cc a day for twenty days, eighty shots of 5 cc into deep muscle. The needle was impressive. I went to the Santa Fe hospital. The nurse bared my bum and looked at the four capsules and said, 'I am not allowed to give so much all at once.'

'You've got to. The doctor ordered it. We have to nuke these parasites'

'Wait. I shall have to ask for permission.'

'Fine.'

She came back.

'Grit your teeth.'

'Owwww!'

Hours later, she said, 'Have a rest. Let it soak in.'

Then my old friend and business partner asked me to spend Easter by the seaside. The waters of the Caribbean lapped the golden beach of Santa Marta, where the Liberator Simon Bolivar retired and died, a century earlier. We swam and dozed and drank and ate paella, and guess who had to stick the needle into my gluteus maximus (bum to you)? Nanette. Her chance of revenge.

'Sorry, not the right place. I'll try again.'

'Owwww! What did I ever do to you?'

The treatment worked and all I have is a scar on my thigh. But it delayed the rebreaking and gluing together of my left wrist, as you can't muck about with bones if you have parasites and chemical warfare zooming around the body. The doctor at the *Instituto* said that he knew of an Israeli military adviser who had injected himself with the Glucantime, while in the forest. He probably ate raw snakes too. I do not aspire to such toughness.

The newspapers carried news of the death of Patricia Medina. She was a tragic case, often heard on the kidnap programmes on the radio. The ELN had her and the family had not heard for a long time. She was found dead with a water bottle in her hand. She must have despaired and run away and been caught up with. Tears came to my eyes. Her poor parents!

I was lent a book about Alexander the Great and his 334 to 330 BC campaign from Greece as far as India. I was interested in warfare, for obvious reasons. His army had been made the most effective fighting force in the world at that time. The secrets included harsh discipline and brilliant logistical organisation. With his army travelled hostages and older Macedonians who guarded them, and women. The troops carried arms, utensils, and food. They did not have servants or carts, so they became the most mobile and light force in the world. In the world of subsistence farming, they had learned to suffer real hunger in the period before harvest, and lose body weight. The staple would always have been grains, which can be stored and are light (dry). But three pounds of grain is insufficient food and leads to demoralisation and excessive rest, so Alexander negotiated (they could not well say 'no') with the inhabitants in his path the purchase of fresh food. Apart from sugar (which did not exist then? The genome of sugar is from Papua), this sounded so similar to our experience. It was not only that I had been kidnapped, but I had been held 'hostage' by a guerrilla army, and had marched and hidden with a fighting force, relying on very ancient means and skills.

Pati and her daughter came round for tea at home. She was dressed in a suit and had lipstick on and had been to the hairdresser. We were out and alive. She could eat the right food for her again. I called on her later at her office in the government building. A queue of constituents lined up to see her about their concerns, concerns that a democratically-elected representative had been elected to resolve. She had not run off abroad, but she told me that her mind was not as fast as it had been before. She forgets the names of people she has known for ages. She is slower. She has lost confidence. She sees people who betrayed her and are on the wrong side, going about freely. She has been hurt badly.

Grandpa came another day, with his daughter. 'Thanks for helping my father so much,' she said.

'Your father is tougher than the rest of us put together,' I said. He sat there with his new glasses, a new dental plate in his mouth, a hearing aid, a suit and tie. He gave us a bag of vegetables from his farm.

I saw him again a year later. He had had his lump cut out of his neck, and the biopsy showed it to be non-cancerous, but he had become deafer. We had all put on weight. He laughed a lot. But he said that for the first year after his release, bad people had walked up to his house and asked for money and threatened to kill him if he told the Army. He had had to hide in another city, but then it got better and they stopped coming.

I rang Papa Noel and went to his office. His daughters were there with their husbands. His son, of course, had been murdered some years before. The door opened and in walked Laureano. He hugged me and sat down, never letting his wife's hand go. His father came in behind him, a father who had sent messages on the radio all the time and had had to pay for his son's life. We went to Papa Noel's house for lunch, prepared by one of his daughters. His wife had died while he was in captivity. His eyes brimmed with tears when he remembered this.

A friend of ours said that he knew the Minister of the Interior. Did I want to speak to him? I made an appointment and went along to his office near the presidential palace. He said, 'This kidnapping. Either we defeat it or it will defeat us.' He listened. 'Did you have to pay?'

'What do you think?' I thought to myself, but only nodded my head. Just before we parted, he lent forward and said, 'You may like to know that the Air Force this morning bombed a camp of 800 *guerrilleros*.'

He was the one who had made so many difficulties about the exchange of prisoners, together with the president. Did they think that war was going to solve the problem? What of the lives of the prisoners and the misery of their families?

Should we tell the world press? They had agreed to shut up about me. It would have been dangerous to make a fuss. The *Daily Blah* had rung and would have offered money to run the story. So no one knew of my predicament. Good. Now I rang the BBC representative, who did a fine story and it started to be printed in the British press. At home, the interest is sentimental. What did you eat? Did they treat you well? What did you do all day? What did it feel like to be free and back home again?

No, I shall never be the same. My dreams, my fears, my body are changed and damaged. I cannot 'forget' nor distance myself from this drama, where so many die.

In June, the bodies of Pablo Helmuth Bickenbach and his wife Doris Gil Santamaria, a former beauty queen, were found murdered near the town of Villeta. They had been kidnapped in December. They had had money and lived well, but were not young any more, nor well off. They were kidnapped from their farm, in the area of influence of *Comandante* Hugo and his *Frente* 22. Apparently an army patrol had come close, without knowing and the *guerrilleros* had had to run, so they murdered the old people, to avoid being slowed down.

The governor of the province of Antioquia, Guillermo Gaviria, and his peace advisor, Gilberto Echeverry, had been taken by the FARC, near Medellin, while on a peace march, just before I had been kidnapped. They were kept with some soldiers, for political exchange, and were still there when I came out. The military found out where they were, by a river in the jungle to the east of Medellin. A request was made to the highest level to rescue them and it was approved. A number of Black Hawk helicopters, loaded with specialist troops, set off and landed an hour away from the place identified as the camp where they were held. The troops hurried through the jungle. It was 5 May 2003. When they arrived at the *caletas*, they found Guillermo and Gilberto murdered, plus all the soldier prisoners of war, except one, who was left for dead, but survived. He recounted how the *guerrilleros* executed the victims at close range, and ran off. I had been trying to find the telephone of Lina, the daughter of Gilberto, someone I had done business with myself, so that I could ring her up, the very day that this awful murder took place. I had had dealings with Gilberto and found him a marvellous, honest man.

I learned that there was a Japanese businessman taken on 22 February 2001, whose company had paid five million dollars and not got his release. The Japanese ambassador was steamed up. It had been his wife that I had heard once on the radio, talking to him in Japanese. His name was Chikao Marumatsu. He was taken by policemen, who sold him to *Frente* 22. In December, while his negotiators were trying to put together the last instalment and shame the FARC into releasing him, his body was found, in Cundinamarca, near Bogotá. This blew a fuse somewhere and the police picked up Hugo in the suburb of Soacha, acting on information. But the kidnappers had been policemen – the gang called *Los Calvos* (the baldies).

On 3 January 2004, the press announced that the Ecuadorian police and a Colombian team had arrested Simon Trinidad in the streets of Quito, the capital of Ecuador. He had a prostate cancer, and leishmaniasis, as I had had. No wonder. We had been only a short distance apart, at the start of the year before. He had gone for medical treatment, with false papers. His real name, as I told you before, is Ricardo Palmera, the son of a lawyer and farmer and himself a former manager of the *Banco de Comercio* in Valledupar, educated and not short of money. As he was marched to the aircraft for the trip to Bogotá, trial and prison, he shook his fist and cried, '*Vivan las FARC – Ejercito Popular.*' He was a member of the Staff (*Estado Mayor*) of the FARC and the most senior man to be captured ever. He was extradited to the USA. The most telling remark that he was heard to make was 'The only thing I ever did wrong in my life was to be born into the oligarchy.' This is the looking-glass nature of the war. Murder and kidnap is all right, but having a decent father and going to a good school is not all right!

The exchange of prisoners has never taken place. Ingrid, the officers and the policemen and the politicians are rotting in the jungle.

What is going to happen? If you read the European press, you may find articles like this. 'Kidnappings fell from 2,908 to 2,300. Killings, captures and desertions in the guerrilla are up. Ordinary people feel more secure.' But the Army has not hit the FARC in Meta and Caqueta, its bastions. An increase in the powers of the president may lead to more torture and disappearances. Human rights groups criticize the amnesty for the paramilitaries. Lasting gains against the guerrilla will be impossible unless the rural communities see benefits in the government campaign. A 'social touch' is necessary if Colombia is to become a peaceful democracy.

At the end of 2003, President Uribe made some criticisms of the NGOs and human rights activists, some of whom are marvellous people, some of whom are far to the left. His friends rushed to tell him not to pick a fight with these organizations.

I suggested to a senior man from Human Rights Watch, afterwards in London, that we should offer asylum to the leaders of the guerrilla, as had been done to so many African despots – a fat pension, several fat wives and a house by Lake Geneva.

'We cannot. Human Rights law is now universal. Anyone could sue them in any jurisdiction.'

The winding up of the paramilitary groups, by amnesty and arms handover, is viewed with incredulity by the human rights people. They want punishment. The road to a general disarmament and 'peace' is very difficult.

The French government tried its damnedest to get Ingrid out. Dominique de Villepin, then Prime Minister of France, flew from Africa to Bogotá in 2003 for a day to see what he could do. In July 2003, there was intelligence that Ingrid was going to come out in Leticia, on the Amazon, in the far south. The French foreign minister sent a Hercules C-130 transport plane with medical and special service forces on board to Manaus in Brazil, without the permission of the Brazilian government. Someone spoke to a Brazilian journalist and it got out and created a diplomatic row. Ingrid never appeared. In September 2003, a video of her was released in which she said that she was in reasonable health, and, strangely, that she agreed with a military rescue attempt to free her. Why? How? We shall have to wait for an explanation. So I got out and this brave young woman stayed. Why me? If I am free, it was due to my wife and children and friends. Back home, I am ruined. We sold the family home, and the savings of years of honest work were wiped out.

A neighbour in the country told me that two bodies had been found near the local town. They were two young men, one 19 and one 14 years old. 'They were extorting money. So someone told the "paras" and they were killed. They had bruising to their faces and bodies, so I suppose that they were asked who was behind them,' the neighbour said. 'They were just the collectors.' In a word, the eternal story of criminals and retribution – 'cleaning up'. The guerrilla in Colombia is by now so entwined with extortion and kidnap that you cannot tell who is a criminal and who is a *guerrillero*. Society either gives in and emigrates or does something about it.